D0204958

MALE-FEMALE
DIFFERENCES

MALE-FEMALE DIFFERENCES

A Bio-Cultural Perspective

Roberta L. Hall
with
Patricia Draper,
Margaret E. Hamilton,
Diane McGuinness,
Charlotte M. Otten,
and Eric A. Roth

PRAEGER

New York
Westport, Connecticut
London

GN
62.85
.H35
1985

Library of Congress Cataloging-in-Publication Data

Hall, Roberta L.
  Male-female differences.

  Includes index.
  1. Sex differences — Addresses, essays,
lectures. 2. Sex role — Addresses, essays,
lectures. I. Draper, Patricia. II. Title.
GN479.65.H35   1985   305.3   85-16924
ISBN 0-275-91335-X (alk. paper)

Copyright © 1985 by Praeger Publishers

All rights reserved. No portion of this book may be
reproduced, by any process or technique, without the
express written consent of the publisher.

Library of Congress Catalog Card Number: 85-16924
ISBN: 0-275-91335-X

First published in 1985

Praeger Publishers, 521 Fifth Avenue, New York, NY 10175
A division of Greenwood Press, Inc.

Printed in the United States of America

The paper used in this book complies with the Permanent
Paper Standard issued by the National Information Standards
Organization (Z39.48-1984).

10 9 8 7 6 5 4 3 2

BARD COLLEGE LIBRARY
Annandale-on-Hudson, N. Y. 12502

To Alice and Nancy,

who have always given encouragement

CONTENTS

1 Introduction   1
   Roberta Hall

2 Two Views of Sex Differences in Socialization   5
   Patricia Draper

3 Sociobiology and the Evolutionary History   27
   of Relations Between Males and Females
   Margaret E. Hamilton

4 Sensorimotor Biases in Cognitive Development   57
   Diane McGuinness

5 The Question of Size   127
   Roberta Hall

6 Genetic Effects on Male and Female   155
   Development and on the Sex Ratio
   Charlotte M. Otten

7 Population Structure and Sex Differences   219
   Eric Abella Roth

8 Issues for the Future   299
   Roberta Hall

Index   307

About the Editor and Contributors   311

1

INTRODUCTION

Roberta Hall

Differences between males and females are so obvious that all of us, even as small children, consider them basic to identifying both self and others. Yet sex differences are in many ways immensely subtle, and are subject to change. The goal of this book is to demonstrate the interrelationships among biological and social factors that produce sex differences and to provide an integrated approach to their analysis.

This book analyzes current studies on sex differences in several important and controversial areas. The effort is interdisciplinary, involving contributions from psychology as well as from human biology and the social sciences. The guiding philosophy is the integrative one of anthropology, which attempts to understand the human animal in its natural setting, that is, its many cultures and environments. What binds the authors is not their commitment to a discipline, however, but a common interest in the interplay of inherited and learned factors in the biology and behavior of human males and females.

The authors have found a gap between popular perceptions of features that distinguish females and males from those discovered by systematic study. Though research has shown sex differences are real, they are not those that our upbringing led us to expect. Most importantly, the implications that these differences offer to society are not those that conventionally have been drawn. Too often, scientists who have promised to provide a natural history, or biological interpretation, of human behavior have provided merely a rationale for the status quo, which frequently includes a rationale for the inferior status of the female sector.

As individuals and as a society, we are repeatedly confronted with questions concerning the biosocial roots of sex differences. These questions are pursued in the following chapters. This book is written for the generalist and for the student or instructor who wants to examine sex differences from the perspective of several disciplines.

Chapter 2 compares two models of how children in different societies learn male and female roles. The sex role-training model, developed primarily from learning theory, regards sex role socialization as the result of interplay between the child's experience and his/her own learning response. This approach is compared with the prepared learning tradition, which emphasizes the child's biological preprogramming toward learning specific roles and behaviors.

Chapter 3 examines the mating strategies of nonhuman primates from the perspective of sociobiology, which construes behavior as an evolutionary adaptation. This chapter applies animal and theoretical models to data on prehistoric humans and examines the nonhuman legacy in our own species.

Cognitive process is an area of sex difference research that has attracted much attention. In addressing the topic, Chapter 4 emphasizes studies of the development of sensory and motor skills that underlie skills such as reading and mathematics — fields in which unexplained sex differences in achievement have been identified. Additionally, the chapter asks us to consider our own responses to these differences.

Size differences in males and females are explored in Chapter 5. The review discusses studies of male-female size differences in other mammals, in our evolutionary predecessors of the human lineage, and in diverse cultures of prehistoric and contemporary periods. Sex differences in body proportions and body composition are considered, in addition to differences in the tempo of growth.

Cellular genetics, hormonal aspects of sex determination, and genetic effects on the sex ratio are presented in Chapter 6. Evidence exists that prenatally, as well as in infancy, childhood, and adulthood, males have a higher natural mortality than do females, and natural selection has responded by producing more males. How this takes place has provided researchers with intriguing problems, which are discussed in this chapter.

The study of one of the most basic male-female differences of all — that of numbers — is pursued further in Chapter 7, which discusses sex ratio differences in various populations. Considered is whether parental preference for children of one sex constitutes a pressure for population growth. The chapter suggests that some of the twentieth century's most outstanding problems — the population explosion and sex discrimination — may be linked through the social system.

Chapter 8 presents the editor's reflections and suggests ways in which the biological and social processes introduced in the book affect individuals.

2

TWO VIEWS OF SEX DIFFERENCES IN SOCIALIZATION

Patricia Draper

The literature on the socialization of human sex differences is likely to remind many students of the parable about the blind men who were grouped around an elephant, each trying to describe to the others what the elephant was like. Several traditions of research in the social sciences have been involved in the study of why the sexes are different. One that emphasizes deliberate sex role training of children owes most of its insights to learning theory and developmental psychology. It regards sex role socialization as the result of interplay between the environmental experience and the child's active learning and imitation. Researchers see the child as one who learns what is being taught and who forms certain evaluations of what is correct or expedient on the basis of experience (Mussen 1973; Maccoby and Jacklin 1974). Unlike the prepared learning tradition, which will be discussed below, systematic consideration is not given to the possibility that girls and boys, *because of* biological sex, will respond differently to the tasks of socialization.

The prepared learning tradition takes as a beginning assumption that girls and boys are born with inherent predispositions to behave in distinctive ways. This tradition accepts the role of learning as necessary for development but assumes that with respect to certain classes of stimuli girls and boys will respond differently. A person who takes this view of sex role socialization will be equally interested in "what children are taught" and "what children choose to learn."

This chapter introduces the reader to findings from these two contrasting approaches and considers the value as well as the limits of each. The discussion will take up a few studies that are good examples of each tradition, but will not attempt a comprehensive review. General features will be presented along with an examination of the differing insights that come from the two approaches. Finally, necessary further information and research will be discussed.

MODEL 1: DELIBERATE SEX ROLE TRAINING OF CHILDREN

According to this way of thinking, girls and boys behave differently because they are reared differently. Parents and adults of human societies everywhere understand that girls and boys will fulfill different social and economic roles, and in anticipation of that fact they put them on different socialization tracks. Children acquire different skills and attitudes owing in part to specific differences in their indoctrination but also because their experiences are different (D'Andrade 1966). An example here would be the common cross-cultural finding that girls receive stronger respon - sibility training than do boys (Barry et al. 1957; Whiting and Whiting 1975). The typical socialization of girls results from the fact they remain close to their mothers and the nature of women's work is such that girls can be incorporated into it at early ages. For example, in most societies women work close to home and do work that can be interrupted and broken into small components that children can master (Brown 1973). Therefore, mothers can simultaneously care for children and, in the case of girls, can instruct them in the skills that they will need as they get older.

Boys are likely to be passed over for responsibility training in early childhood because their adult roles do not require that they learn female role skills. Their mothers tend to their needs but do not expect boys to learn responsibility and obedience to the same degree as girls of the same age. [See Romney and Romney (1965) and Minturn and Lambert (1964) for good ethnographic examples of this aspect of sex role socialization.] Further, the nature of the work typically done by men is such that fathers cannot simultaneously do that work, care for dependents, and instruct the boys (Murdock 1949). Men's work is such that children cannot and should not participate; in many societies, for example, men travel far from home and do dangerous or physically rigorous kinds of work.

Much of this reasoning derives from the study of sex roles in nontechnological societies on which anthropologists have focused almost exclusively until recent years. Among cultures supported by agriculture and/or animal husbandry, differences in sex roles are especially marked. In the case of food producers, families live in large domestic groups (often called "extended families") with larger membership than the nuclear family groups found in foraging societies. In the extended families, senior men and women are in charge of the work of younger, same-sex relatives. This results in a type of domestic labor that is more highly organized and more hierarchical in form. It also entails segregation of the sexes in many aspects of daily life: Work roles are segregated and eating and leisure activities are often done with same-sex individuals.

By contrast, in technologically simpler hunting and gathering societies, this is less likely to be the situation. This is not to say that cultural values regarding differences between the sexes do not exist, nor that functional differences in the work roles of the sexes do not exist. Rather, because hunter-gatherers must remain mobile and at low population densities so as not to exhaust the supply of wild foods, there is an advantage to having the smaller nuclear family be the basic domestic unit. When conditions require, groups as small as one or two nuclear families detach themselves from the larger band and live apart. Under these conditions, men and women must share much in the way of common knowledge, skills, and decision-making ability. Thus, the size of the functioning economic unit may determine the degree of labor specialization — including the degree of sex differences in labor and other activities.

SOCIAL AND ECOLOGICAL INFLUENCES ON SEX ROLE SOCIALIZATION

By paying attention to the social and economic arrangements in the society of which children are a part, one can see that some cultures are likely to maximize the socialization differences between the sexes, while others do not.

Group size and economy are basic aspects of social life that can set a stage for small or great sex role differentiation between children. Bushman children of the !Kung tribe, hunter-gatherers living in the Kalahari

Desert of Southern Africa, receive very little in the way of explicit cultural messages about how girls and boys should do different things. This "lack" is related to both group size and economy. The living groups have about 35 to 40 people and only a small portion of the total are children. In consequence, girls and boys grow up playing in a multiaged peer group of both sexes. Neither sex has an opportunity to play only with same-sex peers, and in the absence of "segregated facilities" there is no opportunity for either sex to engage in stereotypic boy or girl kinds of play (Draper 1976). The idea that same-sex peers play an important part in sex role socialization finds support in various studies of Western children (see Fagot and Patterson 1969; Arganian 1973). Studies of Western children's risk taking are relevant here (Slovic 1966; Ginsburg and Miller 1982). Boys have been found more willing to take risks both in experimental and in natural settings, and it is typically reported that boys prefer to play with peers (preferably same-sex peers) more than girls. The greater opportunity to play with peers (because boys are not put to work) can intensify rivalrous and competitive behavior in boys more than in girls, who have fewer occasions to test themselves against same-sex, same-age playmates.

However, the nature of the economy and the kinds of work that hunter-gatherer adults do exempt girls and boys from being tracked at early ages into sex-differentiated kinds of jobs. Both women and men travel far on foot in the course of gathering vegetable foods and tracking game animals. The adults cover many miles, often crossing areas without drinking water, and they discourage children from accompanying them, knowing that they would slow the work. Girls and boys both stay at the group's base camp under the supervision of other adults who are not working on a given day. All children enjoy a leisured childhood; girls and boys do equally little work.

This brief illustration shows how the circumstances in which children are reared constitute a socialization pressure in and of itself. This occurs regardless of whether adults put an explicit value on their children's socialization in sex roles.

Examples of societies in which girls and boys receive sex-differentiated training and experience are much more common. This is particularly true of the so-called "middle range" tribal societies in which food collecting has been replaced by food producing and surplus accumulation. Along with these economic innovations go institutional changes such as sedentism, increased population density, increased fertility, more numerous subsistence sources and more time-consuming subsistence work, greater sex role specialization, and increased willingness to enlist children into economically useful work.

Societies that derive a large proportion of subsistence from domestic animals provide good examples of the influence of this type of economic progress on the sex role socialization of children. In all such societies, the primary responsibility for the management and defense of herds falls to men. It is boys and not girls who in their middle childhood years begin practicing games and skills that will ultimately make them more successful as herders (and as raiders of the herds belonging to rival groups). Many of the games stress physical prowess, endurance, hand-to-hand combat skills, bluff, and intimidation. Girls in these societies will not undergo this type of anticipatory socialization and one expects (and finds) that female behavior is considerably more muted than the flamboyant style of the men (Edgerton 1971).

An ethnographic description of the Fulani herders of Sub-Saharan Africa provides an apt illustration:

> At about six years of age the boys begin daily herding with their older brothers or fathers. At this time they are encouraged to begin to display aggressive dominance towards the mature bulls and oxen. We were told that initially the boys are often afraid of the bulls. Nonetheless, they are obliged to discipline these animals by charging them or hitting them with herding sticks. Boys who refuse to beat cattle on instruction are usually considered cowards, threatened, and even beaten if they still refuse. After they become accustomed to disciplining cattle, boys often initiate beating without encouragement. Several times at the beginning of a herding day we observed such young herders approaching the dominant bull or ox and hitting him several hard blows with a herding stick. Although the social code apparently discourages such "undeserved" punishment of cattle, these beatings were generally ignored by the older men. . . . The cultural ideal of the fearless, aggressive, dominant personality is fostered by the consistent, and strongly reinforced expectation of all those with whom the boy comes into contact. (Lott and Hart 1977, pp. 181-82)

These arguments suggest reasons for customary sex role allocations and specify the consequences of this sexual division of labor for child socialization. In so doing, they point to the existence of social arrangements that are exterior to the child and prior to his/her existence. Children grow up in a particular social milieu and learn skills that are necessary if they are to join the larger adult society. Depending on the local situation, children may or may not be treated differently primarily because of their sex.

ACQUIRING A GENDER IDENTITY

Various factors besides economics enter into sex role socialization. These depend less on the institutional arrangements of the society into which a child is born and more upon the personal psychological and developmental characteristics of the child. Rather than conceiving the child as responding to the learning tasks provided by the society, it is important to recognize that the child also makes certain discriminations and evaluations among learning tasks. This view incorporates a certain reflexivity in which the child acquires information as a result of experiences but then stores and processes that information in unique ways. The result is behavior that is produced at a later time but that is not simply due to the fact that the child has "learned what he was taught" (Bandura 1977).

Cognitive psychologists have shown that as a child matures intellectually, he/she acquires the language labels and cognitive classification of other speakers. One of the most pervasive distinctions acquired relatively early in the child's life is the category of sex. Once children learn gender labels, they experiment with applying them. As they learn the rules for inclusion in the category "girl" or "boy," they begin to turn the rules on the self in a kind of internal conversation (Kohlberg 1966; Kohlberg and Zigler 1967; Falbo 1980). A boy, for example, reasons, "I'm a boy. Cowboys are boys too. All football players are boys. So I can be a cowboy or a football player. I can practice those roles until I grow up."

An important point that Kohlberg (1966) makes is that children contribute to their own sex role socialization in ways that are not deliberately taught, nor necessarily anticipated by adults. According to this point of view, the role models to which children are exposed can influence their sex role conceptions. For example, the model may deliberately instruct the child and reinforce certain behaviors. If the child sees the model as powerful or attractive, he/she imitates it and in highly active ways tries to incorporate many aspects of its behavior, often going well beyond what the model was consciously trying to convey.

Currently, a number of researchers have predicted that boys who live in households headed by women and lacking a father or other permanent adult male suffer various deficits. Depending on the particular psychodynamic theories to which the researchers subscribe, predictions of deficits due to being reared "father absent" vary (Biller 1970, 1971, 1976; Lynn 1974; Lamb 1981). Earlier researchers believed the origins of homosexuality lie in these family dynamics (Green 1974), but there is no consensus on this topic among researchers in the 1980s (Meyer-Buhlberg 1980). However, some have suggested that father-absent boys will be effeminate as a result of imitating primarily female role models.

Still another set of theoretical and research papers has argued that certain types of "hypermasculine behavior" are a "reaction formation" against an underlying feminine sex role identity. The arguments developed in support of this hypothesis maintain that when boys grow up and contact the larger society, they realize they are expected to "act like boys." In attempting to satisfy the cultural expectations for their gender role, they overcompensate and behave in an exaggerated, stereotypic manner (Miller 1958; J. Whiting and B. Whiting 1975).

In the father-absence literature, analyses of both ecological and psychodynamic factors have been combined. The resulting model portrays a self-perpetuating system for a certain type of sex role socialization. Boys who are born into households headed by women do not have direct contact with adult males who can instruct them in the kinds of skills appropriate to their sex and so they lack direct indoctrination. These boys also may lack close social relationships with adult males, with the result that they do not identify actively at a psychological level with the male role. A further obstacle to developing a positive male self-identity is the fact that women in such social systems may devalue and denigrate males and maleness. The youths not only lack concrete models in their social environment for masculine behavior, but in symbolic ways their mothers and other adult females convey lack of confidence in men in general (Rohrer and Edmonson 1960; Pettigrew 1964; Hetherington 1972).

Children learn many things in the absence of direct, conscious instruction by others. The foregoing discussion of the absence of adult role models for boys illustrates a case in which children are hypothesized as drawing certain conclusions about how to behave as a result of being reared in a particular type of household. Such "conclusions" need not be conscious.

The sex role-training perspective of sex differences has led to the suggestion that if contraception allows women to restrict the number of years they spend in reproduction and child tending, a situation largely confined to modern industrial nations, then for most purposes women and men can assume interchangeable roles (Lancaster 1976). As machines continue to relieve humans of hard physical labor, the male monopoly of certain types of work is expected to disappear. Fundamental to this point of view is the idea that except for obvious reproductive differences between the sexes, males and females are essentially the same. Remove the constraints of reproduction (or reduce them to a minimum) and sex role differentiation will disappear.

SEX DIFFERENCES IN PREPARED LEARNING

The prepared learning view contrasts with the social learning of sex role orientation described above. It is not opposed to all aspects of the training model but it invokes a different set of assumptions about the consequences of reproductive differences between the sexes by considering selective forces that have operated on humans in their evolutionary past.

Studies with laboratory animals and research on pathological development in humans support the idea that during fetal development sex-specific hormones act on the central nervous system of male and female fetuses. As a result, the sexes are differentiated at birth with respect to certain types of behavior. Though boy and girl babies are born equally ignorant, they may display different predispositions for learning, even under the same environmental influences (Stratton 1982). This view is based on observations of laboratory animals in which sexually differentiated behaviors are observable at birth or shortly thereafter. From these have come the conclusion that "learning" as it is usually understood has played little or no role in accounting for the differences. Sex-differentiated behaviors have been observed in higher primates that were reared in captivity and in isolation from other conspecifics from which learning might take place (Gray and Buffery 1975). Reasoning from the animal evidence has led investigators to assume that humans, though relying on postnatal learning to a greater extent than other species, are likely to be similarly organized. Even more convincing evidence of prenatal sex differentiation of the central nervous system has come from published studies of sex differences in brain anatomy (Gorski et al. 1978; Jacobson et al. 1980).

Concomitantly, recent studies of child behavior in many societies report that, in certain ways, girls and boys are different. Boys, for example, tend to show more competitive behavior and a rougher physical manner of play. Boys show more interest in dominance interactions, and, increasingly as they mature, they sort themselves out into same-sex peer groups where they can find like-minded playmates. Girls have a quieter behavior with less energetic displays (Cronin 1980; Omark et al. 1980; Vaughn and Waters 1980). They pick up language at earlier ages than do boys, and, perhaps as a consequence, they gravitate more to adults and into a social environment that places more stress on conformity to adult rules than do the typical surroundings of boys, which include primarily other boys. (See Chapter 4 for a discussion of sex differences in what children pay attention to.)

These different behavior profiles, which show up in children from cultural groups with different values and standards of behavior, lead to the surmise that many of the nonsexual, nonreproductive behaviors of humans are influenced by the same selective forces that operate on fitness. An interpretation of the adaptive advantages of the assertiveness and competition so routinely seen in male-male peer interaction would be that these behaviors are "in place" because of their eventual payoff in reproductive terms. Young men who distinguish themselves in combat or in ritual games look good to young women, and young men who hunt well or show the physical stamina to work hard look attractive to the parents of eligible young women.

This idea has not met with wholehearted acceptance in all social science circles (Sahlins 1976; Chapter 3). The reasons for suspicion and rejection of such assertions are not difficult to understand. Western notions value highly the inherent integrity of the individual and take as a given the ability of the individual to rise above his/her circumstances. In this context, research that includes an irremedial biological given (such as sex or some other congenital or constitutional factor such as race) has been suspect on the grounds that it can or will promote biological reductionism.

Social scientists are particularly uneasy when it comes to the contribution of nonexperiential factors in accounting for individual behavior, for the social science paradigm is premised upon the notion that the environmental component in learning is the most significant. Most data of the social sciences come from empirically observable phenomena, and research designs are geared to recording and quantifying extant events. Therefore, the assertion that differences in behavior are not exclusively the product of learning is avoided on two grounds. In the first place, it conflicts with humanistic and philosophical values of

Western culture. In the second place, it opens up a conceptual "black box" wherein the conventional means of data collection can not be deployed.

Another black box exists for social scientists who contemplate the contribution of biological factors to human sex differences. If sex-differentiated behavior is not "learned" in the usual sense, then how can we understand it? Worse yet, if some behavioral predispositions are prior, then are they malleable? How can we, for example, change sex-differentiated behavior and perhaps interactions between the sexes if girls and boys behave according to a regimen not under environmental influence?

In 1975 E. O. Wilson published *Sociobiology*, a long-overdue account of modern evolutionary theory and its explanation for the adaptive function of both the form and the behaviors of many different species of vertebrates and invertebrates. A smaller portion of the book deals with human behavior from the point of view of the kinds of selective pressures that must have culminated in our present human capabilities. Wilson reasoned that selection would have operated on humans much as it operated on other higher mammals and primates. For all species, broad classes of behavior became intelligible when it was understood that organisms were adapted primarily for reproduction. In species where the reproductive roles of the sexes are highly specialized, as in the case of mammals, theory predicts that males and females will be selected to perform rather different behaviors.

Sociobiology attracted a great deal of attention and controversy, yet many of the ideas contained in it had been current in biological and zoological circles since the 1960s. The difficulty for sociobiology came in the presumption that human behavior could be interpreted in the same manner as the behavior of nonhumans. The alternative position had always been that *Homo sapiens* was unique in the animal kingdom in the unprecedented size and complexity of the brain and in the development of culture. Calling culture "man's extra-somatic basis of adaptation," social scientists built a conception of human cultural variation that stressed that culture was learned and highly arbitrary.

Probably the single most important outcome of the application of evolutionary theory to understanding human behavior was that it forced a telescopic view of human diversity. In the case of scientists working in the area of socialization and sex role acquisition, the evolutionary viewpoint caused people to realize that an overly myopic focus on the proximate causes of behavior could obscure an underlying behavioral structure. Once the existence of such a structure was postulated, and the suggestion was made that the sexes are differently structured (with regard to some classes of behavior), the door was opened to the possibility that individuals of different sex could be expected to perform differently, even under conditions of identical environmental stimulus.

In order to answer the question, How does socialization produce differences in the behavior of males and females?, we need to be clear about the sources of our inferences. In other words, what kinds of factors produce sex-differentiated behavior and what place does socialization play among them? The prepared learning approach assumes that socialization for sex role is but one element in a series of events that humans experience. Socialization for sex role applies more narrowly to the way in which children learn the roles of adult males and females.

Several sources of inference help us understand how girls and boys emerge from infancy into childhood with recognizably distinct behavioral styles. The asymmetry of the sexes in reproductive function and its implications for the way in which natural selection has influenced behavior in the sexes seem an essential starting point. Issues at this level of remove from socialization may be thought extraneous to actual influences on girls and boys. However, the prepared learning model considers that, in addition to reproductive function, the sexes also differ with regard to their underlying predisposition to learn. This forces us to look on the socialization experience not only as "what children are taught" but also "what children choose to learn." This perspective introduces the larger evolutionary and biological context within which sex role socialization operates.

ASYMMETRY OF REPRODUCTIVE ROLES

At the most basic level are the different biological roles played by the sexes. In higher mammalian species, the reproductive roles of the sexes are most distinct. The female nurtures the fetus internally at substantial metabolic cost, births the infant, and then lactates for a sustained postnatal period. The mother's role is not limited to the supply of nutrients, for she is a source of warmth, protection, and instruction for a significant time period in the life of her offspring. In some species of higher mammals, the male plays no role in the nurturing of young beyond that necessary for conception. Other species show an active male parental role; examples are found in a few prosimian species and in the canids, beavers, gibbons, and humans. In many other mammals, including a primate such as the baboon and some of the great cats, males serve a protective function for all the young of the social group, some of whom are their offspring.

It is possible for the significance of the reproductive difference between the sexes to be overlooked. It is so basic that it is easy to assume that it is limited to the tasks of reproduction and that it need have no relevance to other aspects of behavior that are unrelated to copulation, reproduction, and nurturing of young. For example, since in higher mammals females make the heaviest energetic commitment to reproduction, it is females who limit the rate of reproduction. No matter how many males are available, the number of offspring that can be conceived, gestated, birthed, and nursed is limited by the number of females of reproductive age who are physiologically capable of mothering. This condition has been interpreted to mean that, relative to males, females need not worry themselves unduly about how to become inseminated. They can rest assured that natural selection will produce males who will actively seek them. Human scientists, considering the strategies the sexes have been forced to evolve over the eons, can reason that female animals on the average should show less of the masculine urgency and competitiveness in dealings with conspecifics.

The logical outcome of this asymmetry in reproductive role is that natural selection has favored males who can best compete with other males in gaining the sexual cooperation of females. Since humans represent a species that takes such a long time to mature, and since the kinds of skills that characterize an adult take years for an individual to consolidate, one can expect that to the extent this holds, males would be expected to show greater interest in competitive interactions and dominance strivings with other males.

Natural selection has favored a different strategy in females. In the first instance, since human females, like females of other higher mammalian species, make the greatest investment in reproduction, we can expect that females in their parental roles will have been under selective pressure in favor of greater attentiveness to offspring and greater willingness to maintain close proximity to offspring. Various behaviors of a more obvious and proximate sort would be included here: feeding, tending, protecting, monitoring, and socializing offspring. In other ways this view predicts that human females will have undergone selective pressure for what might be called "sociability," or perhaps better stated "selective sociability."

An argument could be made for the notion that the sociability preferences of females are "in place" ultimately because of their relationship to the nurturing of offspring. But to understand the kinds of selective forces on human females only in terms of their immediate consequences for the survivorship of young is to miss an important point. Long-term studies of nonhuman primates and other mammals show that lineages of females constitute the social nucleus of many group-living species (Koyama 1970; Eaton 1976; Hrdy 1981; Daly and Wilson 1983). The fitness of females for millions of years of mammalian evolution has been dependent upon social skills and interaction with other females (typically their kin), though studies that reveal the significance of female-female and female-other interactions have only recently been conducted. Studies by Jeanne Altmann (1981), Sarah Hrdy (1979, 1981), and Jim McKenna (1979) show the extent to which a female's position in a female hierarchy can affect her diet, fertility, and eventually her fitness (see Chapter 3). Coalitions of females, often three or more generations deep, cooperate within the membership and compete with other female lineages for various resources such as rights to drinking water, preferred sleeping places, and the like. A result of within-coalition cooperation and extra-coalition competition is that lineages of females become ranked in a dominance hierarchy. Sociability is thus highly selective.

Research on free-ranging primates has shown the reproductive consequences of such coalitions. Among the yellow baboons of Kenya, long-term studies of the behavior of individual animals that are troop members show that female members of high-ranking coalitions have many advantages (Altmann 1981). They can displace lower-ranked females from desirable feeding places and can drink first among females when the troop moves to a watering place. This advantage is not always of great moment but it becomes so when drought has reduced the water supply below that necessary to sustain all troop members, or when the troop realizes that predators are near the watering place. In this case, the goal is to drink and run, before the predator can draw too close.

Higher-ranking females, probably because of their better diet and less stressful life, enter estrus several months sooner than lower-ranking females, with the result that they potentially will produce more offspring. Further, higher-ranked females are better able to time their estrus so that birth and weaning times coincide with seasons in which the most suitable kinds of forage are available for weanlings. Lower-ranked females are more likely to birth and wean offspring later and in less favorable ecological circumstances, with the result that rates of infant mortality are higher (Altmann 1981).

The concept of selective sociability is relevant in this way: Females have prolonged contact with their own offspring. The relationship is longer and more intense than the relationship that males have with offspring. Females behave as if they have longer memories for kin relations than do males, as indicated by the fact that females interact preferentially with mothers, sisters, half-sisters, daughters, and daughters' daughters. Most primate females, including hominid females in our evolutionary past, have been rewarded for paying attention to bonds with other females and for their ability to maintain complex interactions with other females. Selective sociability is not limited to positive, nurturing behaviors but incorporates hostile, competitive behaviors designed to protect a given female's position against other female challengers. Females that successfully nurture their young leave more offspring in the next generation than females that are less willing to tend and feed dependent young for long periods. Additionally, in species such as *Homo sapiens* in which the male helps in parenting the young, natural selection will favor females who are careful about their choice of mate; a good choice will help more of the young survive. When sex role is conceived in this fundamental manner, it becomes apparent that extensive systems of behavior by males and females are potentially affected by natural selection.

CONNECTIONS BETWEEN REPRODUCTIVE INTERESTS AND BEHAVIORAL PREDISPOSITIONS

The discussion above suggests that the sexes have been distinguished along two dimensions: interest in sexual competitiveness and interest in long-term social relationships. Earlier mention was made of evolutionary biologists' premise that all functions of an organism relate in some way to reproductive ones. The basis of this rather extreme reductionism is that natural selection can work only on individuals. Individuals who do not reproduce themselves (or contribute to the survival of close relatives) stand no chance of having their characteristics transmitted to future generations. Given the reproductive asymmetry between the sexes in all mammals, generally, and in the prolongation of juvenile dependence in humans, specifically, there is the potential for a certain "continental divide" in the behavioral terrain traversed by the sexes.

The reproductive interests of males have been seen to be furthered by the competitive behaviors and preferences that males show in childhood play. A number of studies give empirical confirmation of such a characteristic style in boys (Omark et al. 1980). It remains to outline the same relationship between the reproductive interests of females and the kinds of behavioral schema observable in young girls, schema that may represent preadaptations to a long-term social strategy.

Evidence exists to support such an argument, but the reasoning involves a more complex and subtle sequence of behaviors in the case of females as opposed to males. The difference is related to the difference between coitus (the *sine qua non* for males) and gestation-lactation-rearing (the *sine qua non* for females). While it is true that each sex needs the other, the division of reproductive labor is such that the male responsibility for his posterity is physically satisfied by coitus. In a physiological sense, this is "all the male can do" toward furthering conception, and coitus is achieved in a short time. (We are leaving aside the issue of male parental investment, discussed in Chapter 3. Male involvement affects the probability of infant survival, but does not pertain to the current discussion.) However, competitive interaction with other males and successful courtship displays to females are directly related to whether or not a youth will be in a social position to impregnate a receptive woman.

A woman's physiological responsibility to her posterity is not satisfied in any so direct or momentary a manner as is a male's to his. Indeed, it is not nearly so easy to isolate female behaviors that promote a woman's genetic continuity. Her "success" in this regard is measurable in the number of offspring she rears to sexual maturity (the same as for males), but the behaviors necessary to bring this about lie in the minutiae of hourly, daily, and yearly interactions with those offspring and with other group members whose behavior can affect the offspring. Where should one look for determinants of success?

If the argument that women go for a strategy based on sustaining long-term social relationships is correct, then one would predict the following characteristics. Girls should remain physically close to their mothers and to other females with whom the mother associates. (In many societies, these are likely to be the mother's female kin.) Girls should be attentive to the social interaction of adults and responsible to the social conditioning dealt out by the significant adults in her early years, since the same people are likely to be physically present and socially relevant when girls are reproductively mature themselves. They should be relatively tractable or easily socialized. A girl's close proximity to her mother will mean that aversive behavior on her part toward the mother will be noticeable. If a girl is persistently offensive, her mother may drive her away from the matrilineal enclave, an eventuality that would not promote the girl's welfare. This reasoning leads to the prediction that girls will find it easier than boys to learn the interpersonal tasks of socialization. Additionally, girls should find the society of kindred attractive and rewarding. We need not posit a sixth sense that allows them to detect genetic relatives; rather they should be sensitive to the social lead or guidance of their matrikin.

Several studies point up the greater average tractability of girls; however, these tendencies obscure the considerable variation within the sexes. Behavior observation research on children shows that girls commonly comply with parental requests, whereas similar overtures by parents of boys are more likely to be met with negativism and refusal (Minton et al. 1971; Fagot 1974, 1978a, b). A cross-cultural comparison of children's behavior shows more prosocial behavior on the part of girls (employing social rules to justify behavior) as contrasted with more egocentric behavior by boys (behavior in the service of the self). This suggests that girls are more aware of the influence of social context on their own behavior and the behavior of others, and that they use this knowledge to achieve their goals. Boys resort more directly to unvarnished attempts at assertion and dominance in gaining their objectives (J. Whiting and B. Whiting 1975). Similar findings show up in a study of the social behavior of East African girls and boys (Ember 1973).

Some primate studies indicate that male infants and juveniles wean themselves at earlier ages from close physical proximity to the mother. One suggested mechanism is the greater number of aversive behaviors (pinches, bites, hits) directed at the mothers by male infants and the greater readiness of the mothers to rebuff the close approach of the male offspring except when nursing them (Jensen et al. 1973). Among many primates, mothers may favor female offspring, but in many human societies social and economic practices have changed the odds so that male children more often are favored (see Chapter 7).

CONCLUSIONS

The two views of sex role differentiation in humans stem from different scientific traditions. The sex role-training approach draws on social learning theory, developmental psychology, and an anthro-pological perspective on the requirements posed by social institutions for child socialization. This school of thought considers sex role as one of several learning accomplishments that each new member of society must master. The focus is on postnatal experience, individual maturation, and the implicit and explicit contingencies that shape life in diverse social situations. Social scientists who work in this tradition are likely to view behavior and social role differences between the sexes as primarily acquired and therefore subject to change.

These scholars concede that the reproductive capabilities of the sexes pose different limitations on the nature of the social roles the sexes can fulfill. They expect, however, that under new social, economic, technological, and ideological conditions, the biological differences will fade in significance. The sexes will become functionally interchangeable since, for example, men no longer specialize in roles requiring physical strength or prowess in combat and women no longer expect to spend 20 to 30 years of their adult lives in childbearing and -rearing.

The prepared learning explanation for sex role socialization differences draws on concepts from zoology, evolutionary biology, and ethology. This approach considers that understanding the contemporary behavior of a species requires study of the selective forces that have operated on individuals of the ancestral population. Scholars in this tradition look to the species' evolutionary past for insights into adaptations that would have been favored by selection. The logic behind this apparently reckless disregard of good contemporaneous data about human sex roles is that the forms of social organization, economy, and levels of population density with which *Homo sapiens* now lives are extremely recent innovations in comparison with the tens of thousands (some say hundreds of thousands) of years humans have lived by foraging and at extremely low population levels.

Rather than taking at face value the fact that children undergo specific experiences that bear on their performance as men and women, evolutionists think of each child as partially preprogrammed to carry over behaviors appropriate in another era. Children learn, but they choose what to learn in concert with behavioral schema that have been selected for in past generations (Blurton Jones 1982). Evolution, of course, is an ongoing process. Indeed, if the theory is taken seriously, it implies that the changed pressures on today's males and females will affect the programming for tomorrow's infants.

As is true for any research paradigm, the theoretical assumptions that are necessary at one level to build and test models become obstacles to testing ideas posed from another level outside the paradigm. So there is a potential for the theorists of the two "sides" to continue to operate in separate divisions, talking past each other with separate concepts and vocabulary. Happily, there are signs of rapprochement. Medical and psychological researchers are opening up a new field of neonatology and have uncovered many attributes of infant behavior that represent relatively structured behavior sequences that are seen so early in life that they cannot be tied to postnatal learning. Research on the relationship of sex to these infant behaviors will tell us more about the areas of behavior that are sex differentiated and that may enter into more complex behaviors that we think of as "feminine" or "masculine" in style.

Child development researchers have used the technique of systematic behavior observation for many decades. As interest grows in more "micro" levels of behavior observational analysis, researchers are able to detect much evidence that the child is a major contributor to his/her own socialization. Variables of sex as well as of individual temperament are being evaluated for the role they play in the child's technique for dealing with experience.

We know that the chief distinction of humans is their great capacity for change and for learning. Research in coming years is not likely to contradict this assumption, but we will have more information on why it is that people are able to learn what they do and what kinds of psychological and psychobiological structures underlie human learning readiness. These studies will help us develop more accurate models of the range of sex roles open to human societies and the advantages and penalties that these structures impose upon individuals.

REFERENCES

Altmann, J. 1981. *Baboon Mothers and Their Infants.* Chicago: University of Chicago Press.

Arganian, M. 1973. "Sex Differences in Early Development." In *Individual Differences in Children,* edited by J. C. Westman, pp. 45-63. New York: Wiley.

Bandura, A. 1977. *Social Learning Theory.* Englewood Cliffs, NJ: Prentice-Hall.

Barry, H. III, M. K. Bacon, and I. Child. 1957. "A Cross-Cultural Survey of Some Sex Differences in Socialization." *Journal of Abnormal and Social Psychology,* 55:327-32.

Biller, H. B. 1970. "Father Absence and the Personality Development of the Male Child." *Developmental Psychology,* 2:181-201.

___. 1971. *Father, Child and Sex Role*. Lexington, MA.: D. C. Heath.

___. 1976. "The Father and Personality Development: Paternal Deprivation and Sex Role Development." In *The Role of the Father in Child Development*, edited by M. Lamb, pp. 89-156. New York: Wiley.

Blurton Jones, N. G. 1982. "Origins, Functions, Development and Motivations: Unity and Disunity in the Study of Behavior." *Journal of Anthropological Research*, 4:333-49.

Brown, J. K. 1973. "The Subsistence Activities of Women and the Socialization of Children." *Ethos*, 1:413-23.

Cronin, C. L. 1980. "Dominance Relations and Females." In *Dominance Relations: An Ethological View of Human Conflict and Social Interaction*, edited by R. Omark, F. Strayer, and D. Freedman, pp. 299-318. New York: Garland STPM Press.

Daly, M. and M. Wilson. 1983. *Sex, Evolution and Behavior*, 2nd ed. Boston: Willard Grant Press.

D'Andrade, R. 1966. "Sex Differences and Cultural Institutions." In *The Development of Sex Differences*, edited by E. E. Maccoby. Stanford, CA: Stanford University Press.

Draper, P. 1976. "Social and Economic Constraints on !Kung Childhood." In *Kalahari Hunter Gatherers*, edited by I. DeVore and R. Lee. Cambridge, MA: Harvard University Press.

Eaton, G. G. 1976. "The Social Order of Japanese Macaques." *Scientific American*, 235:96-106.

Edgerton, R. B., ed. 1971. *The Individual in Cultural Adaptation*. Berkeley: University of California Press.

Ember, C. 1973. "Feminine Task Assignment and the Social Behavior of Boys." *Ethos*, 1:424-39.

Fagot, B. 1974. "Sex Differences in Toddlers' Behavior and Parental Reaction." *Developmental Psychology*, 10:554-58.

Falbo, T. 1980. "A Social Psychological Model of Human Sexuality," In *The Psychobiology of Sex Differences and Sex Roles*, edited by J. E. Parsons, pp. 131-42. New York: McGraw-Hill.

Ginsburg, H. J., and S. M. Miller. 1982. "Sex Differences in Children's Risk Taking." *Child Development*, 53:426-28.

Gorski, R. A., J. H. Gordon, J. E. Shryne, and A. M. Southam. 1978. "Evidence for a Morphological Sex Difference Within the Medial Preoptic Areas of the Rat Brain." *Brain Research*, 148:333-46.

Gray, J. A., and A. W. H. Buffery. 1975. "Sex Differences in Emotional and Cognitive Behavior in Mammals Including Man." *Acta Psychologica*, 35:89-111.

Green, R. 1974. *Sexual Identity Conflict in Children and Adults*. New York: Basic Books.

Hetherington, E. M. 1972. "Effects of Father Absence on Personality Development in Adolescent Daughters." *Developmental Psychology*, 7:313-26.

Hrdy, S. B. 1979. "Infanticide Among Animals: A Review, Classification, and Examination of the Implications for the Reproductive Strategies of Females." *Ethology and Sociobiology*, 1:13-40.

___. 1981. *The Woman That Never Evolved* . Cambridge, MA: Harvard University Press.

Jacobson, C. D., J. E. Shryne, F. Shapiro, and R. A. Gorski. 1980. "Ontogeny of the Sexually Dimorphic Nucleus of the Preoptic Area." *Journal of Comparative Neurology*, 193:541-48.

Jensen, G., R. Bobbit, and A. Gordon. 1973. "Mothers' and Infants' Roles in the Development of *Macaca nemestrina*." *Primates*, 14:79-88.

Kohlberg, L. 1966. "A Cognitive Developmental Analysis of Children's Sex Role Concepts and Attitudes." In *The Development of Sex Differences*, edited by E. E. Maccoby. Stanford, CA: Stanford University Press.

Koyama, N. 1970. "Changes in Dominance Rank and Division of a Wild Japanese Monkey Troop in Arashiyama." *Primates*, 11:335-91.

Lamb, M. E. 1981. *The Role of the Father in Child Development*, 2nd ed. New York: Wiley.

Lancaster, J. B. 1976. "Sex Roles in Primate Societies." In *Sex Differences: Social and Biological Perspectives*, edited by M. Teitelbaum, pp. 22-61. Garden City, NY: Anchor Press/Doubleday.

Lott, D. F., and B. L. Hart. 1977. "Aggressive Domination of Cattle by Fulani Herdsmen and in Relation to Aggression in Fulani Culture and Personality." *Ethos*, 5:174-86.

Lynn, D. B. 1974. *The Father: His Role in Child Development*. Monterey, CA: Brooks/Cole.

Maccoby, E. E., and C. M. Jacklin. 1974. *The Psychology of Sex Differences*. Stanford, CA: Stanford University Press.

McKenna, J. J. 1979. "Aspects of Infant Socialization, Attachment, and Maternal Caregiving Patterns Among Primates: A Cross-Disciplinary Review." *Yearbook of Physical Anthropology*, 22:250-86.

Meyer-Buhlberg, H. F. L. 1980. "Homosexual Orientation in Women and Men: A Hormonal Basis?" In *The Psycho-Biology of Sex Differences and Sex Roles*, edited by J. E. Parsons, pp. 105-30. New York: McGraw-Hill.

Miller, W. B. 1958. "Lower Class Culture as a Generating Milieu of Gang Delinquency." *Journal of Social Issues*, 14:5-19.

Minton, C., J. Kagan, and J. A. LeVine. 1971. "Maternal Control and Obedience in the Two-Year Old." *Child Development*, 42:1873-94.

Minturn, L., and W. W. Lambert. 1964. *Mothers of Six Cultures: Antecedents of Child Bearing*. New York: Wiley.

Murdock, G. P. 1949. *Social Structure*. New York: Macmillan.

Mussen, P. H. 1973. *The Psychological Development of the Child*. Englewood Cliffs, NJ: Prentice-Hall.

Omark, D., F. Strayer, and D. Freedman, eds. 1980. *Dominance Relations: An Ethological View of Human Conflict and Social Interaction*. New York: Garland STPM Press.

Pettigrew, T. F. 1964. *A Profile of the Negro American*. Princeton, NJ: Van Nostrand.

Rohrer, H. H., and M. Edmonson. 1960. *The Eighth Generation*. New York: Harper.

Romney, A. K., and R. Romney. 1965. *The Mixtecans of Juxtlahuaca* . New York: Wiley.

Sahlins, M. 1976. *The Use and Abuse of Biology.* Ann Arbor: University of Michigan Press.

Slovic, P. 1966. "Risk-Taking in Children: Age and Sex Differences." *Child Development,* 37:169-76.

Stratton, P., ed. 1982. *Psychobiology of the Human Newborn.* New York: Wiley.

Vaughn, B. E., and E. Waters. 1980. "Social Organization Among Preschool Peers: Dominance, Attention and Sociometric Correlates." In *Dominance Relations: An Ethological View of Human Conflict and Social Interaction,* edited by D. P. Omark, F. Strayer, and D. G. Freedman, pp. 359-80. New York: Garland STPM Press.

Whiting, B., and J. W. M. Whiting. 1975. *Children of Six Cultures.* Cambridge, MA: Harvard University Press.

Whiting, J. W. M., and B. B. Whiting. 1975. "Aloofness and Intimacy of Husbands and Wives: A Cross Cultural Study." *Ethos,* 3:183-207.

BARD COLLEGE LIBRARY
Annandale-on-Hudson. N. Y. 12504

3

SOCIOBIOLOGY AND THE EVOLUTIONARY HISTORY OF RELATIONS BETWEEN MALES AND FEMALES

Margaret E. Hamilton

In some circles, sociobiology is considered the scandal of the sciences. It is lumped with simplistic approaches such as biological determinism and social Darwinism, and it is accused of racism and sexism. People who are uneasy with sociobiology have historical reasons to be wary of biological models that attempt to explain social patterns, for Western evolutionary thought has been plagued with approaches that justify miserable social practices on an assumed biological basis. Hidden under the cloak of scientific objectivity, pseudo-scientists have assured the public that women are biologically destined to stay home and not participate in public life. Yet sociobiology promises to do better.

In 1975, E. O. Wilson's *Sociobiology: The New Synthesis* integrated a diverse body of literature and allowed new insights into the evolutionary basis of animal social behavior. However, the book is marred by a final chapter on humans, which includes comments such as this: "During the day the women and children remain in the residential area while the men forage for game or its symbolic equivalent in the form of barter and money" (p. 553). Wilson thus overlooked the anthropological literature showing that the bulk of human history encompasses small foraging societies in which women made critical contributions to the everyday business of survival. A woman in a gatherer-hunter society is *not* a homebody! This example illustrates what Washburn (1978) described as "the repeated mistake of regarding our culture as synonymous with human nature" (p. 416), in this case the assumption that women are biologically destined to stay at home and not participate in public life.

Instead of accepting the merits of Wilson's book and focusing criticism on the final chapter, some academics rejected the entire book, and its approach. This view was reinforced when *Time* magazine (1977) ran an enthusiastic story on sociobiology that featured an appalling cover photograph of a human couple posed in a stiff puppetlike embrace complete with strings and blank facial expressions. The "Biology-is-destiny" cover was reinforced in the text, which presented the common misconception that evolution has perfected our social behavior. In fact, evolution is enormously tolerant of diverse behavior patterns.

Another obstacle to understanding biological influences on behavior is a tendency to assume that "biologically based" means immutable. Blaffer Hrdy (1981) complained, "If even a portion of the human male's dominance is ascribed to evolutionary causes, an intolerable status quo will have to be condoned as fundamentally unalterable" (p. 2). But Blaffer Hrdy shows this is an error, for change is inherent in evolution. Furthermore, a species' basic biology must interact with the environment. Sex differences, along with other biologically influenced traits, vary with environmental circumstances.

Still, it is a mistake to judge sociobiology on the basis of errors such as Wilson's or misrepresentations such as *Time*'s cover. Sociobiological theories such as inclusive fitness and the parental investment theory of sexual selection are valuable tools in the analysis of social behavior, including our own (Daly and Wilson 1978). Unfortunately, some authors who represent themselves as sociobiologists have used it as a dogma to rationalize their own society's social ideals. [For an example of this, see Van den Berghe and Barash (1977).] However, other studies of human sociobiology have been based on data (see Chagnon and Irons 1978). In this chapter, we will use sociobiological theory to challenge traditional descriptions of sexual interaction and to develop insights into relations between the sexes. We will begin by looking at some common discussions about females and their relationship to males. Following sections will consider relations between the sexes in other primates and in prehistoric human ancestors.

THE NAKED SEXIST

Anthropological discussions of sex differences frequently focus on physical traits in the human female that have been thought to be unique in our species. But traits like continuous sexual receptivity and concealed ovulation are not really as unique as we once thought (Blaffer Hrdy 1981) and merely represent an elaboration of our genetic inheritance from nonhuman primate ancestors. Other traits, such as prominent breasts, truly are unique and presumably appeared at an early stage of human evolution. Because we cannot observe evolution directly, we are confined to speculation based on the human fossil record, evolutionary theory and natural selection, nonhuman primate behavior, and the activities of contemporary foraging societies. As these data sets leave room for interpretation, the term "adaptive story" will be used for our methodology.

Many adaptive stories assume that females were dependent on males for survival and reproductive success, even in the earliest stages of human evolution. [See, for example, Morris (1967, p. 54), Campbell (1970, p. 280), Young (1971, p. 483), Pfeiffer (1972, p. 159), Pilbeam (1972, p. 154), Tiger and Fox (1974, p. 134), Wilson (1975, p. 553), Barash (1977, p. 297), Beach (1978, p. 140), Shepher (1978, p. 260), Fisher (1982, p. 91), Lovejoy (1981, p. 346).] The dependency hypothesis roots on concepts of female vulnerability during pregnancy and the need to carry infants that were more dependent than any known nonhuman primate infant. In the nonhuman primates, infants grasp their mother's hair, usually unaided. This behavior appears almost immediately after birth in monkeys, shows some delay in the earliest stages of ape infancy, and is almost nonexistent in newborn humans. The difference between monkey, ape, and human grasping abilities at birth relates to increasingly prolonged growth periods and different levels of central nervous system maturity at birth. Apes grow more rapidly than humans, and the young ape clings easily without the mother's help within a few months after birth. Modern human infants have an even more prolonged growth period and the ability to cling is further affected by the absence of body hair.

Decline in foot grasping ability occurred with the appearance of anatomical adaptations for bipedalism, which defines the emergence of the human lineage some 4 million years ago. The prolongation of growth and hairlessness are harder to document, though Mann (1975) has shown that the dental eruption sequence of modern humans was also present in some early hominid populations known as the South African Australopithecines. Some paleoanthropologists now place these fossils in a lineage that split from the main line of human evolution about 2.5 million years ago. To the extent that prolonged growth of the central nervous system correlates with tooth patterns, we can postulate helpless human infants by about 2.5 million years ago. Hairlessness has been associated with every feature of human evolution from increased sexiness to the need to sweat while running on the open savanna. We simply cannot say at what point the human infant no longer had a furry parent to grip.

Whether infant helplessness implies female dependency is not as easily answered. There is no doubt that women of the last century have been dependent on men because of exclusion from jobs that pay a living wage (Ehrenreich and English 1978), but is this the "natural" human condition? In some authors' adaptive stories, female dependency based on infant helplessness set up a selective force that favored the evolution of traits that attracted male attention and resulted in favors such as meat sharing. The common female traits cited in this context are continuous receptivity, the ability to have intercourse outside of a limited period of ovulation; concealed ovulation, the lack of physical-behavioral signals that ovulation is occurring; and – in a few scenarios – high female sex drive. In all of these scenarios, the prehuman females start with an estrous (cyclic) sexual pattern that is supplanted by selection for continuous sex behavior as the result of differential reproduction between females. In this story, those females who had sex all year around, or who confused their mates by not signaling that conception had occurred, attracted the most male attention in the form of meat protein and protection from predation. Thus, those females reproduced most successfully because they were better fed and protected. The key weakness in these stories – besides the conjecture that females did not forage on their own – is the assumption that females had to compete for males.

The appeal of the concept of female competition for male attention as an explanation of female sexual traits is rooted in current social conditions, not in primate behavior or in prehistoric evidence, the error that Washburn warned about (1978). The naive reader is left with the impression that our present system of male economic control and female dependency is part of the "natural order of things." Living in the midst of marked social and economic stratification makes it difficult to imagine the character of sexual competition and the quality of male-female interactions in the early foraging societies.

Leacock (1978) provides us with a vivid contrast:

> The tendency to attribute to band societies the relations of power and property characteristic of our own obscures the qualitatively

different relations that obtained when ties of economic dependency linked the individual directly with the group as a whole, when public and private spheres were not dichotomized, and when decisions were made by and large by those who would be carrying them out. (P. 247)

In other words, females in human foraging societies and female nonhuman primates experience a degree of autonomy that is unusual in our society.

SEXUAL SELECTION

Is it "natural" for males to choose while females compete among themselves to be chosen? If we consult biological theory, we find that we should expect the opposite situation: males competing for female interest. In fact, both of these scenarios occur in our society today. The story of how we altered these practices involves dramatic shifts in our history. We will first consider the mammalian pattern of sexual selection, and then examine the modifications that are part of our primate heritage. Finally, we will consider major changes peculiar to hominoids.

Natural selection occurs because individuals with different genetic makeups reproduce at different rates, a picture that is not as dramatic as the popular conception of selection as "survival of the fittest." In the nineteenth century, the term "fitness" often referred to socially desirable qualities that were defined by those in power. By contrast, true biological (or Darwinian) fitness relates only to an individual's (or individual gene's) reproductive success relative to the reproductive success of other individuals or alternative genes. In this sense, fitness is not absolute; it is always measured relative to the reproduction of other individuals (Cavalli-Sforza and Bodmer 1971).

Differences in fitness can occur both because individuals die at different ages and because individuals reproduce different numbers of offspring. These two forms of fitness are differential mortality (people die at different ages) and differential fertility (people have different numbers of offspring). Selection occurs when individual fitness varies because of heritable differences, but a genetic trait that is advantageous in one environment can be neutral or disadvantageous in another.

When mate selection involves one sex favoring certain traits in the other, or competition among members of the same sex for the other sex, it is called "sexual selection." Occasionally, the distinction between natural selection and sexual selection is obvious. For example, the peacock's tail has no apparent selective value in the natural environment, and seems to be related exclusively to the arena of sexual attraction. In some cases, sexual selection and natural selection reinforce each other so that traits that are useful in activities such as predator defense (natural selection) or male-male competition (sexual selection) are favored. In other cases, a sexually selected trait may be ecologically risky.

Most textbooks describe two forms of sexual selection. The epigamic form favors the evolution of traits that are appealing to the opposite sex, and the intrasexual form favors the evolution of traits that are advantageous in competition among members of the same sex. In theory, the two are distinct, but in practice, they often appear as two sides of the same proverbial coin. The male peacock will flash his tail at a rival and at potential female mates. Did the tail evolve because females liked it, or was it selected because owners of large tails could more easily threaten other males?

Fisher (1958) suggested that when one sex competes to be chosen, the sex that makes the choice should favor traits that are already advantageous in the competing sex. A concrete example is provided by male baboons that must compete with other males to obtain high status, which then gives them access to females. Baboon females should tend to favor traits that are advantageous in male-male competition because their own male offspring may inherit them. This helps in considering the large canine teeth in the male baboon, but what about the peacock's tail? Was the tail selected by females because it had value, or was it favored merely because it was different? Are peacocks' tails and other displays simply general indicators of overall health and vigor? These questions are pursued but not resolved in the book *Mate Choice* edited by Patrick Bateson (1983). In spite of such unresolved difficulties, sexual selection is a useful concept.

SEXUAL SELECTION AND PARENTAL INVESTMENT

The parental investment predicts the character of sexual selection based on the resources that each sex contributes to reproduction (Trivers 1972). Parental investment is specifically defined as an activity performed for one (or a set of) offspring that precludes performing the same activity for another (or set of) offspring. When there is unequal parental investment, the sex that contributes the most becomes a limiting reproductive resrource that the other sex must compete for. It is usually the female that contributes the most, and it is usually the male that competes, because the female egg is usually much larger than the male sperm. [For a more detailed discussion of how this basic sex difference in gamete size began, see Daly and Wilson (1978, p. 48), Blaffer Hrdy (1981, p. 21), or Hall (1982, pp. 3-9).] Some people object to the term "investment" by arguing, as Sahlins (1976, p. 72) has, that sociobiology is a form of social Darwinism returned to biology as "genetic capitalism." Bioeconomic terminology in this chapter is not meant to slight the spiritual and psychological dimensions of human reproduction, but simply to follow methodological precedence.

CORRELATES OF SEXUAL SELECTION

Although there are some significant exceptions, female mammals contribute the larger portion of parental investment in most species, that is, spend the most time and energy bearing youngsters. Degrees of variation exist; at one end of the spectrum are species in which males contribute only the sperm, and at the other end are a few examples, such as marmoset monkeys, in which males attend to the young and females provide only the milk. In many others there is a balance between male and female contributions. Where females provide more parental care, they are a limiting reproductive resource for which males must compete. Some males do better than others, and as a group males show greater variation in reproductive success than females. In harem species where large numbers of females are congregated, some males have hundreds of mates while others have none. Females also vary in reproductive success (Blaffer Hrdy 1981), but they show less variation in this feature than males. Systems in which males show much greater variation than females are termed "polygynous."

In species in which males invest less in offspring, the logical mating strategy for males is to seek multiple matings at the expense of other males. Thus, unequal parental investment plus male-male competition leads to polygyny, which is expressed in the social structure. Competition among males excludes some males from the population and results in lowered life expectancies and fewer adult males than females in the population.

Finally, male-male competition creates selection for sexually dimorphic traits, that is, traits that differ in each sex. Differences in size, coloration, hair or other surface features, depth of voice, character of calls, physiology, and behavior displays all suggest that the species has unequal parental investment, unequal variation in reproductive success, and unequal sex ratios. The word "suggest" is used here because sexual dimorphism is not always due to selection affecting males (Hamilton 1982).

As male and female parental investment approaches equality, the expressions of dimorphic traits diminish. With great investment, the male has more reproductive success if he stays with one female than if he competes for additional mates. Pair bonding produced monogamy, defined as equality between the sexes in reproductive variance. Canids, many birds, and some primates such as the gibbons are known for pair bonding and monogamy. Male competition is not intense, sexual dimorphism is slight, and the adult sex ratio is close to equality.

FOOD AND SEX

To fit humans into this theory, we begin with the fact that we are mammals. Wilson (1975) begins his chapter on mammals with the statement: "The key to the sociobiology of mammals is milk" (p. 456). While animals such as birds can share the parental duties of brooding and feeding, pregnancy and lactation in mammals favor male competition and female choice. But biology is not destiny, for mammals vary greatly in the way sexes share parenting chores. The story of how humans have altered this pattern begins with our nonhuman primate ancestors.

The primate order comprises over 200 species that vary considerably in social organization (see Figure 5.2). In the last decade, a number of papers have identified critical environmental features that shape social life (Crook 1972; Eisenberg et al. 1972; Clutton-Brock and Harvey 1977, 1978; Wrangham 1979a; Schaik and van Hooff 1983). Primate social systems are categorized according to sex ratios, mating systems, and group cohesiveness. Schaik and van Hooff's simplified scheme (1983) based on earlier work (Eisenberg et al. 1972) is summarized as follows. First are solitary primates in which individuals forage singly. Male ranges overlap with the ranges of several females, and the result is a polygynous mating system. Second are monogamous species characterized by a mated pair with offspring that are excluded from their parental territory at maturity. Third are polygynous groups, which include several adult females and one sexually active male. Young males may be present, but they are not sexually active. Finally, there are multimale species, in which a group of females and their offspring live with several adult males, all of whom are sexually active in a polygynous mating system. Group size in the multimale society is larger than in the other categories.

Speculation about early human societies usually starts with the multimale society model. Before providing examples, causes of primate structural variation will be considered.

Clutton-Brock and Harvey (1978) have argued that "variation in the distribution, density, and quality of food supplies is largely responsible for species differences in the density and distribution of mammalian populations" (p. 191), and that differences in population density and distribution determine the mating system. Animals feeding on abundant, low-nutrient foods like leaves can tolerate high population densities, whereas feeders on high-nutrient, unevenly distributed fruit forage at lower densities. Further refinements are possible. As Crook (1972) pointed out, if the food supply is evenly distributed and plentiful, such as foliage in the forest, animals may establish a territory and defend resources. Many of the single breeding male social groups follow this ecological arrangement. If the food is unevenly distributed or patchy, animals have to forage over large areas, and territorial defense becomes impossible. Multimale groups are often found in such situations. Body size affects distribution also. For instance, the gibbon (a lesser ape) and the orangutan (one of the great apes) both live in Southeast Asian rain forests and feed largely on fruit, which is unevenly distributed. Because of their small size, gibbon pairs can establish a territory and still have enough food. The much larger orangutan forages over larger distances; orangutans are usually solitary, and polygynous males maintain very large foraging areas that overlap with several female areas.

Wrangham (1979a) recognized that while male reproductive success usually depends on the ability to mate with females, a female's reproductive success hinges on her ability to compete with other females for food. Thus, Wrangham argues that food resources influence female destiny and dispersion, which in turn influence male dispersion. The effect is that a mating system is shaped by the concentration of receptive females in time and space. When females forage on plentiful, evenly distributed food items in an arboreal environment, feeding competition is low and group cohesiveness is high. Under these circumstances, a male may establish an exclusive territory with adequate resources for a number of females. By contrast, if females are dispersed in a terrestrial environment, a male cannot establish a territory or exclude other males. Schaik and van Hooff (1983) suggest that multimale societies result when it is more costly for males to drive away other males than it is to tolerate their presence. Put another way, the gain from exclusive access to females is overshadowed by the expense of excluding other males, an expense including energy used in fighting, risk of injury, and time lost from eating, mating, and watching out for predators. Failure to look after these basic necessities constitutes what Wilson (1975) calls "aggressive neglect" (p. 247), and it is this cost-benefit balance that prevents males from pursuing all-out male-male competition.

MULTIMALE EXAMPLES – BABOONS, MACAQUES, AND CHIMPANZEE SOCIETIES

As we have seen, multimale societies are associated with foraging situations in which females are widely dispersed to exploit small clumps of food unevenly distributed in the environment. This occurs most frequently in terrestrial habitats, which require foraging over large home ranges (that is, 25 square miles). The two most common groups of primates in this habitat today are the African savanna baboon species and their close relatives the Asian macaques, both Old World monkeys. These species provide models of early human social organization because their terrestrial habitat is similar to that of the early humans. Of course, environmental conditions are not identical and these monkeys are very different from humans, early or modern. As they are far less intelligent than humans or chimpanzees, comparisons offer insights into but not replicas of early human life.

Chimpanzees, one of two African species of apes, are not replicas either, but genetically are quite close and can provide clues to the behavioral potential that the earliest humans possessed. Chimpanzee males form stable groups or communities controlling large territories that encompass a number of smaller female foraging territories (Goodall et al. 1979, p. 17; Nishida 1979, p. 79; Pusey 1979, p. 467; Wrangham 1979b). Within each community, males cooperatively patrol boundaries and sometimes defend borders against adjacent communities of allied males (Goodall et al. 1979, p. 123; Nishida 1979, p. 82). Female movement across community boundaries reduces the probability of close inbreeding (Goodall et al. 1979, p. 50; Nishida 1979, p. 96; Pusey 1979, p. 472; Wrangham 1979b, p. 484). Male communities often include siblings, a factor cited as facilitating cooperation, inhibition of male-male aggression, and modulation of competition for females (Bygott 1979, p. 426; Popp and DeVore 1979, p. 319; Pusey 1979, p. 478).

The chimpanzee pattern contrasts with the multimale baboon and macaque societies, which forage in large groups. In these, defense of home range borders is rare and males rather than females change groups as they reach maturity. An enormous literature now exists on these monkeys; the novice may wish to sample an early piece (for example, Washburn and DeVore 1961; Hall and DeVore 1965) followed by more comprehensive long-term studies (Altmann and Altmann 1970; Altmann 1980; Lindburg 1980).

In both the baboon-macaque and chimpanzee societies, males form dominance hierarchies, the function of which primatologists spent years trying to determine. Though considered the vehicle for male reproductive success, counts of copulations per male did not always correlate with dominance. Hausfater (1975) finally demonstrated that the highest-ranking male was much more likely to consort with the female when ovulation was occurring. As this was being clarified, primatologists became aware that females had hierarchies too. By contrast, early baboon studies asserted that a female's status fluctuated with her estrous cycle (Hall and DeVore 1965), rising as she came into estrus and attracted male attention. But as primatologists followed groups through generations, they found that female hierarchies were more stable than those of males (Hausfater 1975). Animals that do not pair bond have no "father," but all know their mother and her kin. Generations of observations showed that the mother's status determines the rank of both males and females. Females use status to compete for food resources needed for successful reproduction (Blaffer Hrdy 1981, pp. 110-16) and organize themselves into matrilineal clans that are ranked internally and externally with each other. This pattern has now been observed in a number of Old World monkeys that live in multimale groups.

Female matrilineal hierarchies are found in chimpanzee societies, but lack the stability of those in monkeys. This is because female chimpanzees are more widely dispersed in their foraging areas, and the female is usually the sex that emigrates.

In multimale societies structured by a ranked set of matrilineages, the degree to which offspring benefit from their mother's rank depends on which sex leaves the natal group at maturity. Generally, male monkeys and female chimps move. This practice prevents close inbreeding

(Harcourt et al. 1976; Daly and Wilson 1978; Greenwood 1980; Cheyney and Seyfarth 1983). Though the sons of high-ranking female monkeys start life with an advantage, in a new group they have to work their way up. This situation is mitigated by the tendency of male siblings to follow each other or emigrate together (Drickamer and Vessey 1973; Enomoto 1974; Cheyney and Seyfarth 1977, 1983).

As with the female matrilineages, closely related males tend to develop alliances and back each other up in fights. Sociobiologists hold that this is because close relatives share certain proportions of genes and thus benefit to some degree from each other's reproductive success. This phenomenon is called "inclusive fitness" (Hamilton 1964). The overlap of common biological interest sets up a force called "kin selection," which facilitates the expression of helping behaviors that usually are directed at close kin.

Chimpanzee females usually wander from their natal area while males remain. The result is that chimpanzee males benefit from their maternal rank throughout their lives. While female chimpanzees apparently maintain some contact with their mothers and siblings, they tend to strike out on their own, and thus do not enjoy the kind of support enjoyed by female baboons. Female chimpanzees compete with each other for food under certain circumstances, but because they are dispersed, their interactions and rank are not as important as they are to monkeys.

Multimale primate societies have provided models of sexuality and assertiveness that have been applied to the human condition. After explaining male-male competition and female choice, many authors suggest that human males should be aggressive and assertive while females should be coy and choosy. "Coy" implies the pretense of being shy and demure. The other word that is used all too frequently is "passive." However, primate studies demonstrate its lack of validity. For example, chimpanzees, baboons, and macaques engage in much higher frequencies of sexual activity than are necessary to achieve conception. Furthermore, females of these species have highly colored swellings (from water retention) around the perineum or simply high coloration, both of which advertise ovulation. These females actively solicit sexual activity and mate with numerous males during the estrous cycle. Some observers have suggested that the physical and behavioral signals evolved so that females might induce intense male competition, allowing them to identify the "best" male (Clutton-Brock and Harvey 1976). But as Blaffer Hrdy (1981, p. 152) notes, daily social interaction provides that information well before ovulation. She speculates that the swelling-coloration occurs because "by pushing a father toward the conservative edge of the margin of error that surrounds paternity a female may forestall direct male interference in her offspring's survival" (p. 153). Infanticide by males, documented in a number of species, is believed to be less likely if a male is familiar with the mother of an infant through previous sexual contact. Additionally, we are beginning to see that male primates provide parental care as well as the legendary cooperative defense of the group (Hall and DeVore 1965), which has been rarely observed. What has been observed as parental investment is the male behavior of holding and protecting individual infants (Altmann 1980; Packer 1980; Taub 1980; Busse and Hamilton 1981).

Baboons form sleeping grove subgroups in which sets of males and females consistently sleep in the same trees (Altmann 1980, p. 66). During the day, females with infants are more likely to be in close proximity to these same males; daytime proximity and sleeping group choice predict previous consort relationships (Altmann 1980, p. 118). Within these groups, males sometimes carry, groom, and defend the infant (Altmann 1980; Packer 1980). Busse and Hamilton (1981) argue that males behave thusly to protect their probable offspring from potentially infanticidal males immigrating into the group. Young males living in their troop of birth show low reproductive activity but perform the same parental service for their matrilineal siblings (Packer 1980). Though males vary considerably in the number of relationships they maintain, females almost always have two such relationships, and if two females have one male in common, they usually share their second male associate as well (Altmann 1980, p. 117).

Chimpanzee males patrol the borders of an area that encompasses several female feeding territories and call the attention of females to food sources outside of their small ranges (Nishida 1979). Chimpanzees show a preference for partners, and both sexes exhibit occasional possessiveness. Sometimes male-female pairs travel together (McGinnis 1979; Nishida 1979; Tutin 1979).

Male baboon and chimpanzee helping behaviors benefit their matrilineal siblings and their (probable) offspring. If their attention is focused upon specific individuals, it limits their mating opportunities – a male caring for an infant can perform this behavior for only a small number of infants. When a male begins to aid young troop members, the question of paternity becomes important. Maternity is always certain, while paternity can be debated. This may be even more true of chimps than of humans!

From the biological point of view, a male should not provide care to young unless certain that he is helping his own genetic offspring. In primates such as monkeys and chimpanzees, there is not enough parental investment to limit mating opportunities or favor monagamy. Males sometimes show behaviors such as defense of a territory or vocal displays calling attention to rich food sources. These behaviors appear parental, but a male can perform them without focusing on one (or a set of) offspring. The behaviors benefit all members of the group, and they do not meet Trivers' definition (1972) of parental investment as an activity that precludes performing the same activity for another (or set of other) offspring.

Chimpanzee males sometimes attempt to control females within a consort, particularly if they have shared food with them (Tutin 1979). Yet male control of females in baboon and chimpanzee social groups is largely dependent on the male's nonsexual relationship with the female and his ability to exclude other males (McGinnis 1979; Tutin 1979; Packer 1980). Tutin (1979) noted that the formation of chimpanzee consorts requires female cooperation "by remaining silent and following the male" (p. 33). Chimpanzee and baboon females and males do not always mate with the most dominant individuals available to them (Hausfater 1975; Tutin 1979). While this may be in part avoidance of sex with close relatives, it also indicates sexual choice based on personalities.

EARLY HUMAN SOCIETIES

Not only have the earliest human societies left few records, the biological species itself is gone. Thus, it is hard to eliminate bias in our speculations concerning such societies. Anthropologists tend to favor models based on patterns of contemporary hunter-gatherer societies, a social type that has characterized 99 percent of our cultural history. Yet neither our cultural nor our biological heritage was fully formed at the time it left the earliest archaeological records, over 2 million years ago, so it is unlikely the hunter-gatherer model of today accurately reflects the past.

The early human life-style is linked to anatomical evidence of bipedalism. According to Lovejoy (1981), one of the reasons that bipedalism evolved as a human specialization was to allow adults, especially males, to gather food and then carry it back to a home base to share. Bipedalism certainly requires an explanation. As an anatomical specialization, obligatory bipedalism, such as *Homo sapiens* practices, does not allow for either great speed or agility, and it created physical vulnerabilities in the foot, ankle, knee, hip joints, pelvic structure, and spine still with us today. The counterbalancing benefits must have been enormous, but, in addition to efficiency in walking, what were they?

To answer that question, we need to go back to 5 to 8 million years ago when there were climatic and geophysical conditions in East Africa that expanded the wooded savanna and open grassland. These changes offered an evolutionary opportunity, but a primate capable of developing an ecological niche within this habitat had to make several adaptations. These produced the first human ancestors.

One of the challenges of this new niche must have been an increased threat of predation. Without the proximity of trees for escape, a primate would have to outrun the predators or face them down. Probably these early humans faced them down by brandishing weapons and producing great volumes of noise. The bipedal stance would aid this strategy because it is inherently threatening (Livingstone 1962); further, bipedalism frees the hands and allows for manipulation of the environment. The ability to carry things was a big gain, but the question of what was carried, and for what purpose, remains open. Initially it was not tools for the hunt, because archaeological evidence for hunting does not appear in the fossil record until 1.5 million years ago, 2 million years after our oldest bipedal human fossils (see Figure 5.3 for an outline of human prehistory). Simpler tools to ward off predators and enhance food foraging, for example, through the use of digging, would benefit both sexes of this marginal hominid. When anatomical adaptations for obligatory bipedalism occurred, an additional advantage may have been gained from the energetic efficiency of human walking – a feature demonstrated in many laboratory tests.

The earliest human fossils, classified as Australopithecines, date from at least 3.8 to 1.0 million years ago. We know that for a portion of this period, there were two separate groups. One evolved into a more human form, called *Homo erectus*, by 1.5 million years ago, and the other persisted in Australopithecine form until it became extinct about 1.0 million years ago.

All of the Australopithecines display, in varying degrees, an array of adaptations that have been related to chewing tough foods. Originally proposed by Jolly (1970) as the "seed eating hypothesis," this complex includes expanded molar areas, thick enamel on the molars, reduced canines for side-to-side grinding, and a biomechanical arrangement of the chewing muscles to enhance grinding efficiency (Wolpoff 1980, p. 90). This complex suggests a diet including seeds, bean pods, roots, and tubers, the latter two of which require digging sticks to obtain.

If we assume that these near-human forebears ate an omnivorous diet that included savanna resources, their food was distributed in a patchy, uneven manner. If females spread out as they foraged, it would have been difficult for a male to monopolize any of them. This picture suggests a baboon pattern of sexual relationships, but it should be modified by chimpanzee data. With their high intelligence, this species clusters at plentiful food sources and practices dispersion when resources are limited. The threat of predation may have influenced how much dispersion took place, for the effectiveness of facing down predators is enhanced by numbers. Yet Altmann and Altmann's analysis (1970, p. 173) of predation on baboons shows that most threats take place near forested areas and waterholes, areas where animals cluster and find safety from numbers. Female baboons, even with young, participate in predator faceoffs (Altmann and Altmann 1970, p. 176). Howell (1979) discounted the need for prehuman male protection, describing !Kung women who "travel widely, without weapons or guards to protect them" (p. 57).

Given the size of the Australopithecines (height estimates of from 3 to 5 feet) and the distribution of their food, they probably ranged over large areas. This suggests that males could not defend home range borders as some primates do. This factor and the potential for female feeding competition observed in monkeys, suggest that social groups were structured around female matriarchies. If this is so, males probably emigrated from the natal troop.

EARLY MALES AND FEMALES

What were the sex roles in Australopithecines, the first known bipedal primates? Many anthropologists have assumed that an elaborate division of labor was in place even in these early societies. Their scenario usually has female foraging activities limited by the burden of helpless infants and dependent children, while males range widely, bringing back meat to share at a home base. Shipman (1983, p. 253) has examined this set of hypotheses through an analysis of animal bone samples. She analyzed the bones for cut marks (as an indicator of meat eating); differential carcass treatment according to carcass size (as an indicator of food carrying); presence or absence of cut marks near joints (as a correlate of food sharing); and clustering of bones (as an indicator of base camps). Shipman compared Australopithecine-age sites with two more recent sites associated with *Homo erectus* – a definite hunter with base camps. She found that the *Homo erectus* sites matched predictions for the kinds of bone treatments expected, while the Australopithecine sites did not, and concluded that a foraging and scavenging pattern predated the establishment of hunting and gathering approximately 1.0 million years ago.

If this kind of analysis holds up, then we need to construct sex roles different from those of contemporary hunters. These will use primate traits, including a mother carrying an infant constantly, and some hunter-gatherer elements. Lancaster (1985) shows that the real difference between nonhuman primate and human development is not so much the period of infant dependency as it is the prolonged juvenile stage. Citing Johnston's work (1982) on learning, Lancaster indicates that the significant costs associated with a prolonged juvenile period are outweighed by benefits. Though a long juvenile stage increases the vulnerability of the individual and delays reproduction, the individual gains the opportunity for increased learning before assuming adult responsibilities.

What were these early humans learning? Lancaster argues that one of the unique aspects of early human adaptation was the development of an "extractive" foraging technology, that is, taking roots and tubers out of the ground with digging sticks. A primate had to learn how to choose material for the digging stick, find resources, identify food plants, and avoid toxic plants. At some point, they learned to use the hammerstone to crack nuts and break down seeds into more edible form. The hominid group that became extinct 1.0 million years ago showed increasing specialization of anatomical features for chewing tough food items, accompanied by an ape-sized brain. The lineage leading to modern humans showed an increase in brain size but no major dental specialization for chewing tough food. These data suggest that our lineage adapted to the diet through cultural as well as physical means.

Chimpanzees show us that tool-using behaviors are fully within the cognitive abilities of Australopithecines. Chimpanzees use twigs to "dip" for ants, and they transport nuts to locations where large rocks are used as hammer and anvil to crack them open (Beatty 1951; Struhsaker and Hunkeler 1971; Rahm 1972). The difference between what chimpanzees do and what the early humans did could be a matter of frequency. Whereas chimpanzees perform these activities occasionally, the earliest humans probably came to depend upon them. Lancaster thinks that juvenile learning works best when the young are released from constant foraging for food. The magnitude of the hominids' "free time" is difficult to estimate, but it was probably between what is known for baboons and contemporary hunter-gatherers, perhaps 2 to 5 hours daily.

How shall we imagine males and females in this early human context? The adaptive stories that focus on female sexuality obscure the fact that the normal condition of adult females in nontechnological societies is lactation. Konner and Worthman (1980) found an average birth space of 3 years and 8 months in a !Kung population and described a pattern of lactation very different from our own:

> Infants are always in immediate physical proximity with their mothers until age 2 years or older, and separations are brief until they are about age 3-1/2, when they are weaned during a new sibling's gestation. (P. 789)

These authors discovered that !Kung infants nursed during bouts that averaged 2 minutes separated by average intervals of 13 minutes! Adult females experienced small periods of sexual cycling that were interspersed with longer periods of carrying and breastfeeding an infant. The length of infant lactation is similar to that in the chimpanzee, but unlike the chimpanzee the early humans probably foraged over larger distances and used more calories to obtain food. Rather than depending on males to provide, it seems clear that females made physical adaptations (Stini 1982). Caloric needs during the first 6 months of lactation go up by at least 500 calories per day, with some estimates approaching 1,000 extra calories (World Health Organization 1965, 1973). Female physical adaptations to these demands include smaller size and relatively less muscle mass (Hamilton 1982) and sexual dimorphism for fat tissue (Stini 1982), a feature apparently unknown in nonhuman primates (Lancaster 1985).

If the early humans provided junveniles with safety, leisure, and some adult help with provisioning food, male involvement beyond the infant carrying observed in baboon-macaque societies or the solicitude of chimpanzee males was required. Evolutionary theory tells us that traits do not appear because they are "needed." There is, however, some flexibility in the system, since the primate pattern includes some male parentlike activity. Adult males probably helped juveniles, some of whom were their offspring – just as male baboons do. Like all young primates, these juve-niles must have spent their leisure time practicing adult skills. Adults who protected them benefited, and natural selection reinforced the pattern.

Shipman's work (1983) suggests that regular meat sharing did not occur until the *Homo erectus* stage, though this does not preclude occasional meat sharing like that observed in chimpanzees (Teleki 1973). Isaac (1982) criticized Lovejoy's thesis that males were provisioning mates and offspring, noting: "The transport of sufficient nuts, berries, and insects poses problems even if one assumes a simple bark tray was used as a carrying device" (p. 295). Isaac advised experimentation to determine the energy cost of behaviors. As it is, our adaptive stories hinge on assumptions about the intensity of predation, the variety of foods that were consumed, and the distributions of food in time and space. Only a time machine could give enough precision to satisfy everyone, but the fields of taphonomy, scanning electron microscopic analysis of dental wear, and trace element analysis offer promise of increased rigor. More comparisons of fossil and contemporary pollen distributions should provide a clearer model of available plant foods (Bonnefille 1976; Carr 1976). Study of microwear patterns in fossils and living animals could allow a better understanding of dietary components (Gordon 1982; Peters 1982; Gordon and Walker 1983; Kay and Covert 1983), and analysis of trace elements in the skeleton should provide data on the relative proportions of dietary meat and vegetables (Boaz and Hampel 1978; Schoeninger 1982). All the behavioral factors acted on the niche and affected how the sexes interacted with each other.

The foraging pattern may have required the dispersion of females accompanied by offspring. If males were not hunting regularly, they probably maintained proximity to the females and may have provided focused parental care; their help in breaking up vegetable material could have increased the likelihood of juvenile survival. The magnitude of male help affects parental investment and the mating system. If males provided a large amount of help, their mating opportunities would have been limited; the result could have been monogamous pairing. If males were providing less aid to any one female and offspring, the mating pattern could have been polygynous. Which is the more likely? One clue is the degree of size sexual dimorphism in the early human population. Johanson et al. (1978) think that the earliest Australopithecine populations, dating from 3.8 to 2.5 million years ago, displayed considerably greater dimorphism than that found in more recent humans (see Chapter 5).

Unfortunately, the nature of human female sexuality does not offer much insight into sex interactions or reproduction strategies. Though human females mate when ovulation is not occurring, so do other primates on occasion (Blaffer Hrdy 1981). Unlike baboons and chimpanzees, humans do not show their ovulation. Traditionally, theorists have made a great deal of this human "deception." Alexander and Noonan (1979) have argued that

> concealment of ovulation evolved in humans because it enabled females to force desirable males into consort relationships long enough to reduce their likelihood of success in seeking other matings, and simultaneously raised the male's confidence of paternity by failing to inform other, potentially competing males of the timing of ovulation. (P. 443)

Blaffer Hrdy (1981) showed that copulation outside of ovulation and during nonconspicuous ovulation occurs in female primates that are not pair bonded (p. 142-46). Combined with an appetite for sexual activity, this may have led females to mate with several males that subsequently would show solicitude toward offspring. Blaffer Hrdy writes: "By pushing a father toward the conservative edge of the margin of error that surrounds paternity, a female may forestall direct male interference in her offspring's survival" (p. 153).

Some observers doubt that human females have the interest or ability to be active and promiscuous in the expression of sexuality. By contrast, Blaffer Hrdy cites the work of Sherfey (1973), which indicates a widespread contemporary view of female sexuality as dangerous and in need of strict controls; the implication is that females would be sexually active if they were not controlled. (Note that the term "promiscuous" in animal studies indicates the absence of pair bonding, not continuous or uncontrolled sex; even in species in which females have sexual contact with a number of males, there is female discrimination.) Sociobiologists have frequently assumed that when males provide a measure of parental care, they are likely to desert the female if she mates promiscuously. Yet the structure of multimale primate societies encourages both sexes to do so.

I believe no one can state with certainty what the mating system of the early hominids was. However, the mammalian and primate heritage, the preliminary evidence for sexual dimorphism, and the nature of human sexuality all suggest polygynous (and promiscuous) mating within a multimale society in the Australopithecine stage. The emergence of hunting and the appearance of *Homo erectus* about 1.5 million years ago changed the economics of subsistence and brought about social conditions that were much more similar to those known in our own species.

RECENT MALES AND FEMALES

Because hunting facilitated increased male parental invesment, evidence for its antiquity provides insights into relations between the sexes. Although the human lineage is at least 4 million years old, there is little evidence for extensive hunting before 1.5 million years ago. Dental adaptations and tools associated with hunting and meat eating appeared gradually (Brace and Montagu 1977; Brace 1979; Wolpoff 1980), with a few of the earliest sites dated at approximately 2.0 million (Isaac 1978) and 2.5 to 2.7 million (Lewin 1981) years. Isaac (1978, p. 102) interprets early bone accumulations as evidence for base camps where females waited to exchange their gathered food for male-scavenged meat, but the assumption that Australopithecine males spent their time scavenging-hunting and depended on females for gathered food seems improbable. Rather, this pattern occurs in contemporary foragers in which part of the woman's role involves preparation and cooking of gathered and hunted food – practices that appear relatively late in the human record.

Scenarios of early hunting usually picture large animals that males cooperate to kill. When this happens in contemporary hunting-gatherering societies, the meat is shared, and it is easy to see why: There are no refrigerators where one person can horde it for later use! To the degree that *Homo erectus* was hunting and sharing meat, kin selection was operating, but we can not confirm parental investment directed at a few recognized offspring. Hunting and meat sharing by males may have parental implications, but as long as males work together, it does not meet the specifications of Trivers' definition (1972) of parental investment.

Zihlman and Tanner (1978) argue that the evolution of hunting was a gradual process:

Meat consumption likely increased, first, by more frequent predation of small animals. Sharp implements began to be used to dress scavenged meat and butcher large animals trapped in swamps. Eventually, hominids developed to the point of killing animals at close range with various artifacts and only much later, pursuing and killing them with specialized tools. (P. 59)

At 1.5 million years ago, we have evidence for meat eating, food carrying, food sharing, and base camps, as Shipman (1983) has shown, but fire and cooking are conspicuously absent. Without cooking technology and an elaborate division of labor, there is less reason to assume that the socioeconomic arrangement called "marriage" was present. Zihlman and Tanner (1978, p. 59) place the advanced techniques of "pursuing and killing" game with specialized tools after 500,000 B.C.

As the technology associated with subsistence became more complex, tasks associated with obtaining food multiplied. This included food preparation and cooking, food preservation, the preparation of animal skins, the production of clothing, the building of temporary or permanent shelters, and the construction of specialized tools and containers. Tools such as hammerstones for food preparation are evident from the earlier stages of human evolution (Isaac 1978; Lewin 1981), but fire for cooking was not established as a certainty until 450,000 years ago at the French site of Terra Amata (DeLumley 1975, p. 745) and approximately the same time at Chou-Kou-Tien, near Peking, China. [An earlier date for fire of 1.4 million years ago from East Africa involves burnt clay (Gowlett et al. 1981) and needs to be confirmed before its implications can be assessed.] Also at Terra Amata is evidence for temporary shelters and use of animals' skins, wood containers, and an awl, which may have been used to work leather. It seems reasonable to hypothesize the onset of the institution of marriage at approximately 500,000 B.C., since most of the crucial elements are in place by this time. However, a sample of *Homo erectus* specimens dated at 700,000 to 400,000 B.C. (Wolpoff 1980) shows physical adaptations to cultural activities ancestral to the cultural adaptations recorded for Terra Amata; these and other finds may push the date back. Regardless of the exact date, the argument remains the same: A division of labor based on cultural complexity implies an institutionalized pair bond (Gough 1975; Lancaster 1976).

The establishment of marriage escalates female competition for mates, because it represents an intensification of male parental investment. But the level of formality may vary. Howell (1979) notes that among the Dobe !Kung, "the criterion of a 'real' marriage seems to be social acceptance" (p. 228). Socioeconomic elements, such as lack of property transfer, contribute to marital informality in this group.

The distribution of food through overlapping kin networks as described by Friedl (1975) tends to diffuse the focus of male effort. This factor counteracts assumptions about the importance of nuclear families, which function in industrialized societies as isolated units valued for their consumer habits, privacy, and the "haven" they offer from the insensitive and competitive marketplace (Ehrenreich and English 1978). This contemporary emphasis overlooks the importance of kin networks that support the stability of the marriage alliance in foraging and nonstate societies. As Friedl (1975) has commented:

> Marriage enlarges the network of kin from whom food can be received and to whom it will be distributed. Marriage reduces the risk of starvation for any one individual. In this sense, marriage is a system of recruiting the labor of men and women outside the nuclear family in a society in which other forms of recruitment, such as slavery, serfdom, or wage labor, are not possible. (P. 20)

In such societies, extended kin networks are as important to survival as nuclear families. Here the human pair bond does not seek isolation for stability; rather, stability depends upon connections with large supportive structures. Thus, the emergence of the pair bond-marriage in itself did not lead to the high levels of female isolation and dependency that have been documented for industrial-based families today (Ehrenreich and English 1978). In order to produce the modern levels of competition among females, marriage and focusing had to be combined with the exclusion of females from subsistence activities, female dependency on male-provisioned resources, variation in male ability to provide these resources, and limited opportunities for females to find mates (Hamilton 1984). Yet these features have occurred only in some of the agricultural societies that developed in the last 10,000 years. Carol Ember (1983) relates female exclusion and dependence to intensive agricultural systems that involve plowing and irrigation, arguing that these traits result from increased domestic work along with greater fertility, which introduces female isolation. Because of the dependence, monogamy is the norm. The agricultural transition is also associated with the development of economically based social classes, differences that are most pronounced in intensive agricultural or industrial societies. A class system affects mating patterns by increasing male variation in the ability to provide parental investment.

Although societies have been known where adult males outnumbered adult females, females 19 years and older have outnumbered males in Western societies for approximately 1,000 years (Herlihy 1978). Thus, in the twentieth century, we have monogamous marriage, female isolation (and in some classes little female participation in the workforce), low wages for women in the workforce, enormous variation in male ability to provide resources, and fewer males than females for mates. It is not surprising that female competition has eclipsed male competition!

Biologically, this is a bizarre situation. In spite of all of the cultural and physical changes that have occurred over the course of human evolution, females still make an enormous physical investment in reproduction. The fact that females compete despite this huge investment suggests that the male contribution to rearing young is theoretically critical to female reproductive success. Yet the human father's contribution is not "built in" like the brooding pouch of the male seahorse or the innate parental behavior of some male birds. Human males must learn parenting behavior, though in unstable eras such as our own the social process for such learning tends to break down. Thus, females are "locked in" to their reproductive costs while males are not, a difference that has produced a great deal of tension in modern sexual relationships. The "sexual revolution" has liberated women from the stigma of freedom in sexual relationships, but it has not liberated them from the biological costs of reproduction. In this light, it is ignorant as well as ludicrous for *Playboy* magazine to publish an article (Morris 1979) that ignores 1.5 million years of cultural evolution by arguing that sociobiology justifies the double standard. Our biological and cultural system rests on monogamous pairing. It requires focused economic and social investment from males and offers unreasonable risks for females involved in double-standard adventures. Examination of debates about day care, divorce laws, affirmative action, paternity leave, equal pay, and parttime or interrupted careers reveals the instability of our social structure. Whether the instability will be resolved is the crucial question, but one our highly varied primate background cannot answer.

CONCLUSION

This chapter has provided a sociobiological analysis of the evolution of mating relations between the sexes. I have criticized authors who misinterpret sociobiology by using it to justify the status quo, and also those who reject an evolutionary approach, and sociobiology, out of hand. Data on the ecological and intersex patterns of other primates were examined for clues to the human pattern. Archaeological data on early human societies provided insights on roles and mating patterns, and a brief examination of sex roles in industrial society was included.

It is hoped this analysis will help the reader to relate contemporary upheavals in intersex behavior to our sexual heritage, and to appreciate contemporary efforts by women to recover the flexibility enjoyed by our earlier ancestors. We cannot return to the days of the hunter-gatherer society, but we can seek humane solutions that provide the nurturance and social support – for and by both sexes – that our evolutionary history suggests was once a key adaptation.

REFERENCES

Alexander, R. D., and K. M. Noonan. 1979. "Concealment of Ovulation, Parental Care, and Human Social Evolution." In *Evolutionary Biology and Human Social Behavior*, edited by N. A. Chagnon and W. Irons, pp. 436-53. North Scituate, MA: Duxbury Press.

Altmann, J. 1980. *Baboon Mothers and Infants*. Cambridge, MA: Harvard University Press.

Altmann, S. A., and J. Altmann. 1970. *Baboon Ecology*. Chicago: University of Chicago Press.

Barash, D. P. 1977. *Sociobiology and Behavior*. New York: Elsevier.

Bateson, P., ed. 1983. *Mate Choice*. Cambridge: Cambridge University Press.

Beach, F. A. 1978. "Human Sexuality and Evolution." In *Human Evolution: Biosocial Perspectives*, edited by S. L. Washburn and E. R. McCown, pp. 123-53. Menlo Park, CA: Benjamin Cummings.

Beatty, H. 1951. "A Note on the Behavior of the Chimpanzee." *Journal of Mammalogy*, 32:118.

Blaffer Hrdy, S. 1981. *The Woman That Never Evolved* . Cambridge, MA: Harvard University Press.

Boaz, N. T., and J. Hampel. 1978. "Strontium Content of Fossil Tooth Enamel and Diet in Early Hominids." *Journal of Paleontology*, 52:928-33.

Bonnefille, R. 1976. "Palynological Evidence for an Important Change in the Vegetation of the Omo Basin between 2.5 and 2 Million Years." In *Earliest Man and Environments in the Lake Rudolf Basin*, edited by Y. Coppens, F. C.

Howell, G. L. Isaac, and R. E. F. Leakey, pp. 421-31. Chicago: University of Chicago Press.

Brace, C. L. 1979. "Biological Parameters and Pleistocene Hominid Lifeways." In *Primate Ecology and Human Origins*, edited by I. S. Bernstein and E. O. Smith, pp. 391-438. New York: Garland.

Brace, C. L., and M. F. A. Montagu. 1977. *Man's Evolution. An Introduction to Physical Anthropology*, 2nd ed. New York: Macmillan.

Busse, C., and W. J. Hamilton. 1981. "Infant Carrying by Male Chacma Baboons." *Science*, 212:1281-83.

Bygott, J. D. 1979. "Agonistic Behavior, Dominance, and Social Structure in Wild Chimpanzees of the Gombe National Park." In *The Great Apes,* edited by D. A. Hamburg and E. R. McCown, pp. 405-27. Menlo Park, CA: Benjamin Cummings.

Campbell, B. G. 1970. *Human Evolution, An Introduction to Man's Adaptations.* Chicago: Aldine.

Carr, C. J. 1976. "Plant Ecological Variation and Pattern in the Lower Omo Basin." In *Earliest Man and Environments in the Lake Rudolf Basin*, edited by Y. Coppens, F. C. Howell, G. L. Isaac, and R. E. F. Leakey, pp. 432-67. Chicago: University of Chicago Press.

Cavalli-Sforza, L. L., and W. F. Bodmer. 1971. *The Genetics of Human Populations.* San Francisco: W. H. Freeman.

Chagnon, N., and W. Irons, eds. 1978. *Evolutionary Biology and Human Social Behavior.* North Scituate, MA: Duxbury Press.

Cheyney, D. L., and R. M. Seyfarth. 1977. "Behavior of Adult and Immature Male Baboons During Intergroup Encounters." *Nature*, 269:404-06.

____. 1983. "Nonrandom Dispersal in Free-Ranging Vervet Monkeys: Social and Genetic Consequences." *American Naturalist*, 122:392-412.

Clutton-Brock, T. H., and P. H. Harvey. 1976. "Evolutionary Rules and Primate Societies." In *Growing Points in Ethology*, edited by P. P. G. Bateson and R. A. Hinde, pp. 195-237. Cambridge: Cambridge University Press.

____. 1977. "Primate Ecology and Social Organization." *Journal of Zoology*, 183:1-39.

____. 1978. "Mammals, Resources, and Reproductive Strategies." *Nature*, 273:191-95.

Crook, J. H. 1972. "Sexual Selection in the Primates." In *Sexual Selection and the Descent of Man 1871-1971*, edited by B. Campbell, pp. 231-81. Chicago: Aldine.

Daly, M., and M. Wilson. 1978. *Sex, Evolution and Behavior.* North Scituate, MA: Duxbury Press.

DeLumley, H. 1975. "Cultural Evolution in France in Its Paleo-ecological Setting During the Middle Pleistocene." In *After the Australopithecines*, edited by K. W. Butzer and G. L. Isaac, pp. 745-808. The Hague: Mouton.

DeVore, I., and E. R. L. Hall. 1965. "Baboon Ecology." In *Primate Behavior*, edited by I. Devore, pp. 20-52. New York: Holt, Rinehart, and Winston.

Drickamer, L. C., and S. H. Vessey. 1973. "Group-Changing in Free-Ranging Rhesus Monkeys." *Primates*, 14:359-68.

Ehrenreich, B., and D. English. 1978. *For Her Own Good.* Garden City, NY: Anchor Press/Doubleday.

Eisenberg, J. E., N. A. Muckenhirn, and R. Rudran. 1972. "The Relation Between Ecology and Social Structure in Primates." *Science*, 176: 863-74.

Ember, C. R. 1983. "The Relative Decline in Women's Contribution to Agriculture with Intensification." *American Anthropologist*, 85:285-304.

Enomoto, T. 1974. "The Sexual Behavior of Japanese Monkeys." *Journal of Human Evolution*, 3:351-72.

Fisher, H. E. 1982. *The Sex Contract*. New York: William Morrow.

Fisher, R. A. 1958. *The Genetical Theory of Natural Selection* , 2nd Rev. Ed. New York: Dover.

Friedl, E. 1975. *Women and Men: An Anthropologist's View*. New York: Holt, Rinehart, and Winston.

Goodall, J., A. Bandora, E. Bergmann, C. Busse, H. Matama, E. Mpongo, A. Pierce, and D. Riss. 1979. "Intercommunity Interactions in the Chimpanzee Population of the Gombe National Park." In *The Great Apes*, edited by D. A. Hamburg and E. R. McCown, pp. 13-53. Menlo Park, CA: Benjamin Cummings.

Gordon, K. D. 1982. "A Study of Microwear on Chimpanzee Molars: Implications for Dental Microwear Analysis." *American Journal of Physical Anthropology*, 59:195-215.

Gordon, K. D., and A. C. Walker. 1983. "Playing 'Possum: A Microwear Experiment." *American Journal of Physical Anthropology*, 60:109-12.

Gough, K. 1975. "The Origin of the Family." In *Toward an Anthropology of Women*, edited by R. R. Reiter, pp. 51-76. New York: Monthly Review Press.

Gould, S. J. 1977. "Darwin's Delay." In *Ever Since Darwin*, edited by S. J. Gould, pp. 21-27. New York: W. W. Norton.

Gowlett, J. A. J., J. W. K. Harris, D. Walton, and B. A. Wood. 1981. "Early Archaeological Sites, Hominid Remains, and Traces of Fire from Chesowanja, Kenya." *Nature*, 294: 125-29.

Greenwood, P. J. 1980. "Mating Systems, Philopatry, and Dispersal in Birds and Mammals." *Animal Behavior*, 30:1140-62.

Hall, K. R. L., and I. DeVore. 1965. "Baboon Social Behavior." In *Primate Behavior*, edited by I. DeVore, pp. 53-110. New York: Holt, Rinehart, and Winston.

Hall, R. L. 1977. "Paleobiology and Systematics of Canids and Hominids." *Journal of Human Evolution*, 6:519-31.

___. 1982. "Introduction: Consequences of Sexuality." In *Sexual Dimorphism in Homo sapiens: A Question of Size*, edited by R. L. Hall, pp. 3-9. New York: Praeger.

Hall, R. L., and H. S. Sharp, eds. 1978. *Wolf and Man: Evolution in Parallel*. New York: Academic Press.

Hamilton, M. E. 1982. "Sexual Dimorphism in Skeletal Samples." In *Sexual Dimorphism in Homo sapiens: A Question of Size*, edited by R. Hall, pp. 107-63. New York: Praeger.

___. 1984. "Revising Evolutionary Narratives: A Consideration of Alternative Assumptions About Sexual Selection and Competition for Mates." *American Anthropologist*, 86:651-62.

Hamilton, W. D. 1964. "The Genetical Theory of Social Behavior, I, II." *Journal of Theoretical Biology*, 7:1-52.

Harcourt, A. H., K. S. Stewart, and D. Fossey. 1976. "Male Emigration and Female Transfer in Wild Mountain Gorilla." *Nature*, 263:226-27.

Hausfater, G. 1975. *Dominance and Reproduction*. Basel: S. Karger.

Herlihy, D. 1978. "The Natural History of Medieval Women." *Natural History*, 87:56-67.

Howell, N. 1979. *Demography of the Dobe !Kung*. New York: Academic Press.

Isaac, G. L. 1978. "The Food-Sharing Behavior of Protohuman Hominids." *Scientific American*, 238:90-108.

___. 1982. "Letter to Science." *Science*, 217:295.

Johanson, D. C., T. D. White, and Y. Coppens. 1978. "A New Species of the Genus *Australopithecus* (*Primates: Hominidae*) from the Pliocene of Eastern Africa." *Kirtlandia*, No. 28.

Johnston, T. D. 1982. "Selective Costs and Benefits in the Evolution of Learning." *Advances in the Study of Behavior*, 12:65-106.

Jolly, C. J. 1970. "The Seed Eaters: A New Model of Hominid Differentiation Based on a Baboon Analogy." *Man*, 5:5-26.

Kay, R. F., and H. H. Covert. 1983. "True Grit: A Microwear Experiment." *American Journal of Physical Anthropology*, 61:33-38.

Konner, M., and C. Worthman. 1980. "Nursing Frequency, Gonadal Function, and Birth Spacing Among !Kung Hunter-Gatherers." *Science*, 207:788-91.

Lancaster, J. B. 1976. "Sex Roles in Primate Societies." In *Sex Differences. Social and Biological Perspectives*, edited by M. S. Teitelbaum, pp. 22-61. New York: Anchor Press/Doubleday.

___. 1985. "Evolutionary Perspectives on Sex Differences in the Higher Primates." In *Gender and the Life Course*, edited by A. Rossi, pp. 3-27. Chicago: Aldine.

Leacock, E. 1978. "Women's Status in Egalitarian Society: Implications for Social Evolution." *Current Anthropology*, 19:247-75.

Lewin, R. 1981. "Ethiopian Stone Tools Are World's Oldest." *Science*, 211:806-07.

Lindburg, D., ed. 1980. *The Macaques: Studies in Ecology, Behavior, and Evolution*. New York: Van Nostrand-Reinhold.

Livingstone, F. B. 1962. "Reconstructing Man's Pliocene Pongid Ancestor." *American Anthropologist*, 64:301-05.

Lovejoy, C. O. 1981. "The Origin of Man." *Science*, 211:341-50.

Mann, A. E. 1975. *Paleodemographic Aspects of the South African Australopithecines*. University of Pennsylvania Publications in Anthropology, No. 1. Philadelphia: University of Pennsylvania Press.

McGinnis, P. R. 1979. "Sexual Behavior in Free-Living Chimpanzees: Consort Relationships." In *The Great Apes*, edited by D. A. Hamburg and E. R. McCown, pp. 429-39. Menlo Park, CA: Benjamin Cummings.

Morris, D. 1967. *The Naked Ape*. New York: McGraw-Hill.

Morris, S. 1979. "Darwin and the Double Standard." *Playboy*, August 1979.

Nishida, T. 1979. "The Social Structure of Chimpanzees of the Mahale Mountains." In *The Great Apes*, edited by D. A. Hamburg and E. R. McCown, pp. 73-121. Menlo Park, CA: Benjamin Cummings.

Packer, C. 1980. "Male Care and Exploitation of Infants in *Papio anubis*." *Animal Behavior*, 28:512-20.

Peters, C. R. 1982. "Electron-Optical Microscopic Study of Incipient Dental Microdamage from Experimental Seed and Bone Crushing." *American Journal of Physical Anthropology*, 57:283-301.

Pfeiffer, J. E. 1972. *The Emergence of Man*, 2nd ed. New York: Harper and Row.

Pilbeam, D. 1972. *The Ascent of Man*. New York: Macmillan.

Popp, J. L., and I. DeVore. 1979. "Aggressive Competition and Social Dominance Theory: Synopsis." In *The Great Apes*, edited by D. A. Hamburg and E. R. McCown, pp. 317-38. Menlo Park, CA: Benjamin Cummings.

Pusey, A. 1979. "Intercommunity Transfer of Chimpanzees in Gombe National Park." In *The Great Apes* , edited by D. A. Hamburg and E. R. McCown, pp. 465-79. Menlo Park, CA: Benjamin Cummings.

Rahm, U. 1972. "L'emploie d'outils par les chimpanzees de l'ouest de la Cote-d'Ivoire." *Terre et Vie*, 25:506-09.

Sahlins, M. D. 1976. *The Use and Abuse of Biology. An Anthropological Critique of Sociobiology*. Ann Arbor: University of Michigan Press.

Schaik, C. P. van, and J. A. R. A. M. van Hooff. 1983. "On the Ultimate Causes of Primate Social Systems." *Behavior*, 85:91-117.

Schoeninger, M. J. 1982. "Diet and the Evolution of Modern Human Form in the Middle East." *American Journal of Physical Anthropology*, 58:37-52.

Schoeninger, M. J., M. J. Deniro, and H. Tauber. 1983. "$^{15}N/^{14}N$ Ratios of Bone Collagen Reflect Marine and Terrestrial Components of Prehistoric Human Diet." *American Journal of Physical Anthropology*, 60:252.

Shepher, J. 1978. "Reflections on the Origin of the Human Pair Bond." *Journal of Social and Biological Structures*, 1:253-64.

Sherfy, M. J. 1973. *The Nature and Evolution of Female Sexuality*. New York: Vintage Books.

Shipman, P. L. 1983. "Early Hominid Lifestyle: Hunting and Gathering or Foraging and Scavenging?" *American Journal of Physical Anthropology*, 60:253.

Stini, W. A. 1982. "Sexual Dimorphism and Nutrient Reserves." In *Sexual Dimorphism in Homo sapiens: A Question of Size* , edited by R. L. Hall, pp. 391-419. New York: Praeger.

Struhsaker, T. T., and P. Hunkeler. 1971. "Evidence of Tool-Using by Chimpanzees in the Ivory Coast." *Folia Primatologia*, 25:212-19.

Taub, D. 1980. "Female Choice and Mating Strategies Among Wild Barbary Macaques (*Macaca sylvanus* L.)." In T*he Macaques: Studies in Ecology, Behavior, and Evolution*, edited by D. Lindburg, pp. 287-345. New York: Van Nostrand-Reinhold.

Teleki, G. 1973. *The Predatory Behavior of Wild Chimpanzees*. Lewisburg, PA: Bucknell University Press.

___. 1974. "Chimpanzee Subsistence Technology: Materials and Skills." *Journal of Human Evolution*, 3:575-94.

Tiger, L., and R. Fox. 1974. *The Imperial Animal*. New York: Dell.

Time Magazine. 1977. "Why You Do What You Do." *Time*, August 1, 1977, pp. 54-63.

Trivers, R. L. 1972. "Parental Investment and Sexual Selection." In *Sexual Selection and the Descent of Man 1871-1971*, edited by B. Campbell, pp. 136-79. Chicago: Aldine.

Tutin, C. E. G. 1979. "Mating Patterns and Reproductive Strategies in a Community of Wild Chimpanzees (*Pan troglodytes schweinfurthii*)." *Behavioral Ecology and Sociobiology*, 6:29-38.

Van den Berghe, R. P., and D. P. Barash. 1977. "Inclusive Fitness and Human Family Structure." *American Anthropolgist*, 79:809-23.

Washburn, S. L. 1978. "Human Behavior and the Behavior of Other Animals." *American Psychologist*, 33:405-18.

Washburn, S. L., and I. DeVore. 1961. "The Social Life of Baboons." *Scientific American*, 204:62-71.

Wilson, E. O. 1975. *Sociobiology: The New Synthesis* . Cambridge, MA: Harvard University Press.

Winterhalder, B. 1981. "Hominid Paleoecology and Competitive Exclusion: Limits to Similarity, Niche Differentiation and the Effects of Cultural Behavior." *Yearbook of Physical Anthropology*, 24:101-21.

Wolpoff, M. H. 1980. *Paleoanthropology*. New York: Alfred A. Knopf.

World Health Organization. 1965. Nutrition in Pregnancy and Lactation. W.H.O. Technical Report Series No. 302, Geneva.

___. 1973. *Energy and Protein Requirements*. W.H.O. Technical Report Series No. 522. F.A.O. Nutrition Meetings Report Series No. 52, Rome.

Wrangham, R. W. 1979a. "On the Evolution of Ape Social Systems." *Social Science Information*, 18:335-68.

___. 1979b. "Sex Differences in Chimpanzee Dispersion." In *The Great Apes*, edited by D. A. Hamburg and E. R. McCown, pp. 481-89. Menlo Park, CA: Benjamin Cummings.

Young, J. Z. 1971. *An Introduction to the Study of Man.* London: Oxford University Press.

Zihlman, A., and N. Tanner. 1978. "Gathering and the Hominid Adaptation." In *Female Hierarchies*, edited by L. Tiger and M. Fowler, pp. 53-62. Chicago: Aldine.

4

SENSORIMOTOR BIASES IN COGNITIVE DEVELOPMENT

Diane McGuinness

When a chimpanzee goes fishing for termites, she first finds a slender twig, strips its leaves, makes her way to the termite nest, and plunges the twig into the opening of the nest. Then, slowly and gently, she withdraws the stick and devours the clinging insects.

This behavior encompasses all of the ingredients of a cognitive operation. First, the chimpanzee must be able to discriminate between termite nests and other similar-looking objects (perceptual discrimination). Second, she must observe that termites will climb up sticks (inference). Third, she must devise a means of using the natural behavior of termites toward her desired goal (insight). She does this by constructing a tool (invention). Finally, she is able to transmit this learned behavior to her offspring through the mechanism of imitation (communication). Thus, the great apes are capable of quite complex problem-solving behavior; cognition is not unique to human beings.

Cognition can be considered to be problem-solving behavior that is not part of the inherent repertoire of the species, and that requires "cogitation" and invention. This means that language, a species-specific aptitude of *Homo sapiens*, is not necessarily a cognitive process. It is a device or a tool that can be used cognitively, that is, to achieve a desired purpose such as effecting a change in the world or interpreting other people's feelings and desires.

This leads to a first principle of the nature of sex differences: The sexes do not differ in overall cognitive ability. They differ only in the choice of "tools" they employ to solve problems and in the type of problems they choose to solve.

This chapter is about sex differences in the nature of these choices. The most characteristic differences relate to perceptual and motor abilities and to what boys and girls choose to learn about their environment. Though biases in aptitude and interest exist from birth, both the environment and social factors shape development, for biological biases are not immutable. However, one of the functions of the brain is to sift out, from all the signals impinging on the senses, those events that are most useful. If males and females have different predispositions, they will pay attention to different events (see Chapter 2).

Because sex differences research is in its infancy, one is faced with a tantalizing conglomeration of research reports that have to be systematized. This procedure is identical to constructing a jigsaw puzzle with no prior knowledge of the picture on the cover of the box. For those who like to be secure about their knowledge of the world, sex differences research is an anathema; for those who are challenged by ambiguity and can suspend the need for certainty, it is fascinating. Before the evidence on behavioral differences is reviewed, several assumptions and pitfalls in interpreting this research must be pinpointed. The social sciences must rely heavily on statistical analyses. This is because it is impossible to impose rigorous experimental constraints on human beings. A statistical test provides a means to reach an approximation to a totally controlled experiment, and also compensates for small populations. Statistics are extremely important, but it must be remembered that each study is only an approximation to the truth.

For this reason, I have emphasized throughout this chapter the notion of a data set, a body of experimental results taken as a whole. It is important that the data set have a common frame of reference, or address the same level of performance. For example, it has been stated in a large review of the sex differences literature that there are no sex differences in "vision." This was concluded after the authors had assembled a list of all experiments remotely related to vision, and found that in some the males were more sensitive, in others the females, and in still others no sex differences emerged. Therefore, the authors concluded that the results largely canceled out. This conclusion ignores the fact that vision is an immensely complex set of processes, and there are sex differences in some of these processes but not in others. The problem, then, is one of comparing equivalent studies in a data set.

A related problem is the statistical process itself. In the sex differences literature, there are two difficulties in establishing the meaning of a statistically significant result. One is the common problem of statistical power, which relates directly to how many subjects participated in the experiments. Behavior scientists have established a set of arbitrary criteria of probability values based upon small sample sizes. Most psychologists, for example, work with groups of 20 to 50 individuals, and the cutoff point to establish a result that is significantly different from chance has been set at 5 percent. This means that if an experiment is carried out 100 times, the same result will occur purely by chance only 5 times out of that 100.

When this 5 percent cutoff is applied to large samples, such as an entire school district, a "statistically significant" result can emerge that might be quite meaningless in terms of the practical importance of the effect. For instance, in a longitudinal study by Ross and Simpson (1971) in Great Britain carried out on every child born during 1 week in 1946, "highly significant" sex differences were reported on a number of cognitive tests. However, the average scores for the boys and girls in this sample of over 4,000 children differed by only a few points out of a possible 100.

A second difficulty posed by statistics concerns distribution of the various scores. It is quite usual that the distributions for males and females are dissimilar. They exhibit what statisticians call "skew," shown in Figure 4.1. In this example, students performing poorly on a test are more often male, but the sexes are identical in the middle and upper ranges, a pattern seen often in research on reading in young children. In mathematics, the evidence is for the opposite case, with the sexes looking very similar at the low and middle portion of the curve, but with the males overrepresented at the high end.

Almost without exception, psychologists do not publish an account of the distribution of their results, reporting only average scores and the probabilities of the difference being due to chance. Probability values are important especially if they represent a very robust effect, but it is also important to consider whether the sex differences make a difference in the real world. If, as is indicated by the evidence, boys outnumber girls in remedial reading populations by three to one, then this is a difference that makes a difference.

In the first part of the chapter, I have set out the data from three categories of research findings: sex differences in interest between objects and persons; research findings on sex differences in auditory and visual sensory processing; and studies reporting sex differences in motor skills. In the second part, evidence on sex differences in cognitive tasks is presented.

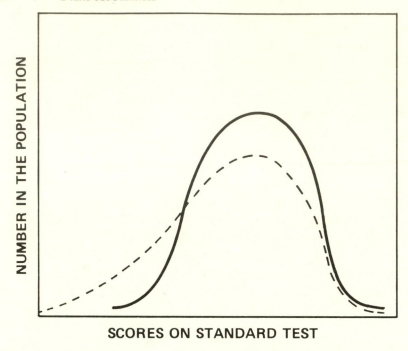

SCORES ON STANDARD TEST

Figure 4.1. Hypothetical curves showing one population with a "normal" and one with a skewed distribution.

THE OBJECT-PERSON DIMENSION

One day I was sitting beside a hotel swimming pool watching a group of about eight children playing in the water, the sons and daughters of several families vacationing together. About half an hour into their game of tag, one of the parents appeared with an infant in her arms. At once all of the girls abandoned the game and leapt out of the pool, leaving the boys in the water.

This anecdote highlights one of the most intriguing differences between the sexes: Females are more attracted to people and males to the world of objects. But is this behavior a result of social conditioning or of some inherent predisposition of females to be responsive to people? In this section, we will look at situations in which this object-person dichotomy can be demonstrated, first reviewing the results from experiments on nonhuman primates.

Nonhuman Primates

Female mammals give birth to offspring and provide initial nourishment and care. Studies on humans and other animals have shown that the mother is hormonally primed at birth to bond to her infant. The mechanism appears to be the enormously elevated levels of female sex hormones that are found shortly after parturition. Should this releasing mechanism be thwarted (as it regularly is in most hospitals), then a second mechanism goes into operation, though this process takes considerably longer. Here, proximity to an infant produces bonding. Maternal behavior can be induced even in the lowly rat by placing a rat pup in a cage with a nonlactating female.

In many primate species, when an infant is born in the wild, both sexes become excited by the event. In general, the mother will not permit the infant to be held by anyone until she feels it is safe. During this period, juvenile females make repeated attempts to steal infants, sometimes successfully, and a mother often has to resort to cunning to retrieve her infant. Lancaster (1979) has described the behavior of the vervet monkey:

> The small black infant acts as a magnet to a juvenile female regardless of her age and social position. It is common to see each new mother acquire an entourage who follow her about during the day waiting for a chance to touch the infant. Even older infant females which are only 9 months old and not yet weaned themselves show greater interest in newborns. No male of any age was seen to direct any maternal behavior such as hugging, carrying, or grooming toward a newborn infant. (P. 167)

This conclusion drawn from a study on the vervet monkey is generalizable to other nonhuman primates that live in social groups, with the possible exception of two species of baboon. Experimental studies on rhesus monkeys, carried out by Harry and Margaret Harlow in Wisconsin (Harlow et al. 1969), showed that when the infants were reared in isolation, all forms of social behavior, including mothering, were grossly maladaptive. Isolate-reared mothers were often brutal and maimed their first infant, though their behavior became more normal with the secondborn.

Armed with this and similar evidence, some psychologists have argued that all social behavior is learned. But the social deprivation studies cannot explain the spontaneous emission of interest expressed by females and not by males in the wild. What these studies indicate is that there is a special type of interaction between biology and the environment. A relationship exists between a biological predisposition and the opportunity to act on it. Without a period during which a female can observe caretaking behaviors, she may not display them spontaneously at a later period when they are needed. On the other hand, males without this biological predisposition need much more experience and training.

In a series of studies on the rhesus monkey carried out in the laboratory by Mitchell (1979), juvenile females were more likely to respond with nurturing behavior when they were placed in cages with infants. The males, by contrast, treated their charges to hostility and abuse. Vocalizations signaling desire for contact were observed exclusively between the female pairs.

Brandt and Mitchell (1973) had this to say about the behavior of juvenile females housed with isolate-reared infants: "It was the authors' subjective impression (and is quite noticeable on our films) that the female preadolescents in particular were therapeutic for the isolate infants" (p. 227). They found the adult males ignored or abused their charges; however, after a while, the male caretakers began to form strong attachments. On separation, the adult males reacted violently, often resorting to self-inflicted wounds. Similar but less violent distress was displayed on the part of the infant. Brandt and Mitchell noted that in male-infant bonding, dependency may increase over time, in contrast to the female-infant relationship, where the infant is gradually encouraged to be independent. Nevertheless, the social behavior of the male-reared infant was completely normal, and they concluded that there is a "surprising potential for behavioral change in the primate."

Taken as a whole, the data on the nonhuman primate indicate that though there is little biological predisposition for male caretaking of infants, males can learn to be nurturant. Females, on the other hand, require normal exposure to infants for them to begin to learn variations on an inborn theme.

The Human Primate

Cross-cultural studies in humans support these conclusions. Unlike most nonhuman primate species, human males carry out an important parental role. However, the capacity for parenting appears to be strongly influenced by environmental factors. For example, P. Berman (personal communication) notes a relationship between the human male's tendency to be nurturant and the number of siblings in his family, but no such relationship has been demonstrated for girls. West and Konner (1976) report that male nurturance in several traditional societies is related to the amount of time spent in warfare or in hunting or work-related activities, polygyny, and the degree of male-female intimacy. Female nurturance is unaffected by these factors.

Studies in our own culture indicate that empathy develops earlier in girls and is consistently higher at all ages. The definition of empathy used by Hoffman (1977) in his review of these studies is "a vicarious response to affect"; it does not mean sympathy, nor an intellectual interpretation of what another is feeling. Rather, it is feeling "as if" you were that other person. This capacity develops into an ability to take the other's perspective, to do for that person what would be appropriate for their needs, a sort of higher-order "Golden Rule."

These sex differences, which have been reported for children and adults of various ages, might be attributable to biological as well as social factors. If there is an inherent capacity in females to be more socially responsive, then differences might appear very early. How might this be investigated? In an ingenious set of experiments, Fagan (1972) tested infants aged 4 to 6 months on their ability to recognize faces represented by three-dimensional masks, photographs, and line drawings, by recording the amount of visual fixation on each of a pair of images. After the infant sees a series of the same pair over and over again, the infant's fixation begins to decline, a process called "habituation." After a time, Fagan changed one member of the pair and recorded shifts of attention. If the child looked at the new item, this indicated that he/she noticed the difference.

At 4 months of age, neither males nor females shifted their gaze to new items, though both sexes noticed the difference between an upright and an inverted photograph. Between 5 and 6 months, however, both males and females discriminated between the masks, but only females showed differential responses to the photographs. Further, females discriminated between photographs of two people who were highly similar in appearance. In a control study, Fagan could find no difference between the sexes in visual function, thus ruling out effects due to over-all developmental differences.

Other studies on very young infants show that females distinguish between realistic and unrealistic faces earlier than males, and they give highly appropriate social responses to faces. Females smile and vocalize only to faces, whereas males are just as likely to smile and vocalize to inanimate objects and blinking lights (Lewis et al. 1966; McCall and Kagan 1967; Lewis 1969).

The sociability of females continues in early childhood. Jacklin and Maccoby (1978) studied pairs of toddlers aged 33 months dressed in look-alike dungarees in a laboratory playroom. The highest levels of positive social behavior were exhibited by the girl-girl pairs and the least in the mixed-sex pairs, where the girls frequently responded to the boys with fear and passive withdrawal. Girls paired with girls were also more likely to offer toys to each other than children in the other pairs.

Girls are less likely to show fear of young boys when the boys are in need of social support. McGrew (1972), working with preschool children, introduced newcomers one at a time over a period of several weeks. Girls consistently exhibited positive social behavior (empathy) to the strangers, whether they were male or female, whereas the initial response of the boys to male newcomers was indifference or rejection. The evidence is consistent in demonstrating that females are more interested in social events, more adept at interpreting them, and more effective in nurturing or caretaking roles. If this is the case, what interests males?

From very early ages, males are attracted to nonsocial stimuli, especially if it is three dimensional or visually interesting. In several studies using a similar methodology to the habituation experiment of Fagan, infant males showed more interest and better discrimination of nonsocial stimuli (Kagan and Lewis 1965; Meyers and Cantor 1967; McCall and Kagan 1970; Pancratz and Cohen 1970; Cohen et al. 1971; Cornell and Strauss 1973). Also, as noted above, they directed verbal and nonverbal behavior toward people and objects alike.

Goodenough (1957) asked children aged 2 to 4 years to illustrate a story. About 45 to 60 percent of the girls included people as opposed to 11 to 18 percent of the boys. The majority of boys drew objects such as cars, trucks, and fire engines. In another experiment, children were asked to invent stories about a mosaic pattern they were shown. Girls consistently included persons (see Figure 4.2).

In a study eliciting stories from elementary school children about exciting or upsetting episodes in their lives, Feshbach and Hoffman (1978) scored the stories according to what agents or events produced various emotions. Girls were more likely than boys to attribute the source of happiness in their lives to their parents. By contrast, objects made

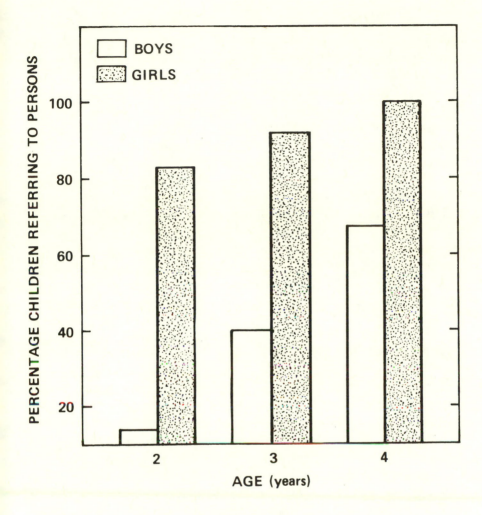

Figure 4.2. The percentage of boys' and girls' stories that contained people. The children were asked to invent a story in response to an abstract pattern. (Redrawn with permission of author and publisher from Goodenough, E. W. "Interest in persons as an aspect of sex differences in the early years." *Genetic Psychology Monographs*, 1957, 55:287-323.)

boys happy, with "possession" a close runner-up. Boys felt "proud" when they did something that made them feel competent; girls felt "proud" when they received socially sanctioned rewards such as grades or praise. Males were not immune to social factors, however, for the boys were more likely than girls to report fear during social isolation. People were important sources of comfort, more from the negative impact of their absence than the positive impact of their presence. On the other hand, girls were more likely to attribute fear to events or to the withdrawal of parental affection.

Male attraction to the world of objects has been demonstrated in one of my own experiments (McGuinness and Symonds 1977) in which college students were asked to look into a viewer at pairs of colored photographs and describe what they saw. Each pair consisted of a picture of people and a picture of a common object, for example, a wristwatch, images that were likely to be encountered equally often by both sexes. The visual field was divided so that one image was presented to one eye, and the other to the opposite eye. This produces "rivalry" between the images, hence the name of the effect: "binocular rivalry." Studies have shown that the most interesting item predominates and the brain actively suppresses the least interesting. Females reported seeing the pictures of people more often than pictures of objects, while males showed the opposite effect (Figure 4.3). Note that females were not as biased toward seeing persons as males were biased to reporting objects.

The reader who has a strong commitment to a socialization position may try to explain these findings as due to social reinforcement for appropriate sex role behavior, but a sex role theory does not seem a valid explanation for the data on social behavior in monkeys, chimpanzees, and very young infants. Those with a biological preference feel more comfortable with the fact that the data are "all of a piece"; that is, there is almost no contradiction in the findings across age, culture, and species. However, it must be noted that so far no biological mechanism has been discovered to account for these differences, that is, to show why females, even in infancy, show differential behaviors to persons and to objects whereas males do not. Post-infancy development biases males away from interest in both persons and objects toward objects. What sort of neural organization might predispose human males to become biased toward an interest in objects?

At this stage, it is wise to keep an open mind on these issues until we have better explanations than currently exist. No doubt there is a powerful interaction between biological and social factors, but apart from

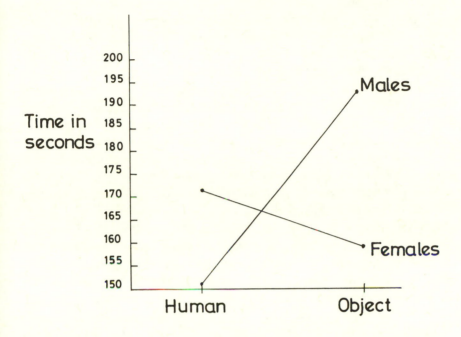

Figure 4.3. The amount of time that subjects reported seeing objects or persons when they viewed slide pairs. One slide contained a picture of objects and the other of persons. They were presented simultaneously in a divided visual field. n = 40. (Reprinted with permission from *Perception.*)

some very rudimentary data on sex differences in neural and hormonal organization, we are far from understanding how these differences influence behavior.

SENSORY TOOLS

The distinction between males and females in their attention toward objects and persons is one set of facts considered in this section. One might ask: Are these sex differences the "ground" upon which all else becomes manifest; that is, are they in some way causing other differences? Or, is the object-person dichotomy just one of many sex differences found in sensory, motor, and cognitive realms? Taken as a whole, do they represent a higher-order process, such as selection pressures for efficient child care and territorial behavior?

Evidence will be presented to show that females are more attentive and discriminating in certain auditory tasks. Does this have something to do with paying attention to people, who speak, or does their auditory facility produce their interest in people? Conversely, do attention to people and sensitivity to sound (especially speech), reflect a deeper process, perhaps one related to maintaining the young?

One can be tempted to answer these questions prematurely. While they should not be disregarded, there is a danger in seeing relationships where none may exist. One danger is the evolutionary trap, in which each new finding is attributed to natural selection. Take, for instance, the fact that females are more sensitive to the volume of sound and have better sound localization. It could be argued that this is important for survival because it might allow a mother to locate her wandering infant. But suppose instead you were told that males had better sound localization. Immediately an explanation springs to mind: Males have been selected for hunting and need to localize their prey!

The Auditory System

Sensory systems function much the same, but are distinguished in responding to different forms of energy: electromagnetic energy for the eye and mechanical energy for the ear and skin. The responses of brain cells to patterns of energy are activated by only three properties of the signal to which they are sensitive: frequency, amplitude, and phase. These dimensions, singly and in combination, give rise to qualitatively different forms of subjective experience.

In the auditory system, changes in the frequency or wavelength of mechanical energy create changes in pitch. Variations in amplitude are perceived as changes in volume or loudness. The interaction between combinations of frequencies produces signals that are either in or out of tune. Simple harmonic relationships in musical performance produce consonance, whereas complex harmonic relationships are heard as noise or dissonance. Changes in amplitude and phase help us localize sounds in space. Finally, in speech perception, the complex ratios of frequencies produced by the voice create each individual's characteristic timbre or voice quality, while phase relationships determine the characteristic sounds of words and syllables.

Training can increase efficiency in processing certain of these parameters and not others. For instance, musical training improves pitch discrimination, but attempts to train subjects to detect sounds of very low volume (threshold tests) have proved unsuccessful. These results contribute to our understanding of the impact of the environment on biological function, and are also highly relevant in the study of sex differences.

Amplitude

In studies investigating sensitivity to amplitude (loudness), subjects can be asked to respond in one of three ways: detect the smallest amplitude levels across a range of frequencies (threshold); set subjective levels of loudness comfort; discriminate between differences in loudness.

The response of the human ear at threshold to a variety of frequencies is a U-shaped function with a maximal sensitivity at about 1,000 cycles per second (Hertz). This is approximately "high C" on the piano. On either side of this frequency, sensitivity falls off, and hearing becomes impossible below about 20 and above 20,000 Hertz. When the sexes are compared, females show a greater sensitivity at threshold for sounds above 4,000 Hertz, and their sensitivity relative to males improves with higher frequencies. These effects become more pronounced with age, and women suffer much less hearing loss than men (Corso 1959; Eagles et al. 1963; Hull et al. 1971; McGuinness 1972; McCoy 1978), results that are independent of environmental factors. Corso (1959) studied 500 males and females, aged 18 to 49 years, who had been screened for a history of proximity to noisy environments and for auditory problems. Females were found to have lower thresholds above 3,000 Hertz. Evidence from psychophysics shows that high-frequency sensitivity is important in sound localization, and studies on speech perception show that these upper frequencies are important in discriminating between people's voices and in the accurate perception of consonants, especially c, h, s, t, x, and z.

Tests of comfortable loudness find sex differences that are most pronounced. When 50 college students were asked to increase the volume of sound until it reached its maximum level of comfort

(McGuinness 1972), females set lower levels of volume than males for all frequencies tested. The difference between the sexes was a constant 7 to 8 decibels across the entire frequency range (see Figure 4.4). Previous research has shown that when subjects are asked to set the volume of sound to levels that are "twice as loud" or "half as loud," the subjective doubling of loudness is about 9 decibels. At levels of maximum comfort, women hear the same physical amplitude of sound as subjectively twice as loud as men.

Some have suggested that this sex effect is due to social factors in which males are permitted to make loud noises and females are not. If this were the case, loudness tolerance would be expected to increase in males and diminish in females during the socialization process, for example, with age. However, Elliott in 1971 reported the identical difference in comfortable loudness levels as those in my experiment (McGuinness 1972) for schoolchildren at both 5 to 6 years and 10 to 11

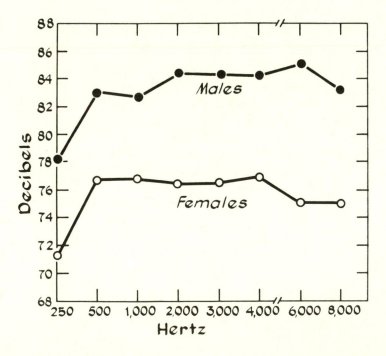

Figure 4.4. The levels of comfort set by male and female college students to a series of pure tone frequencies. n = 50. (Reprinted with permission from *Perception.*)

years of age. In an experiment on comfortable loudness levels using three types of rock music, college males preferred to set the volume at an average of 84 decibels, whereas females set the volume at 73 decibels (D. G. Hays and J. A. Lienau, personal communication). These values, produced by U.S. college students, were nearly the same as the values obtained in my own study on English college students (McGuinness 1972). Because this effect is pronounced and consistent across age and culture, there is a plausible case for a biological predisposition in males and females to show differential sensitivity to the volume of sound.

In the third category of loudness measure, subjects are tested on their ability to discriminate between changes in volume between one sound and another. The greater sensitivity found in females ought to predict better discrimination, and this is exactly what has been found. Three separate experiments indicate that this discrimination capacity is found across all ages. Zaner et al. (1968) tested 50 schoolchildren aged 4 to 8 years, asking them to listen to a series of sounds and detect when a change appeared in duration (short and long), loudness, and pitch. The girls were much more accurate at detecting changes in loudness, while boys were better in judging changes in pitch.

Pishkin and Blanchard (1964) used a similar approach in adult subjects who were asked whether the change had occurred at the left or the right ear. No sex differences were found on measures of duration or frequency, but the women were consistently more accurate in detecting changes in loudness and were also accurate in labeling the ear where the various changes had occurred. The men's performance hovered at chance with error scores at 50 percent (see Figure 4.5).

In a followup study, Pishkin and Shurley in 1965 tested 120 adults aged 25 to 50 years on a more complex version of the same type of task. Here the number of dimensions varied simultaneously, and the tasks varied in difficulty from 0 to 3 dimensions. The results are presented in Figure 4.6, where it can be seen that females were particularly adept in handling complex auditory signals.

Shuter (1968) tested 200 students at London colleges of music on the Wing battery of musical aptitude, which includes a variety of tests of musical discrimination and of memory. She then carried out a factor analysis, a statistical manipulation in which the scores from a number of tests are intercorrelated and the tests that are related grouped together in clusters called "factors." The sexes proved similar in the ways in which their abilities grouped together, except that the women had an extra factor produced by their performance on all tests of musical dynamics.

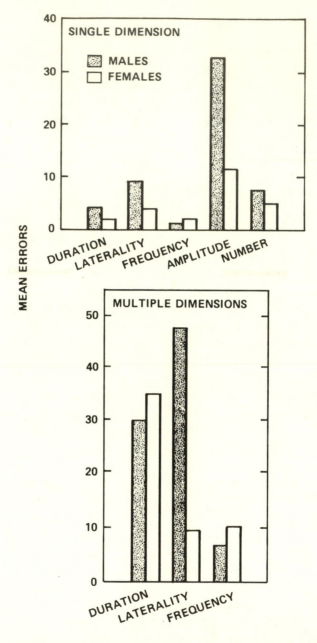

Figure 4.5. Error scores for men and women on tasks in which they had to determine whether a particular dimension of auditory input had varied. n = 134. (Reprinted with permission of the authors and publisher from Pishkin, V., and Blanchard, R. "Auditory Concept Identification." *Psychonomic Science,* 1964, 1:177-78, Figures 1 and 2.)

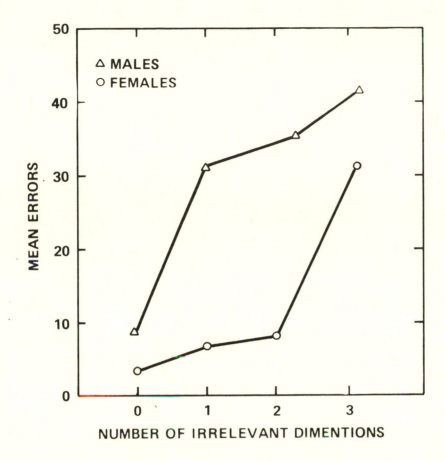

Figure 4.6. The error scores for overall performance in determining whether a particular dimension had varied in a set of complex signals changing in pitch, duration, or laterality. n = 120. (Reprinted with permission of the authors and publisher from Pishkin, V., and Shurley, J. T. "Auditory Dimensions and Irrelevant Information in Concept Identification of Males and Females." *Perceptual and Motor Skills* , 1965, 20:673-83, Figure 1.)

Dynamics refers to the changes in loudness that create an emotional reaction in the listener. Once again, this points to a female sensitivity to loudness.

Frequency

Apart from the effect found in Zaner et al.'s experiment (1968) showing boys slightly better in the discrimination of pitch, no study has shown any sex difference in this ability. Pishkin and his colleagues found no sex difference in the ability to judge whether a sound was varying in pitch. In my own experiment, cited above, the same subjects were asked to carry out extremely difficult pitch judgments between increments that varied in frequency from one-eighth to a whole tone of the musical scale. (The smallest increment on the piano keyboard is a half-tone.) The results showed that the amount of musical training had a marked effect on the student's performance, but that there were no sex differences whatsoever. This result contrasted with the threshold and loudness tests described above, where musical training had no effect on performance.

To date, no one has investigated sex differences in the perception of phase, in part because complex apparatus is required to carry out these experiments. It could be hypothesized that females would prove superior because phase shifts are important in speech production and perception, in which females have precocity.

Speech Perception

The perception of speech is a complex phenomenon because it involves discriminating between speech sounds and comprehending the meaning of words, as well as the capacity to monitor nonlinguistic cues such as inflection, voice quality, and rhythmic stress. Research in this area of sex differences is limited, but evidence points to a greater facility in females. It corresponds with results in the more numerous studies of speech production, which are reviewed in the section on motor behavior.

Mittler and Ward (1970) reported on a study of English children assessed on the Illinois Test of Psycholinguistic Abilities, which had previously been standardized on U.S. children. One hundred 4-year-old children were tested on a number of different tasks. Girls were superior in the comprehension of meaning, in auditory-vocal memory, and in applying linguistic categories to objects. Mirabile et al. (1978) tested 150 children aged 7 to 15 years on a complex discrimination task involving pairs of consonant-vowel-consonant syllables, presented to each ear. The experimenters varied the presentation time between the ears from 0 to 90 milliseconds. The girls were more accurate over all except the simultaneous condition, and their superiority increased with longer and longer lag time between the ears. The effect was strongly age dependent, suggesting that the girls were accelerated in their development of speech perception.

It often is not possible to chart these sex effects longitudinally, but an experiment by McCoy (1978) illustrates that the facility in females for speech perception is not merely the result of a developmental acceleration. McCoy tested 60 subjects over the age of 50 years, none of whom had any known hearing deficit. The men were found to perform significantly worse both on a test of speech discrimination and in a dichotic listening task in which the subject had to attend to one of two messages presented simultaneously to each ear.

As we saw earlier, the sexes do not differ in tests of pitch discrimination, nor have I found any sex difference in high school students in the perception of rhythm (unpublished data). This suggests that males are as attentive as females to the world of sound, but they might choose to attend to sounds other than speech. In a series of tests on 80 children aged 5 to 8 years, Knox and Kimura (1970) studied memory for digits and the ability to identify environmental noises and animal sounds. The sexes did not differ in digit span, but the boys were uniformly better in identifying both the environmental and animal noises. This sex effect appeared to increase with age, with the boys showing a much greater developmental acceleration than the girls.

This finding is of particular interest because it indicates that one of the popular theories concerning sex differences is wrong. This theory, called the Global Developmental Lag Theory, holds that girls are uniformly accelerated with respect to boys by as much as 2 years in every type of task. The data indicate otherwise. It is possible that girls are accelerated in some tasks, but not all, and there is currently no way to determine whether this finding is due to a biological predisposition or to use. That is, the girls might be accelerated in language because they use language for social interaction and schools teach skills related to language.

The Visual System

Although the fundamental properties of the signals that are analyzed by the visual system are the same as in audition – that is, amplitude, frequency, and phase – visual processing is considerably more complex. This is because there are several primary visual capacities, each responsive to different domains of electromagnetic energy. The major distinction is between the peripheral and central visual systems. The cells in the periphery of the retina (the rods) are more sensitive to movement and to low levels of light, whereas cells that are located centrally in the region called the "fovea" (the cones) are sensitive to color and fine detail and function only in medium to high levels of light. An additional complexity is binocular vision, which allows us to see objects in three dimensions. Sex differences have been mapped for most of these functions, and the evidence indicates that there are strong sex differences in many aspects of primary visual processing.

Amplitude

The visual system, unlike the auditory system, processes patterns of light waves dispersed over space, as well as energy that is transmitted over time. Spatial analysis requires the discrimination of differences between varying degrees of brightness or luminance in the visual field. This information is carried by the differences in amplitude of various combinations of light waves. It has only recently been discovered that cells in the visual portion of the brain cortex are sensitive to a particular width or band of these variations in luminance. This has given rise to a new term in vision, "spatial frequency," an unfortunate choice of terminology on two counts: The word "frequency" means changes over time, not space; and the term obscures the fact that the critical physical dimension is the spatial arrangement of amplitudes and not frequencies. Experiments have shown that without variations in amplitude, we would be functionally blind, even if we were bombarded with light rays.

Results from studies on men and women in different conditions of luminance indicate that females have an advantage in low-light conditions, whereas males have greater sensitivity in normal or daylight conditions. In one of my studies (McGuinness 1976), I found that females are better than males in detecting a very dim patch of light in a completely dark field. Not only this, but visual persistence (the duration of the after-image) in the dark-adapted state is longer in females, thus providing them with a double advantage. Results from experiments on the dark-adapted eye are presented in Figures 4.7 and 4.8. In industrial societies, there is little advantage to highly developed dark vision, but it must have been extremely useful before the invention of artificial light.

When light levels are increased to match our everyday experience of normal daylight conditions, males are found to be more sensitive. First, they show significantly less tolerance for bright lights, the opposite to the result on the loudness test (McGuinness 1976). Second, they are able to detect much finer differences between contrasts than females. This is called "visual acuity," most typically measured by an optician's eye chart. This sex difference has been found at most ages tested, which is down to about 5 years of age. Conversely, tests of visual acuity on older subjects show that females are more susceptible to the effects of aging than males (Roberts 1964; McGuinness 1976; McGuinness and Pribram 1978; Ross and Woodhouse 1979). However, it must be pointed out that the results on visual acuity are not robust, and usually require a large number of subjects to produce a reliable difference statistically. In other words, the degree of average difference is small.

A more striking sex difference in visual acuity appears in tests in which a target is in motion. This tests what is called "dynamic acuity." In two surveys (Burg and Hulbert 1961; Burg 1966) involving about 18,000 people, the California Department of Motor Vehicles employed two psychologists to test men and women for dynamic acuity, and to compare this to static acuity measured in the traditional way. The test required the subject to indicate which corner of a rapidly moving square contained a checkered pattern. The square was reduced in size over trials and was displaced at various speeds ranging from 20 to 180 degrees per second. Only a moderate relationship was found between static and dynamic acuity, and the men were overwhelmingly superior at each level of speed and over all ages. The men were so much more accurate that there was little overlap between the two sets of scores.

Spatial Frequency

The sexes have also been compared on static and dynamic tests of contrast threshold for "spatial frequencies" (Brabyn and McGuinness 1979). Here the subject sees a series of fuzzy gratings, or stripes, of various widths. As the amplitudes of the dark and light portions of the stripes are gradually made more and more similar, the field appears a uniform gray. The subjects are asked to determine when the stripes

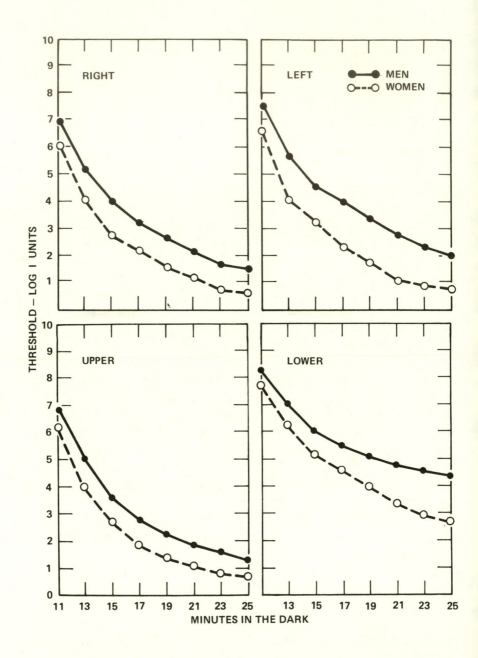

Figure 4.7. Threshold curves for men and women during dark adaptation. Measurement began after 7 minutes of initial dark adaptation. n = 50. (Reprinted with permission from *Perception.*)

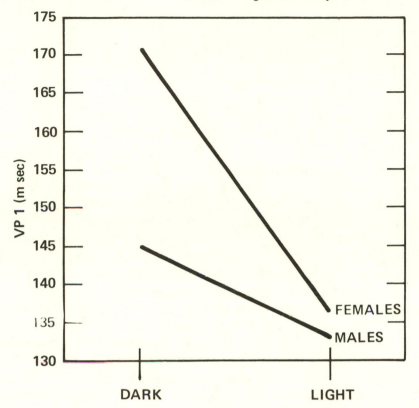

Figure 4.8. The persistence of the visual image (VP) in the dark- and light-adapted eye in men and women. n = 50. (Reprinted with permission from *Perception.*)

disappear and reappear. Our results showed that females were consistently more efficient in detecting low spatial frequencies (wide stripes), but males were more efficient in detecting high spatial frequencies (very narrow stripes). Men and women were equally efficient in tests involving the midrange frequencies, and the results were the same whether the stripes were stationary or in motion. These findings confirm what has been reported above. The detection of wide patterns (low spatial frequencies) requires sensitivity over the entire retina, especially the peripheral region, whereas the detection of very fine patterns (high spatial frequencies) is part of an acuity mechanism and requires sensitivity in the central or foveal visual system. Females appear to have an advantage in peripheral vision and males in foveal vision.

Temporal Frequency

In the visual system, changes in frequencies over time, corresponding to the wavelength of light, give rise to the perception of color. It is widely assumed that there are sex differences in color vision, yet the evidence to support this comes from a small fraction of the population who are "color blind" or have what is more accurately described as anomalous color vision. The trait is carried on the X chromosome, and since females have two X chromosomes and males only one, females have to inherit a defective X chromosome from both parents to exhibit this deficiency. (See Chapter 6 for a discussion of X-linked inheritance.) However, no sex differences have been observed in people with normal color vision. In a study on children aged 5 to 6 years, Gaines (1972) found no consistent differences between boys and girls on a series of complex color discrimination tests.

Ian Lewis and I investigated visual persistence in 50 college students in two tests using colored and noncolored stimuli (McGuinness and Lewis 1976). We screened all our subjects using the Ishihara color discrimination test, which was specifically designed to detect anomalies in color vision. Not one of our 50 subjects failed any items on this test. We did discover some rather unusual color sensitivities in our subjects, however. In one experiment, we pasted plastic diffusers over subjects' eyes and placed them in a room completely bathed in colored light. This has the effect of eliminating contours in the visual field, creating what is called a "Ganzfeld" – it produces a gradual loss of the sensation of color and a feeling of being shrouded in a gray mist. We found that men were much less likely to report a loss of color in the time limit (20 minutes), whereas all of the women did so within about 12 minutes, a result that was opposite to the persistence effect in the dark. Also, there was a striking difference in the response of women to the red and green lights. The women lost the sensation of green much more rapidly than red, whereas the men responded identically to both (see Figure 4.9).

A special sensitivity to red in the women was also found in a second experiment in which subjects were required to stare at a black pattern of a cross pasted on a bright white lamp for 2 minutes. After this, they were instructed to stare at a white wall and report their experience. This produces an after-image, which is the same sensation experienced after having your picture taken with a flash bulb. Gradually the black pattern begins to fragment and the white background turns multicolored as the color-sensitive cells recover at different rates. This effect is described as

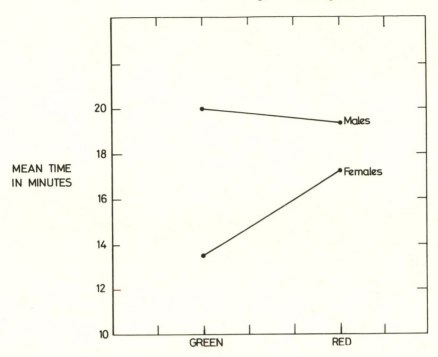

Figure 4.9. The amount of time taken to lose the experience of color during an experiment in a Ganzfeld. n = 40. (Reprinted with permission from *Perception*.)

the "flight of colors." We found that the men reported seeing the pattern of the cross for much longer than the women (longer persistence), and that 100 percent of the women, as opposed to 50 percent of the men, reported seeing colors in the red end of the spectrum. The sexes did not differ in reporting other colors. Since this experiment was carried out, Jacobs (1977) has shown that the female squirrel monkey is significantly more red sensitive than the male. The sensation of red is produced by sensitivity to long wavelengths (650 to 700 millimicrons). It appears that females have more long wave receptors than males.

Binocular Vision

All of the experiments described so far refer to monocular vision; that is, the same effects could be demonstrated with only one eye. Binocular vision, involving coordinated visual reception in two eyes, allows us to see objects in three dimensions. You can demonstrate this effect by covering one eye and walking around the room for a few minutes. Now uncover your eye and notice the sensation. Everything appears much more solid, and you have the feeling that you can see around the edges of objects. The experience of seeing in depth results from the image of the same object falling on different parts of the two retinas. This principle has been employed in stereograms, in which two identical photographs are placed side by side in such a way that the major contours are displaced; this makes two pictures appear as one three-dimensional image.

Brabyn and I (1979) carried out several experiments on binocular vision with male and female college and high school students. Sex differences appeared only in the tests of stereopsis, measured as the amount of time it took each subject to identify a figure, or figures, in depth. Males were more efficient, and results were unrelated to eye muscle control or to the ability to judge the distance of real objects in space. Rather, it seemed to reflect a high-level process called "central binocular fusion," which is carried out by the visual cortex of the brain.

Motion Perception

Motion perception is dependent upon the brain keeping track of information about the displacement of objects across the retina, information that is coded as changes in phase. As mentioned, males are able to maintain central visual fixation to a rapidly displaced target and to discriminate the fine detail on the target surface. This occurs not only because of their superior acuity, but also because of their skill in visually guided tracking, an ability that is in contrast to the peripheral motion detection system. In young infants, the earliest visual skill is the detection of movement in the peripheral visual field. As an infant develops, this sensitivity gradually increases in range until it covers over 180 degrees of visual angle. We noted that females have a more efficient peripheral visual system that provides more sensitivity in the dark, and they have greater sensitivity to low spatial frequencies.

These differences point up two fundamental properties of the visual motion system. One involves the active tracking of targets in motion, so that the center of the retina (the fovea) is continuously stimulated by the target. The second system, in which a stationary eye is stimulated by something moving in the visual field, involves only the detection of motion. From the evidence above, females would be expected to be more sensitive to movement in the peripheral visual field and more susceptible to illusions involving movement. This is exactly what was found in a study by Johansson (1955) on the effect of an illusion called "motion track enlargement." In this experiment, targets are displaced across a screen and the subject has to operate a pointer to indicate the place where a moving target disappears from the screen. Johansson found that all subjects overestimated the distance of the moving target. However, females overestimated this distance considerably more than the males. Results from these experiments may provide an explanation as to why some females might have difficulties in certain sports. This could occur because they are more sensitive to movement but are less able to track a moving target, which means that they would be more likely to overrespond to a rapidly moving object.

Currently we do not know whether these sex differences arise because of inherent differences in the organization of the visual system or because of differential use (for instance, males typically engage in more sports). However, certain of these tasks – specifically the finding that females have more efficient dark-adapted vision and that they are more sensitive than males to low spatial frequencies – are hard to explain in terms of an experiential model. Similarly, it would be hard to argue that males are socialized to avoid bright lights but to seek out noisy environments.

Conclusions on Sensory Differences

This analysis has been restricted to the auditory and visual systems, which play a predominant role in human behavior and are more likely candidates for involvement in cognitive development than sex differences in other sense modalities, such as taste, smell, and touch. Yet differences exist there; in general, the findings support the conclusion that females are more sensitive in the domains of touch and taste. Their greater tactile sensitivity may be important in performing tasks that require the participation of what is known as "the fine-motor system." Sex differences in motor performance will be considered next.

MOTOR SYSTEMS

One of the most striking sex differences in physical dimorphism is the proportion of body weight devoted to muscle (see Chapter 5). In males muscle makes up about 40 percent of the total body weight, whereas in females this value is approximately 23 percent. These figures are for the young adult, and do not apply to children; but despite the belief that girls and boys do not differ noticeably in muscle development before puberty, tests of performance indicate otherwise. The Youth Sports Institute of Michigan State University has followed 550 boys and girls from the age of 2 to 18 years. The director of this research, Vern Seefeldt, reports that boys outdistance girls in running by the age of 2.5 years (see Monagan 1983). In five of eight tests of strength, speed, and agility, boys were superior by age 7.5, and their superiority increased with age. Girls were superior on only one of the tests: muscle flexibility.

The motor system involved in whole-body movement, especially that requiring speed and force, is referred to as the "gross-motor system." This system is part of a central neural mechanism called the "extrapyramidal motor system." The second major motor system, responsible for fine-motor control, is called the "pyramidal motor system." These two systems regulate very different forms of motor activity: The gross-motor system is responsible largely for total organization of the limbs and torso, whereas the fine-motor system regulates the distal muscles, specifically fingers, toes, and tongue, and is engaged primarily in the fluency of action, or sequential motion. As might be anticipated from the discussion of primary sensory functions, females are biased toward fine-motor skills and males toward gross-motor skills.

The Gross-Motor System

Infants develop control over their bodies in two directions. First, the development proceeds from the body midline to the periphery, and second from the upper limbs to the lower. It is not known whether males have an edge on the developmental progression of the gross-motor system, that is, the control over the movement of limbs and torso. No one, for example, has reported that males walk sooner than females. But then, until Seefeldt's research, it would not have been predicted that 2-year-old boys could outrun girls.

What is known is that boys engage in a type of large-muscle play, called "rough-and-tumble play," that is uncommon in girls. The word "play" suggests that no one is seriously hurt; however, mock fighting can erupt into real aggression. Rough-and-tumble play appears around the age of 2 years, is triggered by male conspecifics, and continues throughout childhood. It has been suggested by primatologists and ethologists that since rough-and-tumble play is a universally male behavior in many species, its function is to train the individual for subsequent combat in later struggles for dominance. Certainly, it seems clear from a number of field studies that confidence in one's skill in combat stems from early experience, and confidence is a critical factor in establishing dominance.

In many nonhuman primate species, adolescent males must fight for the right to belong to a social unit. Many die in this attempt, especially in those species in which males transfer out of their natal troop. Evidence suggests that rough-and-tumble play and the subsequent greater aggressivity in human males may be a holdover from the evolutionary period in which they constituted a surplus population. Infant mortality in the wild in all species, including many traditional human cultures, is extremely high. Reproducing females are essential to species' maintenance, whereas a surfeit of males is simply a drain on resources.*

The combative and competitive nature of sports can be seen as a formalization of rough-and-tumble play. For this reason, sports tend to be a male domain, and despite the attempts to integrate the sexes on the playing field, one major concern of the boys is that they may be beaten by a girl. The Israelis reported that enemy soldiers refused to surrender to Israeli women officers. In other words, real or ritual combat is seen as the province of males. Females not only are irrelevant, but they get in the way; furthermore, if a man cannot beat a woman, who is anatomically the weaker sex, this casts considerable doubt on his masculinity. In biological terms, male dominance stands for survival: Nondominant males may not survive. This might promote a strong psychological dimension, including a sensitization to and a fear of any threat to status.

---

*Over the last 4,000 years, this problem has reversed because we have become too efficient in maintaining life. As Harris (1974) has pointed out, warfare, rather than reducing the population, actually increases it, because the females increase their reproductive efforts. The logical solution, given the exploding population, would be to send women into battle and leave the men at home. The problem is that this solution is contrary to our biological heritage. Not only this, but warfare has come to be seen as an irrational solution to the problem of overpopulation, especially in view of the destructive capabilities of nuclear weapons.

The Fine-Motor System

The pyramidal motor system, which regulates skilled action especially of the distal musculature, is a distinct neural system in the brain. One of the primary aspects of this system is the capacity for fluent sequential movement. This typically refers to the action of the fine muscles, especially the fingers and tongue, but this system may also regulate whole-body sequential action, including activities such as dancing and gymnastics. For ethical reasons, neurophysiological experiments are restricted to the behavioral repertoire of subhuman species. This rules out any possibility for a direct understanding of the motor systems involved in complex human behavior such as piano playing, singing, speaking, and dancing. Indirect evidence is available from brain-damaged patients in which the precise involvement of specific neural pathways can never be determined.

In one of the most enlightening experiments carried out on brain-damaged patients, Kimura (1977) investigated men and women who had lesions of either the right or the left hemisphere. In the left hemisphere-damaged group, the patients exhibited varying degrees of aphasia, or deficits in receptive and productive language. Kimura taught these patients a number of simple motor tasks, such as opening a latch. When the patients had learned each task to a predetermined degree of efficiency, she then asked the subjects to carry out all of them in a fixed order. Her original hypothesis was that the patients with aphasia would fail to remember the sequence. Instead, she found that the aphasic patients were deficient in fluent action. They hesitated, and persevered, repeating the same action many times, but carried out the sequence perfectly. Furthermore, the inefficiency of the behaviors correlated with the degree of aphasia, being much less common in patients with only minimal language deficits. Equally important, it did not seem to matter whether the patients had lost speech or receptive language skills – a deficiency in sequential fluency was found in either case.

Kimura concluded that the left hemisphere of the brain is more involved than is the right in developing skilled performance, especially that requiring fluent sequential action. Using normal subjects, Lomas and Kimura (1976) found that speaking interfered dramatically with finger tapping involving sequences, especially of the right hand, but had little effect on tapping speed using one finger. This is the same problem encountered in attempting to talk while playing the piano. Unlike the extrapyramidal system, the pyramidal system is a late phylogenetic development that is absent entirely in lower vertebrates and even in some species of higher vertebrates. Lomas and Kimura's results might indicate that in humans, at least, the cortical control over this system has shifted to the left hemisphere.

Earlier the findings on sex differences in the perception of speech were discussed, where females were found to be better temporal processors than males and had a more accurate memory for sequences of speech sounds. Shortly, I will take up evidence for a female advantage in speech production. Studies on fine-motor skills independent of speech also demonstrate a female superiority, results that are more surprising because they are not predictable from a socialization hypothesis. Annett (1970) asked 220 English children, aged 3 to 15 years, to shift pegs rapidly along the holes in a peg-board task. The girls were significantly faster overall, especially with the right hand, which was better than their left. The boys were better with their left hand.

Denckla (1973, 1974), testing several hundred children between the ages of 5 and 10 years, found that in both hands girls were consistently faster at a task that required a rapid sequence of finger-thumb oppositions. The girls showed a consistent improvement over the age range, whereas the boys appeared to reach a plateau at age 8. When the boys and girls were compared on single repetitions of thumb or fingers, speed of repetitive hand pats, speed to pronate and supinate the arm, and speed of foot tapping, no sex differences emerged. However, when heel and toe sequences were measured, females were faster at every age. The youngest girls, aged 5 and 6, showed a marked difference between the feet, with the right foot considerably faster. Though this asymmetry largely disappeared with age, it indicates that young girls are considerably more biased toward left hemisphere activation than boys. Overall, the results indicate that the girls' advantage is specific to rapid sequential action, or fine-motor fluency.

Speech Production

Speech is a species-specific characteristic of all human populations. While it has been found that the great apes understand speech, they are not able to produce it, and even when taught sign language they show a reduced vocabulary and almost no syntax. Apes are not prototype humans locked into a silent world, but appear to have no inclination to employ a signaling system as complex as human language, even when they are given the opportunity.

This does not mean that humans are superior to the apes – it means only that we are different. Speech is just as much a part of our repertoire as the vocalizations and gestures of chimpanzees are of theirs. What has proved surprising about human language is that it develops if at least two species members are interacting with one another. Only in conditions of extreme deprivation in which a child is isolated from human discourse does the development of language fail to occur, with the most recent evidence coming from a UCLA study of "Genie," a 12-year-old girl rescued from confinement in a Los Angeles bedroom. Genie had never heard speech, and even after several years of training she had language skills that seemed indistinguishable from the great apes: a severely restricted vocabulary, no syntax, and telegraphic utterances of only two to three words in length. Taken in conjunction with other reports of similar cases, these findings strongly suggest that language development has a "critical period," and that some human interaction is required before the age of 5 to 7 years for normal language to develop. Nevertheless, for 99.99 percent of the human race, including the mentally retarded, speech develops between any two individuals whether they have an existing language system or not. Many accounts have been given of twins who establish a completely new language that is totally unintelligible to everyone but themselves.

Normal, ordinary human speech is not primarily a "cognitive" ability but is as much a part of human behavior as a bipedal gait and aimed throwing. It is a motor skill in the sense that speech production can be efficient or inefficient, but becomes cognitive only when it is used for some intellectual purpose, such as persuasion and reasoning or in the service of art, as in literature and poetry.

The sex difference that has been reported is that females, advanced relative to males at most ages throughout childhood, appear to have a greater facility in producing accurate speech sounds. They employ more words in phrases or sentences, a measure referred to as the "mean length of utterance." However, in most studies across a wide age range and across cultures, no sex differences exist in tests of vocabulary.

Despite the assumption that the female superiority is merely a product of greater precocity, a detailed analysis of the data reveals that the sex difference is much more complex. First, it is difficult to demonstrate any consistent effect of sex before about 18 to 24 months. Up to this period, both sexes are extremely variable in speech development. Second, after the age of about 24 months, the sex difference seems to become more noticeable with age up until middle childhood. Both of these findings suggest that the female aptitude is not just a matter of developmental acceleration. The overall advantage in speech development in females has been found in longitudinal studies both in the United States (Cameron et al. 1967) and in England (Moore 1967). A reliable sex effect appeared by about 12 to 18 months along with a strong correlation between early language development in girls and later verbal and intellectual ability, a relationship that was not found for boys in either study. In a somewhat more exact report of language development, Paynter and Petty in 1974 investigated the accuracy with which 90 young children produced consonants and the number of consonants in the child's repertoire across the ages of 24 to 30 months. The sexes were noticeably different only at 30 months, with the girls having seven consonants (measured as being accurately produced by 90 percent of the 45 girls) and the boys having five.

Speech surveys are generally begun at 4 to 5 years of age, at which time most children have an adequate ability to produce all of the speech sounds of a native language with a reasonable degree of accuracy, and in general to speak fluently. In all of the surveys examined, it has been found that males produce more dysfluencies and more inaccurate articulation, and show considerably more pronounced speech defects, such as stuttering (Hull et al. 1971; Brownell 1973; Ingram 1975). Verbal fluency, as measured by the absence of hesitations and by mean length of utterance, has been found to be greater in females not only in English-speaking countries but in places with dramatically different languages such as Nepal and Czechoslovakia (Gaddes and Crockett 1975; Potsova 1975; Spring 1975; Thomas et al. 1978).

More recently, studies on the uses of language by men and women, specifically with reference to sex roles, have revealed that women in various countries around the world speak more accurately than men, as for instance in using appropriate word endings such as "ing" instead of "in." This has been explained as due to males being "socialized" to speak badly, but it seems just as likely to be the result of the females' greater skill in speech production.

The superiority of females in the motor production of speech sounds may be due more to a general capacity for "fluency" than to a special aptitude for language or to special environmental circumstances. Two sets of findings bear on this statement. First, it has been demonstrated that mothers do not speak differently to their sons and daughters, in terms of either their clarity of speech or difficulty of vocabulary (Phillips 1973; Fraser and Roberts 1975). Despite this, a greater vocal interchange is often found between mothers and daughters than between mothers and sons, and this difference appears to reflect the interest of the female child in her mother's speech, as was pointed out earlier. Also, Potsova (1975) found the same female advantage in 5-year-old children reared on a collective in Czechoslovakia. Second, females show the striking aptitude for fluency in nonverbal vocalizations, suggesting that their skill is not restricted to language per se, but is due to a general aptitude for sequential fluency. Research in England on monotonism (the inability to sing in tune) has revealed an extremely robust sex difference, with male monotones outnumbering females by at least six to one. Furthermore, female monotones are almost never found past the age of 8 to 9 years, whereas male monotones are common well into the teenage period (Bentley 1968; Roberts 1972).

Finally, it appears that the function of vocalization is a relevant factor. Smith and Connolly (1972) found that when the utterances of preschool children were categorized into "play noises" and "conversations," the boys were overwhelmingly more likely to make play noises and the girls to talk to other children and adults. This result occurred despite the total vocal output of the boys and girls being identical. Here we see an example of the importance of the function of language with respect to the object-person dimension, with boys spending more time imitating objects and animals and girls communicating with people.

Considering these results on speech production, it is clear that the essential differences between males and females relate more to motor skills and the function of language than to cognition. However, as will be seen later, sensory and motor skills as well as the object-person dimension are important in biasing the type of cognitive skill that will be favored over others. These factors predict "cognitive style" rather than cognitive ability.

CROSS-MODAL INTEGRATION

Cross-modal integration refers to the way in which the brain combines information from the senses with the motor system, as well as to the capacity to integrate different modalities of sensory input.

Examples of sensorimotor integration are aiming a baseball bat at a moving ball and mimicking the voice quality of another person. Combining information from two or more senses not only provides a richer experience of events and objects in the world, but is essential to many cognitive skills such as learning to read. In this section, we take up the evidence for sex differences in both types of cross-modal integration.

Sensorimotor Integration

When the speed of motor sequencing is combined with a verbal or visual task, female ability is pronounced. Majeres (1977) tested 204 college students on the time to process items from one list and to tap the matching item in an adjacent list. The pairs were word-word, color-color, directional symbols, shape-shape, and shape-name. The sexes were equal in the shape-shape condition, but the females were superior in every other case. Reasoning that the females may have memorized the response card sequence, Majeres scrambled the response cards in the second column on every trial. This manipulation actually improved the women's performance, which accelerated by 1 to 2 seconds, and women subjects were now an astonishing 5 to 7 seconds faster than the men in every trial block. Similar results were found in a population of over 1,000 subjects by Decker and DeFries (1980) where females across a wide age range were overwhelmingly superior in a test of coding speed.

Majeres concluded that the female superiority is due to the ability to make a rapid translation from a visual to a verbal code – that it is in cross-modal sensorimotor coding that their superiority is to be found. This conclusion is debatable because many of the tasks, such as the color-color task at which the females were particularly outstanding, did not require verbalization. Similarly, the directional symbols task was performed best by females. Majeres's conclusion is based on the view that naming colors and directional symbols would occur automatically while labeling abstract shapes would be far less likely.

Evidence from my own laboratory tends to disconfirm the notion that females automatically translate all visual input into verbal codes. In a series of studies on 240 students aged from 7 to 11 years, Amy Olson and I (unpublished) investigated incidental learning for words and pictures that were rated on either a meaningful or a meaningless dimension. Without warning, the students were then asked to recall the items. The girls remembered considerably more than the boys in all conditions where there was verbal recall for the lists of both pictures and words, but were no better than the boys when they were asked to draw the list of pictures from memory. If the girls were automatically coding the pictures into words, one would expect that their memory would be superior to the boys, as it was in the pictures-words condition.

The critical factor in the studies that show a sensorimotor facility in females appears to be sequencing speed, especially in generating sequential motor programs that are independent of changes in the visual environment. Kimura (1977) has called this type of motor behavior "movement without objects," or internally programmed motor acts. In contrast to females, males appear to excel in externally programmed motor acts, responses triggered by sudden changes in the visual environment.

The primary sensorimotor integration that shows a striking superiority in males is visuomotor tracking. Experimenters have measured the speed and accuracy with which subjects self-correct their movements to shifts in the position of objects in a visual display. In general, males are superior at all ages tested, which is down to approximately 5 years. In the early childhood period, their skill is due largely to accuracy and not speed. By the early teens, boys' responses are also much faster, and the combination of speed and accuracy produces quite an overwhelming superiority (Ammons et al. 1955; Shephard et al. 1962; Noble et al. 1964).

Sensorisensory Integration

The data on cross-modal sensory integration points to a solitary sex difference in which females show a facility in tests of auditory-verbal to visual translation. Haptic cross-modal tasks, where subjects have to match items by touch with pictures of those items, revealed no sex differences in a study on 99 6 year olds (Gurucharri 1974). However, young boys tend to show a left hand superiority at these types of task, whereas girls have equal ability with either hand (Witelson 1976). Rae (1977) could find no sex differences on the Birch and Belmont auditory-visual cross-modal task, in which a series of tones is matched to a series of blinking lights.

In an extended test of phonetic-visual cross-modal matching (McGuinness and Courtney 1983), we found a striking sex effect on the auditory but not the visual component of a search task. We asked college students to search for target letters of phonemes (A or I) in either a visual or an auditory presentation of a series of five-letter words. When the subjects were looking for a target letter or a target sound in the series of visually presented words, no sex effect emerged. However, when the same subjects were asked to listen to a similar set of words and judge whether they contained a particular sound or letter, strong sex effects appeared for both the sound and the letter conditions. Males were much poorer in detecting the presence or absence of a target sound, but, even more remarkable, half of the male subjects were found to perform at chance levels (50 percent correct, 50 percent incorrect) when they were asked to determine whether the target letter was present or absent in a word they heard. The males were not only poorer in receptive auditory processing, but were particularly disadvantaged in creating a visual image of a word they heard – one reason, perhaps, why males have greater problems in spelling. It came as a surprise that college men had difficulty on these relatively simple tasks.

Clearly, this account of sex differences in cross-modal integration suffers from a lack of data. From the evidence reported later in this chapter, we know that cognitive development is particularly dependent upon the ability to make rapid connections between sensory modalities. So far, it is not clear just how sensorimotor integration is involved in cognition. We are only at the tip of the iceberg in our understanding of the importance of how these interrelationships develop, and whether or not the sexes differ in the way information is integrated between the senses and the motor systems.

COGNITIVE ABILITY

The "cognitive revolution" in psychology represents the movement away from strict behaviorism. As formulated by B. F. Skinner and others, behaviorism holds as a fundamental tenet that it is impossible to investigate internal psychological processes. One can only measure an event in the world (stimulus) and the observable effect (response) and correlate these two phenomena. Dissatisfaction with this approach resulted in several landmark publications including *Perception and Communication* by Broadbent (1958), *Plans and the Structure of Behavior* by Miller et al. (1960), and *Cognitive Psychology* by Neisser (1967). They all have as a common theme that the brain is engaged in selectively filtering information available to the senses, and that it operates a conscious, voluntary control over both input and behavior. In short, the brain constructs its own reality. Only in extremely impoverished environments, such as a Skinner box, would this active selective process be less likely to be observed.

However, use of the word "cognition" has proved problematic because it is so vague. Cognition can refer to "plans" and "decisions," to "perception," or to "selective attention." One problem with these definitions is that the mentally retarded may exercise very stringent plans in highly obsessive behavior or pay undivided attention to some totally trivial set of events, behaviors that do not qualify as true "cognitive" ability.

This is not to say that the cognitive revolution is unimportant. The new approach pried open a Pandora's box of internal psychological processes, and permitted a detailed analysis of what has come to be called "information processing." The result is that the study of human capacities has become infinitely more refined and precise. But it is important to bear in mind that the word "cognition" in and of itself is not a magic key to new understanding, and I might add neither is the expression "information processing."

Many psychologists prefer to retain the more general meaning expressed in the dictionary definition of cognition: "The intellectual process by which knowledge is gained about perception and ideas." Note that this definition introduces the concept of the intellect and raises the thorny problem of defining "intelligence." As psychologists have been arguing for over 100 years about the meaning of intelligence, a new term scarcely seems an advance! For this reason, in the opening pages of this chapter I outlined my own particular definition of cognition, where the distinction between species-specific behavior and the degree of skill or inventiveness with which they are employed are emphasized.

Cognitive ability appears to be enhanced by two fundamental capacities. The first is the ability to integrate or reorganize information within and between sensory modes or between sensory and motor processes. This ability produces an entirely new level of ability, one that would not be predicted from the basic sensorimotor repertoire. For example, composing or performing music transforms auditory images into motor acts. Intelligent listening involves restructuring or categorizing musical phrases and storing them in memory for comparison later in the piece.

Second, the "intellectual process by which knowledge is gained" is due to the capacity to evaluate the efficacy of one's endeavors before an act takes place. This introduces the concept of "insight," which refers to the ability to predict the success or failure of a solution to a problem. This capacity requires a higher-order attention, in which a portion of attentional capacity is devoted to the entire milieu including oneself as actor. To put this another way, it involves a thoroughly conscious awareness of what one is aware of, and even why one is aware of it. The capacity for self-conscious reflection is the criterion that demarcates most human beings from most animals and the severely mentally retarded.

An additional conceptual problem has plagued the study of intelligence and individual differences. Over the last 20 to 30 years, when intelligence quotient (IQ) tests were standardized for different populations, the field became a battleground for the nature versus nurture controversy. Arguments pro and con are predicated on the assumption that there are two distinct phenomena: "nature" as opposed to "nurture." Some offer the apparent solution that these two phenomena "interact," rather like combining two ingredients in a mixing bowl. The most sophisticated solution to this problem is Scarr's suggestion (1981) that we abandon the concepts of nature and nurture and think instead of what is *easy* and what is *difficult* for any species member to learn. What is easy is more biologically based, and what is difficult is more influenced by the environment, but the two aspects are always present in any behavior. For example, even the most striking characteristic of the human species, the bipedal gait, can be subverted by unusual experiences. The Wild Boy of Avignon was found crawling around on all fours in imitation of his adopted wolf parents.

An important but little known fact in the history of intelligence testing is that during the construction of IQ tests, a number of important sex differences were eliminated in the early stages of test validation. In Paris at the turn of the century, Binet and Simon found in their initial testing that boys were less "intelligent" than girls, a finding that turned out to be due to an excess of test items that favored the skills of girls (see McGuinness 1985 for review). Since these early beginnings, the items have been carefully balanced so that sex differences never emerge in overall scores. In part, the solution was to balance tests like symbol substitution, which favor girls, with those like block design, which favor boys. The major portion of the verbal section was restricted to tests of vocabulary, the only aspect of verbal ability that has never shown any sex difference. A review of the evolution of the unisex IQ has been presented by Kipnis (1976).

It will probably never be possible to know whether one sex is more "intelligent" than another, nor is this even the right question to address. There are innumerable types of intelligence, but formal tests tap only a fraction. One of these, which has been consistently ignored by almost everyone, is "behavioral intelligence," a concept discovered by Spearman (1927) early in this century and more recently by Guilford. Guilford (1967) describes behavioral intelligence as the capacity to interpret and to respond accurately and appropriately to behavioral cues. He found that females consistently showed greater "intelligence" in tests of this type, a result that is consistent with the studies showing females to have higher levels of empathy. Of course, behavioral intelligence is neither valued in our culture nor taught in schools, nor have any items like those employed by Guilford been incorporated in intelligence tests.

Because of the lack of research, I will have to omit consideration of behavioral intelligence. A related process that cannot be dealt with here is moral judgment. Unfortunately, research on this topic is plagued by an overdose of deductive theories, arising from a set of prior assumptions about stages of moral development. This emphasizes the ages at which these stages are supposed to be reached, rather than the characteristics of moral reasoning per se. Had this research been integrated with the studies on empathy, it might have been shown that the most advanced form of morality stems from a capacity to comprehend the totality of another person's needs and wishes.

The remainder of this chapter focuses on the sex differences that "make a difference." These turn out to be the tasks that are considered to be highly relevant to the needs of our culture: the cognitive abilities of reading, writing, and mathematics. In the language arts, females are found to excel, but in higher mathematics, especially geometry, males are superior. The important issue is not the negative one, Why are females or males bad at any one set of tasks?, but rather, What particular aptitudes make each of them efficient in specific tasks?

WHAT IS READING?

Reading is a superlative example of the integration of the sensory and motor systems, and involves the visual and auditory senses, memory, and the capacity to use a spoken language. A series of transformations, ranging from the primitive to the complex, occur at each level from the sensory input to the motor response. At the most basic level, various letters must be discriminated one from another. The next task is to memorize each letter name and its corresponding sound or phoneme. But first a child must be able to discriminate phonemically; that is, he/she must be able to hear the difference between b and p or t and d, as well as produce these sounds in speech. When phonemes are combined into morphemes, or syllables, short-term memory comes into play. Short-term memory involves the ability to hold a series of items in a temporal sequence: fa-mi-ly is not the same as fa-ly-mi. As short-term memory is particularly vulnerable to interference and declines rapidly over time, the speed at which each individual item can be decoded is extremely important.

So far we have reached only the level of the word. When words can be decoded fluently, the reader needs to bring in his/her knowledge of the language. A child must be able to anticipate the structure of sentences on the basis of grammatical rules and to determine the meaning from the context of the story. The capacity to comprehend the meaning of spoken language and to be able to utter grammatically correct sentences appears essential to this process.

It is now generally acknowledged that the two earliest stages in the reading process, visual discrimination and learning letter names, seldom cause problems in learning to read. Children with either of these problems are rare, and difficulties with these tasks are rapidly outgrown. For a few poor readers, problems can begin when learning sound-letter correspondences, but for the majority the major stumbling block occurs at the stage where visual symbols are combined into syllables.

For the last 10 years, evidence has been accumulating that reading problems are less related to orthography (the structure and arrangement of visual symbols) than to auditory perception, specifically the ability to decode speech sounds. Currently, studies of children with reading problems lead to two major conclusions. First, reading success is highly dependent upon linguistic competence in all its varied domains, and second, it is dependent upon short-term memory for temporal sequences. Specifically, these break down into the following categories of skills:

1. Phoneme-syllable decoding
2. Phonological coding
3. Naming fluency
4. Short-term memory

5. Fine-motor fluency
6. Language comprehension

Phoneme-Syllable Decoding

In a study investigating the relationship of auditory processing to reading aptitude, Calfee et al. (1973) tested 660 children aged 5 to 11 years on a test devised by the Lindamoods (1971) called the Auditory Conceptualization Test. The test involves assigning phonemes to colored blocks and arranging the blocks in various sequences. Part 1 of the test identifies subjects who have severe auditory problems, and almost everyone does well on this part. Part 2 requires the subjects to combine phonemes using the blocks, and is particularly discerning in identifying reading-retarded subjects. For example, a child may be asked to assign the phonemes a, s, and p to three blocks of different colors and arrange them in the order just given, "asp." Next, the child will be asked to rearrange the blocks in a different order: "If that is 'asp,' show me 'aps.' " This form of the test is generally failed by poor readers of all ages. As this test requires the child only to remember phonemes assigned to colored blocks, there can be no doubt that the deficit is specific to auditory decoding and not to problems with the English alphabet.

In children followed from 4 to 6 years, Liberman and Mann (1981) found a strong developmental progression, beginning with the ability to segment words into syllables and followed somewhat later by the ability to segment syllables into phonemes. The child's ability to segment speech sounds into syllables and phonemes at 4 and 5 years of age was highly related to subsequent success in learning to read. This same relationship was found by Lexier (1979) in a study of 48 children, in which auditory blending and phonemic segmenting were highly related to the child's scores on a reading test. As in the Lindamood and Lindamood study (1971), Lexier also found that the ability to discriminate between individual phonemes did not distinguish between good and poor readers.

It has been inferred from the results of these studies that the major distinction between good and poor readers is a general facility in spoken language. For a certain proportion of children, this is true. Tallal and Stark (1982) found that when children have difficulties in language development, one of the most discerning tests is a syllable discrimination test. When two syllables such as "be" and "bi" (ba-by) are presented rapidly (less than 500 milliseconds apart), language-delayed children often report the sequence in the reverse order. When the rate is slowed down to more than 500 milliseconds, the same children have no difficulty with this task. These authors found that there was a very strong relationship between the scores on the syllables test and those on a reading test.

When Tallal and Stark separated the reading-delayed children into two groups, those with and without language problems, they found that the poor readers with normal ability in receptive and expressive language still had difficulties in discriminating between certain vowels, such as "dab" and "daeb," and in categorizing consonants. This group also had problems with serial memory.

Phonological Coding

Phonological coding refers to the capacity of some individuals to be particularly attentive to language sounds. These people automatically translate letters into sounds and are almost inevitably good readers, whereas poor readers are much more influenced by the visual appearance of the letters. Sensitivity to sound produces confusion in experiments where subjects are asked to remember lists of items that sound alike. Liberman and Mann (1981) reasoned that if good readers automatically decode letters into sounds, they ought to be disrupted when trying to remember letters or words that are similar phonologically. A series of experiments with 7-year-old children indicated that when lists of items had to be memorized, the good readers were always superior to the poor readers unless the items rhymed. It did not matter whether the items were letters, words, or sentences, or whether they were presented to the ear or to the eye, the interference produced by rhyming was considerably greater for the good readers. What is especially interesting about these results is that poor readers had nearly identical scores for the lists of rhyming and nonrhyming words or sentences, showing that they were completely unaffected by phonological similarity.

Naming Fluency

A number of experiments have shown that poor readers are slower in tasks requiring rapid naming, but it does not make any difference whether the items are letters, pictures, or colors. For example, Denckla and Rudel (1976) tested good and poor readers on the time it took to name lists of pictures of objects, colors, letters, or digits. On the color-naming test alone, it was possible to identify 70 percent of the poor readers. These results confirm the earlier work of Jansky and de Hirsch (1972), which indicated that performance on letter- and picture-naming tasks was the best predictor for reading failure. In a test of naming speed using children of different ages, Spring and Capps (1974) found that naming speed for digits, colors, and pictures improved with age, but that even the youngest good readers, aged 7 to 10 years, were superior to the oldest poor readers, aged 12 to 13 years.

Short-Term Memory

In a series of tests involving memory tasks, Tallal and Stark (1981) investigated good and poor readers, aged 7 to 9 years, who were identical in expressive and receptive language. Testing these children on a large battery of items, they found that a major difference between the two groups was their ability to remember items in a particular order. The poor readers were significantly worse in tests of nonverbal auditory memory (a series of tones), visual-verbal memory (a series of letters), and nonverbal cross-modal memory (a series of tones matched to a series of lights). As two of these tests are unrelated to language, it can be concluded that some poor readers have particular difficulty with temporal organization in auditory memory and with intermodal flexibility. No differences were found between the two groups in nonverbal visual memory, confirming other results showing that poor readers have no difficulty in remembering visual information.

When memory is investigated using a series of lists, performance typically declines with trials. After hearing or seeing the same type of material over and over again, it becomes increasingly difficult to remember it. If there is a sudden change in either the category of the items, for example, from lists of furniture to lists of plants, or a shift to a new modality, such as from a visual to an auditory presentation, performance instantly returns to the original level. Farnham-Diggory and Gregg (1975) studied this effect in good and poor readers by presenting 40 lists of four-letter words to the eye or to the ear, switching the modality at the end of each series. At the beginning of the test, the results were similar for the two groups. Both began with highly accurate performances, but declined to about 65 percent accuracy. However, when the modality was switched, the good readers rebounded to their initial levels of performance, whereas the poor readers scarcely improved or actually got worse. This suggests that poor readers find it difficult to shift from one mode to another, an ability that is essential in reading. Once engaged in either a visual or an auditory mode, poor readers seem locked into that particular mode.

Fine-Motor Fluency

Fine-motor fluency is the capacity to perform rapid sequences of movements, especially with the parts of the body controlled by the fine-motor nerves: fingers, toes, vocal chords, and tongue. We have already seen that rapid naming is important to reading skills. What has only recently been discovered is that tests involving control over the fingers and hands are also related to reading. For example, Badian (1982) discovered that drawing ability was highly related to reading performance, and Smith (1982) reported that one of the key predictors of reading failure was poor performance on a peg-board task in which pegs have to be shifted to different holes as rapidly as possible. These results suggest that part of the naming fluency effect may be due to the ability to sequence a series of rapid movements, specifically those involving the fine-motor system.

Language Comprehension

Finally, a number of studies have reported that language comprehension is a critical factor in reading fluency. Jarvis (1974) tested 183 7 year olds on such items as digit span, auditory blending, and auditory discrimination and comprehension. The strongest predictor of scores on three reading achievement tests was auditory comprehension. This same effect was reported by Jackson and McClelland (1979) on college students. They asserted that, apart from naming speed, the most critical factor in a student's reading skills was the accurate comprehension of spoken language.

At this time, we do not know how all of these skills are related. It is possible that each of the tests described above is but one cog in a complex of aptitudes called "language." There have been only a few attempts to relate these tests in any systematic fashion. Using the data collected by Liberman and Mann (1981) as well as new data on approximately 100 more children, Blachman (1982) studied the relationship between the ability to segment syllables and phonemes, the ability to produce rhymes, and performance on rapid naming tests. She found that segmenting and rhyming were only moderately related, and that naming speed was independent, both for kindergartners and first graders. The best predictors of reading success for the 5-year-old children were the rhyming test and rapid naming of colors. By age 6 the best predictors were phoneme and syllable segmenting and rapid naming. These abilities could predict the rank order of the first-grade pupils on reading achievement with 68 percent accuracy. When short-term memory tests were added, the prediction rose to 74 percent. This indicates that short-term memory is partly independent of the other factors.

Smith (1982) has been studying families who have a history of reading disorders. Using a complex battery of tests, she discovered that four tests were particularly discriminating and that each was relatively independent: auditory discrimination of phonemes, short-term memory for digits (digit span), naming speed, and speed on the peg-board task. Although performance on these four tasks could separate nearly all of the poor and good readers, the accuracy of classification improved when tests of visuoperceptual organization and visual memory were added. It appears that severely dyslexic individuals were actually superior on these tests, suggesting that they are biased toward the visual mode and that this interferes with learning to read.

Finally, in one of the most comprehensive tests to date, Badian (1982) tested 180 children aged 4 years, 9 months, on the Holbrook Screening Battery, which consists of 15 different tasks. She followed these children through to the end of the third grade. The best predictors of reading ability were, in order, the Wechsler IQ subtest "information" (involving a verbal report), counting out loud (verbal fluency), the draw-a-person test (fine-motor skill), another Wechsler subtest called "sentences" (auditory comprehension), and letter naming. Scores on these five items could predict reading success 4 years later with 92 percent accuracy.

Although these comparisons have been made using different batteries of tests and different sets of assumptions about what the tests are measuring, the results point in the same direction. It is clear that visual processing has nothing to do with reading; in fact, a strong reliance on the visual mode is often antagonistic to progress in learning to read. Serial short-term memory appears to be independent of the purely linguistic tasks. Naming fluency seems more related to a general fine-motor fluency than to decoding or to retrieval skills.

Reading Skills and Sex Differences

Badian's tests (1982) were successful in pinpointing those children who had trouble in learning to read; 83 percent were boys. In addition, Smith (1982) reported that all of the dyslexic persons in the family study were male. Even when reading scores were below normal in the female family members, the males were considerably worse. Earlier it was mentioned that even by the most conservative estimates, 75 percent of the reading-disabled population is male.

In the first part of this chapter, the sex differences in various auditory and language tasks were reviewed. The conclusions on the basis of the available data were that females are more attentive to speech sounds than males, more accurate in decoding speech, and more accurate and more fluent in speaking; have better skills in temporal sequencing; and finally exhibit noticeable superiority in fine-motor fluency. Thus, it is not at all surprising, if one is familiar with the literature on sex differences, that girls show a decided advantage in learning to read. What is surprising is that although reading achievement test batteries have been independently standardized by race and by socioeconomic class, no such standardization has ever been carried out for boys and girls. This means that the remedial reading population is selected on the basis of the combined scores of both sexes and will inevitably single out males at the expense of females. The issue is that it is perfectly normal for boys to lag behind girls in reading ability. This does not mean that they are "disabled" or have brain damage, as has often been suggested.

The problem in learning to read lies in the ability to make the translation from text to phoneme to word at sufficient speed. Sex differences in reading appear to be determined in large part by the speed at which these transformations are carried out. This is equally true if a child is faced with a page of text or is asked to write out a word after hearing it. Spelling is partly the mirror image of reading, a point also made by Montessori (1972) when she discovered that it was far easier to teach reading if you taught a child to write first. It might also be mentioned that Montessori reported that after a child was able to decode letters into sounds, she repeatedly urged: "Say it faster. Say it faster." This reminds me of a sign that hung over a swimming pool where Olympic athletes trained: "The only way to swim fast, is to swim fast."

It is not surprising that children will tend to favor those particular perceptual or motor skills that come easily and to avoid those that are difficult. This helps to explain why females tend to persist in adopting verbal problem-solving strategies even when they are inappropriate, such as in learning algebra and geometry. Mathematics, a language devised for dealing with the world of objects, is related to syntax and not to phonetics. It is difficult to "talk" mathematics or even communicate mathematical concepts in conventional language.

THE MYSTERY OF MATHEMATICS

The current status of research in arithmetic and mathematics is approximately the same as that for reading 20 or 30 years ago. For example, Steeves (1982) points out that although 4,000 research reports on the nature of reading appeared during the late 1970s, there were only 8 on mathematics. Clearly, the cognitive revolution has not found its way here.

This means that the cognitive processes involved in mathematics are almost completely unknown. A further complication is that the proper study of mathematics must be carried out by people who not only are mathematically sophisticated but who are also concerned with the psychological processes involved in learning math. These people are very rare indeed. People like Steeves in the United States and Richard Skemp in England agree that even simple concepts in arithmetic are far more complex than had been believed. In teaching remedial mathematics, Steeves has discovered that Jean Piaget's description of the process of addition and the nature of numbers is essentially correct. First, children must be able to grasp the concept of topological space, that is, to identify and classify objects and object relations. Next, they need to comprehend the concept of serial order, by which objects can be ranked according to some criterion such as height or weight. When these concepts are understood, then numbers come to have meaning. Learning to count is no guarantee that a child will automatically know what a number system represents.

Perhaps the most original approach to unraveling the mystery of mathematics is that of Patricia Davidson, who is currently developing a series of test batteries in which a child's strategies can be discovered. Davidson's tests (1982) are framed in one of three modes: concrete, pictorial, and abstract. Each child is given a choice of using any one or more of these modes in solving mathematical problems, in both the form of the test items and the form of the answer. Theoretically, this could give rise to nine possible mathematical strategies in which the form of the problem and the preferred solution could differ along three by three dimensions; for example, a student might prefer to see a problem in graphic form, but solve it with an equation. As yet, it is too early to know which particular strategies are most common and which produce the best results.

Meanwhile, Davidson has been studying children who have difficulty in math. She has found that these children fall into two distinct categories. The first type attends to detail and solves all problems in a serial order, or stepwise fashion. These children are better at addition and multiplication and worse on subtraction and long division; they are particularly bad at estimating and do not seem at all bothered when their answers are wide of the mark. The second type of child is better at subtracting and dividing than addition and multiplication, and relies on a wholistic grasp of the entire problem, quickly recognizing when an answer is incorrect. These children fall down on multistep procedures and word problems. It seems likely that females would fall into the first category, because of their verbal and rote memory skills, and males the second. However, this has not been tested.

So far, the evidence on sex differences in mathematics indicates that boys and girls perform identically on tests of arithmetic computation, but that girls begin to fall behind when algebra and geometry are introduced. This appears to be entirely due to the subject matter and not to other factors, because the age at which the sex difference appears varies between ability groups and between cultures, and depends entirely on the time at which algebra and geometry are introduced. In studies on mathematically gifted children, it has been found that despite the girls' interest and ability in math, they rarely score in the top 10 to 20 percent on advanced math tests. In the Johns Hopkins talent searches begun in 1972, the ratio of boys to girls is five to one in the 100 children scoring 600 or higher on the mathematics portion of the Scholastic Aptitude Test (Benbow and Stanley 1980).

Several hypotheses concerning these effects have been suggested. The most popular is the socialization theory, which states that girls fall behind in advanced mathematics because of social pressures or societal expectations. The social pressures theory cannot be maintained on logical grounds because it would predict that girls would be reluctant to compete with boys in all subjects, not just mathematics. Yet girls do not fall behind in subjects such as history, English, social sciences, biology, zoology, art, and music, where higher math is not required.

Societal expectations are relevant, and it is clear that girls receive less encouragement to continue in math. However, contrary to popular belief, this is not the same thing as saying that societal expectations are causing the girls to have problems in mathematics. Rather, it indicates that when they do have problems, parents and teachers are more likely to allow them to give up. Conversely, boys are not permitted to give up learning to read.

Socialization and Mathematics

Do societal expectations create the sex difference in higher math? Because we cannot carry out experiments in which children are reared with different sets of expectations, we cannot answer this question directly. Instead, we must rely on correlational statistics until it becomes clear which sets of aptitudes and attitudes bear any relationship to performance in mathematics. Correlational studies are largely for the purpose of mapping out a terrain, discovering what things go together and which do not, but they cannot assess directly questions of causation. This is especially true in any investigations that attempt to compare performance on a cognitive task with attitudes. Is a child poor at math because he/she does not like it, or does he/she dislike it because he/she is poor at it?

A further problem that is particularly vexing with many studies testing a socialization hypothesis was mentioned earlier in the discussion on inductive and deductive theorizing. Investigations initiated from a socialization perspective are largely questionnaire studies. These demonstrate that girls from the age of 13 or so, depending upon which country is involved, show an increasing dislike for math and are more likely to drop out of math classes. However, a second crucial research step, comparison between a child's scores on an attitude questionnaire and his/her performance in mathematics, is rarely taken.

To my knowledge, there have been only four surveys in which this vital comparison was made: those by Benbow and Stanley (1980),

Fennema and Sherman (1977), Stallings (1979), and Entwhistle and Baker (1983). The Benbow and Stanley study (1980) found no relationship between attitudes and ability, but this might be expected because they used a high ability population. Fennema and Sherman (1977) found that the strongest relationships to performance in math in high school students were vocabulary, visuospatial ability, confidence in mathematics, and the student's perception of his/her teacher's attitude, a pattern of relationships that was identical for both males and females. Sex differences were found in math ability in three of four high schools, and the combined data across all four schools in the study showed a highly significant sex effect. Girls were also found to be less confident about mathematics than the boys.

The Fennema and Sherman study (1977) suggests that ability is more important than attitudes, as the two strongest relationships to mathematics performance were vocabulary and visuospatial ability, but it would be nonsensical to state that vocabulary skills are causing mathematical ability. The relationship between the two arises because both represent a higher-order aptitude called "general intelligence." Similarly, it is also erroneous to argue that attitudes are causing mathematical performance, when the reverse is equally likely to be true.

In a longitudinal study carried out by Sherman (1980), students were tested first in eighth grade and again in the eleventh. Sex differences were found in math ability in the older groups but not in the younger. The best predictors of math performance at grade 11, on the basis of testing at grade 8, were tests of ability, involving knowledge of math concepts, problem-solving skills, and spatial ability. These were followed by the number of math courses taken. The only attitude measure to show any meaningful relationship was confidence, a result that confirms those from the 1977 survey.

Stallings (1979) reported large sex differences in geometry, analytic geometry, calculus, and algebra I, but found no sex differences in algebra II or trigonometry and a female advantage in arithmetic. For both sexes, there was a strong relationship between visuospatial ability and higher math, but not with arithmetic. The major differences between girls continuing in high school math and those dropping out were visuospatial ability, math anxiety, difficulty in learning math concepts, and greater parental support for those girls who were continuing. Again, we cannot determine whether difficulty in math is being caused by attitudinal factors, or whether the attitudes are caused by problems in math. The socialization theory receives support from the finding that the girls who continue in math report greater encouragement from their parents than the girls who quit.

Entwhistle and Baker (1983) investigated parental expectations and student performance in arithmetic in elementary school children. Boys and girls were identical in performance. Middle-class parents expected the sons to be better than daughters, whereas lower-class parents expected the reverse. The relationships of these expectations to performance only marginal, and in view of the opposite effects for social class and the absence of sex differences in performance, it is difficult to interpret these results.

In general, attitudes have not been found to be good predictors of math achievement. This result suggests that socialization may not be the critical factor in producing the sex differences in math. Other hypotheses, reviewed below, appear more fruitful.

Visuospatial Ability and Mathematics

Stallings's data (1979) indicate that visuospatial ability alone accounts for 50 percent of the variance regarding analytic geometry. This means that scores on a geometry test will predict scores on a spatial test with 50 percent accuracy, and vice versa, perhaps the strongest relationship that has been found between any one test and mathematical performance. As females have greater difficulty in geometry than in algebra (Dwyer 1979) and also tend to be poorer in visuospatial tests, this finding has focused research on visuospatial ability.

The type of tests in which the sex differences are most pronounced requires the subject to imagine movement in static representations of objects or movement among parts of objects. Most typically, the tests designed to measure this aptitude are two-dimensional line drawings of three-dimensional forms. The subject is asked, for example, to compare an unfolded diagram with several examples of what it might represent when it is folded. Many experiments using tests of this type and similar problems, such as mazes in two and three dimensions, have been reviewed elsewhere, with the consensus that, on average, males are superior in their performance on them (Maccoby and Jacklin 1974; Harris 1976; McGuinness 1976; McGuinness and Pribram 1978).

For a time it was believed that these sex differences emerged only in late childhood, but this was largely because most of the tests of visuospatial ability cannot be solved by children of either sex much before the age of 11 or 12. Other data show that problem solving with real three-dimensional objects is more advanced in males from quite early ages. In one of my own experiments, Cindy Morley and I asked preschool children to solve problems using jigsaw puzzles and Lego blocks. We found no sex differences on the two-dimensional jigsaw tasks, but the boys were much faster in constructing replicas of three-dimensional models from the age of 4 years. A similar result was found by Jahoda (1979) in two different cultures, in Ghana and in Scotland, with boys consistently ahead in both countries. Problem solving using three-dimensional material was also superior in boys in a New Guinea population (Shea and Yerua 1980). Once again, these results are striking confirmation that boys are not developmentally retarded with respect to girls.

So far, we have little information on which factors contribute to the development of spatial ability. My own data indicate that this aptitude has nothing to do with properties of the visual system involved in perceiving depth or distance, despite the fact that males have more efficient binocular vision. One possible explanation is that spatial ability arises because of the integration between the binocular visual system and the gross-motor system. This would predict that visuospatial imagery would develop after a lengthy period in which a child manipulated objects. To date this hypothesis has not been tested. The only evidence in its support is that males are consistently found to manipulate objects more than females (McGuinness and Pribram 1979).

Bent Twigs and Interest

Sherman suggested in 1967 that one of the reasons why girls may have difficulties in both spatial ability and mathematics is that they rely too heavily on verbal problem-solving strategies. She described this as the "bent twig" hypothesis. People who have investigated visuospatial problem solving often ask their subjects how they solved the problems. Females are far more likely to describe their strategy as one of labeling parts of the figure and comparing them one with another. Males are much more likely to report that they made the diagrams "move." These reports are suggestive, but they cannot explain whether the females' excessive reliance on verbal strategies is due to necessity or to choice. They may be forced back on verbalizing because of an underdeveloped capacity for visualization, or they may lack visual skills because they opt for verbal solutions, as these have worked for them previously. Whatever the reason, it seems obvious that when faced with a discipline such as geometry, which has been devised to map the spatial relations between planes and surfaces, the absence of a visual strategy could cause problems.

Finally, the object-person dimension must play a role. Higher mathematics is about objects and not about persons or indeed anything living. It is not so much that the study of higher math seems irrelevant (too many people have told girls that it is useful), but that it seems meaningless. For many girls, not only is the study of triangles, rectangles, cubes, and spheres quite pointless, but when faced with a formula, the most urgent question is: What does it mean? This is the question that is most difficult to ask and most difficult to answer.

BIOLOGICAL THEORIES

I have suggested that the sex differences that appear in subsequent cognitive development arise because of certain predispositions and biases between the sexes in both sensory and motor processing, as well as in selectivity in attending to people and to objects. If this is the case, then one might expect to find some evidence on differences in neural organization between males and females. Similarly, one might expect to find certain abilities or disabilites to be genetically determined.

To begin, two theories that are currently most popular, but that are nonetheless incorrect, must be discarded. First is the suggestion that sex differences in language and in visuospatial ability or higher mathematics are due to differences in the lateralization of the brain. Second is the theory that spatial ability is due to the inhibitory effects of a particular gene on the X chromosome (X-recessive hypothesis), which has been finally put to rest by Vandenberg and Kuse (1979). The evidence on sex differences in brain organization and some more promising genetic theories are discussed below.

Sex and the Brain

In hundreds of experiments on hemisphere laterality, the conclusion is overwhelming that both males and females have language localized in the left hemisphere and rapid pattern analysis in the right hemisphere. The more complex the pattern, the less accurate the right hemisphere and the more accurate the left; this is equally true for both men and women (McGuinness and Bartell 1982). There is some marginal evidence, inferred from brain-damaged patients, that females may have slightly more language skills represented in the right hemisphere (McGlone 1982), but this is tempered by the fact that right hemisphere damage generally does not affect language in either men or women. In contrast to McGlone's suggestion, Kershner (1978), in a study on 110 6 year olds using various measures of laterality, found that there was no sex difference in the degree of lateralization in his subjects. However, Kershner's results did reveal that boys who had a high concordance of hand, eye, foot, and ear, whether right or left, were most often the poorest readers. When these children were followed up at 9 and 11 years, the highly lateralized boys were consistently inferior in reading at both ages. No such relationship emerged for the girls.

Though we are on the threshold of some exciting new discoveries, the data do not permit a comprehensive picture of what is involved. The evidence on sex differences in the brain indicates that females have two major advantages for language and cross-modal integration. First, they appear to have a more complex organization within the left hemisphere. Studies carried out by Mateer et al. (1982) showed that when patients undergo cortical stimulation prior to brain surgery in order to locate crucial language areas, both receptive and productive language is considerably easier to disrupt in males over a much wider region of brain tissue. This finding helps to explain not only the females' advantage in language, but also why they are much less likely to suffer from aphasia following brain damage. Confirmation of a more precise nature has been presented by Kimura (1983) who carried out a study on 216 patients with damage to the left hemisphere. Overall, 51 percent of the men versus 31 percent of the women were identified as aphasic. However, the men were aphasic following damage to both the anterior and posterior regions of the left hemisphere, whereas in the female patients, aphasia was produced largely by anterior damage. Only 2 (11 percent) aphasic women emerged out of 19 women patients who had lesions known to be restricted to the classic "language system" (Wernicke's area) of the posterior left hemisphere.

Kimura's recent data indicate that there are some verbal functions also assigned to the right hemisphere in females only. The functions are verbal short-term memory and verbal retrieval in vocabulary tests. These data are reviewed in Kimura and Harshman (1984). Some right hemisphere verbal functions would give females an advantage in integrating verbal and visual information, which has been found in a study on the imaging of letters in spoken words (McGuinness and Courtney 1983).

So far we have little solid evidence on the neural organization involved in complex visuospatial and mathematical ability. My own evidence, cited above, shows clearly that difficult visuospatial problems are solved more accurately by the left hemisphere, just the opposite to popular theory. Furthermore, older data indicate that the frontal lobes of the brain may be involved in rotational imagery (Teuber 1974).

Other scraps of evidence are less related to human populations, but nevertheless intriguing. Diamond et al. (1981) have found a large sex difference in the cellular organization of rats' brains, with the males having thicker right hemispheres and the females thicker left hemispheres. The left-right differences in the male rat are present at birth, but the left hemisphere changes come later in the female and seem to be under hormonal control. The only sex difference in rat behavior that might be relevant to the human situation is the male's advantage in running mazes (a spatial ability).

In addition, it has recently been discovered that sex hormones are critically involved in neural transmission in the brains of rats and monkeys, and these regulate functions that are quite unrelated to reproduction. For example, sex hormones are found at every sensory relay and in limbic structures of the brain that control attention (see McGuinness and Pribram 1978).

A Genetic Link to Dyslexia?

The neural systems in the brain are both preprogrammed at birth and modifiable by the environment. Because young infants are unable to use language systems that take some 4 to 5 years to develop, one cannot argue from the neurological evidence that sex differences in language and reading are due to biology or to the environment. It is necessary to turn to additional data to support either claim.

Two major studies have been set up to study the genetic determinants of reading disability. One is the Colorado Family Reading Study carried out by J. C. DeFries and his colleagues at the University of Colorado at Boulder, and the second is being conducted at the Boys Town Institute in

Omaha, Nebraska. The first study involves over 1,000 subjects, half of whom are poor readers, and their immediate families; the other half is a control group of normal readers and their families. The ratio of male to female poor readers is 3.3 to 1. Decker and DeFries (1980) outlined their results on tests of reading achievement, visuospatial ability, and coding speed, which showed conclusively that reading problems run in families. The siblings of the poor readers were inferior to the siblings of the control group, and the same effect was found for the parents of the two groups. However, this does not prove a biological basis for the reading problems, because the effect could just as well be due to environmental factors, for example, the number of books in the house or whether or not the parents read to their children. Further analyses of their data reported by DeFries and Decker in 1982 revealed an interesting effect. When the sexes were studied separately, the male siblings of the poor readers were considerably worse than the female siblings. In fact, the female siblings of the dyslexic children had normal reading skills. This result suggests that the environment alone cannot be responsible for creating dyslexia, and that severe reading difficulties are heritable. However, despite the fact that heritability was clearly involved, a simple Mendelian model did not fit their data.

Investigations of familial traits may involve analyses of trait distributions in families, as in the study above, or a biochemical approach, which was the method used in the second study carried out at Boys Town. Eight families of learning-disabled boys were investigated, involving 70 people over three generations, all with a history of severe reading difficulties. Blood samples were taken from each subject and were tested for a host of genetic markers including the classification of blood groups and the measurement of chromosomal staining patterns known to be heritable.

Smith et al. (1983) reported that a common pattern that emerged in these families was a pronounced staining of chromosome 15. The protein beta-2 microglobulin situated on this chromosome is known to be influenced by the sex hormone testosterone, and is also involved in the lateralization of the brain, as well as the immune system. It is possible that the beta-2 microglobulin is somehow connected with factors that also influence the acquisition of reading skills, but much more refined assessment of the correlation between this staining pattern and precise sensorimotor performance will have to be carried out. As in the Colorado project, the brothers of the probands in this study were all significantly more severely retarded in reading than sisters. In addition, the reading skills of the adult males in this population were indistinguishable from those of the male dyslexic individuals. As noted earlier, these subjects, like other children with reading problems, were found to have poor performance on the following tasks: digit span, auditory discrimination, and the peg-board test, especially with the nondominant hand. The severely dyslexic boys were superior in tests of visual memory and visuoperceptual organization when compared with matched controls.

It is difficult to integrate the findings from these two studies as one uses both boys and girls in one-generation families and the other tests boys and three generations of their families. Both suggest, however, that there is a heritable component to reading disorders. The data confirm general population studies that show that males are much more at risk to factors that predispose against the easy acquisition of reading skills. On the other hand, girls with reading problems are rarer and their problems are much less influenced by the environment.

If boys are more at risk for reading disorders, the performance of males should be more affected than the performance of females in unstable environments. In a normal school environment, the sex ratio for dyslexia is approximately three to one, but in clinical populations or in special schools for the learning disabled, these ratios shift to five or six to one (Finucci and Childs 1981). Furthermore, in males, but not in females, there is a correlation between behavior disorders and reading difficulties. These facts in conjunction with the genetic studies suggest that both biological and environmental factors are involved. The clinical data indicate that males are more vulnerable to environmental factors, so that when the environment is not supportive, male reading ability declines even further with respect to the performance of females. Females in similar situations exhibit fewer deficiencies in reading skills when compared with normal populations.

Teachers have long recognized the importance of the influence of reading material on reading success. If the material is interesting, then reading performance improves. However, it turns out that this is true largely for males. In an attempt to specify the importance of high-interest material on girls' and boys' reading progress, Asher and Markell (1974) tested 87 fifth graders on reading performance using material specifically suited to the interest of each individual child. Over time, it was found that the boys' and girls' reading scores did not differ. However, in the control population, which read material of equal difficulty but selected to be of no interest to 10 year olds, sex differences reappeared, with the girls significantly better than the boys.

Additionally, it appears that males are penalized in classrooms where silent reading is the norm. Rowell (1976) tested 240 children in the third and fifth grades in three types of schools in Connecticut. In each school, reading comprehension for the boys in the oral reading condition was significantly better than when they read silently. For the girls, it made no difference whether they read silently or aloud. Males also appear to have more difficulties than females in open-classroom environments. Gies et al. (1973) found that the greatest sex difference on tests of vocabulary, reading, and language arts emerged in an open-classroom setting, in which females did particularly well. Sex differences were less pronounced in the closed-classroom condition in his sample of 108 sixth graders, where the males surpassed the females on the vocabulary portion of the test. It is not clear from this analysis whether it is the lack of distraction that is important to males, or whether they respond to the greater structure in the closed-classroom setting. The implications of these two findings are that males might do well in a highly structured environment where there is stress on oral reading, whereas females work somewhat more effectively with greater independence.

Low socioeconomic class combines with minor birth complications to further depress male reading scores. This finding has been reported by Hesselholdt and Aggerholm-Madsens (1974) in a sample of 184 10-year-old children in Denmark. A strong relationship existed between reading problems and these two factors for males, but not for females. Yule and Rutter (1968) reported a high correlation between antisocial behavior in English schoolboys and reading difficulties, with no such relationship found for girls. A similar finding has been reported for a U.S. population by Lanthier and Deiker (1974).

Not only does severe environmental stress influence male but not female aptitude, but male performance can also suffer from minor and more immediate environmental stressors. Cotler and Palmer (1971) studied 120 children in the fourth through sixth grades on tests of reading comprehension by asking students to match paragraphs for meaning. The children were put under mild pressure by inducing anxiety through praise or criticism. Though girls were consistently superior at this task, the sex effect was enhanced by the manipulation involving criticism, which strongly affected the performance of the boys.

In Lanthier and Deiker's study of 117 adolescent inpatients referred for behavior disorders (1974), a strong relationship was found between reading and math test scores for the 66 males and their mothers, but no relationship between test scores for 51 adolescent girls and either parent.

Meanwhile, the girls were significantly ahead on the language achievement test and the total test battery with respect to the boys. Heritable factors that are transmitted from mother to sons tend to be sex linked (on the X chromosome). But as this model has so far failed to find support, a more likely alternative is an environmental explanation involving the impact of a more academically demanding mother on her male offspring. The latter explanation seems more likely in the light of a large investigation by Cicirelli published in 1967.

Cicirelli studied 600 middle-class white families and the sex constitution of the siblings. Daughters were superior to sons on the verbal elaboration subtest of the Minnesota Creative Thinking Battery and on the California Language Achievement Test. When Cicirelli examined the sex of the siblings in families with two to four children, the general finding was that boys' performance, as well as their IQ scores, increased noticeably if they had at least one female sibling. Male children were particularly at risk when their siblings were male, especially in families with three or four children. In 90 two-child families, the highest average IQ was for firstborn girls (118) and the lowest was for firstborn boys (108), with second born boys and girls being more similar (114 and 111, respectively). The findings for three-child families showed little effect of the sex constitution on IQ or reading for girls, but both IQ scores and reading scores increased if boys had at least one sister. The average IQ for boys with two brothers was 109.6, with two sisters 118, and with one brother and one sister 117. Reading test scores also reflected this trend.

Cicirelli did not report the ages of the siblings. It is possible that his results would be even more striking if the boys with older versus younger sisters were compared. However, the data strongly suggest that both mothers and sisters are very important to a boy's language development. It does not seem to matter a great deal to the girls' language development whether they are in a large or small family or whether they are surrounded by brothers or sisters.

These results bring us to the crux of the nature versus nurture issue. Given an adequate environment, sex differences are found to emerge, indicating a biological basis to these differences. In stressful environments, the performance of boys deteriorates markedly. Males appear at risk during the early school years, leading one to ask: Is the predisposition to risk also biological? The interaction between the environment and biology is thrown into high relief by these findings, and the meaninglessness of a nature versus nurture argument becomes apparent. Scarr's insight (1981), discussed earlier, is of obvious importance here: What is easy to learn is most rooted in biology and least influenced by the environment; what is difficult to learn is most upset by environmental stressors and least biologically fixed. We now have considerable evidence that females have a greater biological predisposition to develop linguistic competence. Hence, the environment is less relevant.

What remains as a tantalizing question is whether there is a trade-off between verbal ability and spatial-mathematical ability. Steeves (1982) reported that approximately 25 percent of the severely dyslexic boys she studied were gifted in mathematics, scoring in the same range as boys in the mathematically gifted program in a normal school environment. Smith (1982) also reported a relationship between extreme dyslexia and high spatial ability. Therefore, it is entirely possible that many boys who have been rejected by the school system as unteachable might have developed into brilliant inventors or mathematicians. One need only think of people like Henry Ford, who had extremely poor language skills, to see the danger of this practice.

SUMMARY

This is a difficult chapter. It asks the reader to assimilate a host of findings on sex differences in various perceptual and cognitive tasks and compare these findings with our current knowledge about development in the language arts and mathematics. The important fact about these two sets of findings is that though they have come from entirely independent research programs, there is a remarkable similarity between the data. This was first brought home to me when I was asked to prepare a paper on sex differences for a conference on learning disabilities. I had little detailed knowledge of this field, and so went to the library computer center to request a literature search. As I began to read the results of various experiments, especially those on reading, I was astonished at the parallel between the two sets of data, especially the fact that the key sensorimotor skills involved in reading, writing, and spelling are almost identical to the perceptual and motor abilities that differentiate males and females. My aim in this chapter has been to illuminate these parallels.

However, this process also uncovers some interesting corollaries. First, these parallel findings imply that there are biological or genetic reasons why girls and boys develop different sets of abilities in cognitive tasks. The brunt of this chapter has been devoted to demonstrating that it is entirely normal for boys to lag in reading, but to be accelerated in higher math. What we need to ask, as stated earlier, is: What are the girls doing when they learn to read, write, and spell that makes them so efficient, and what are the boys doing in algebra and geometry that makes them efficient? We now have some of the answers for the language arts, but so far nothing but speculation for mathematics.

But more importantly, this comparison of the sexes highlights a philosophical position in our culture that has been completely overlooked. This relates to the problem of how and why children come to be designated "learning disabled." It is necessary to go beyond the discovery that boys lag behind in some skills and girls in others, to ask a more fundamental question: In what situations is the term "learning disabilities" applied? It turns out that this label is reserved entirely for children who are slow to acquire habits in a particular writing system or who misbehave in classrooms. It is never applied to children on the playing field, in arts and crafts, woodwork, or music classes. This tells us something about our culture. We value literacy and numeracy more than we value anything else. When certain skills are valued so excessively, there is enormous pressure on children to acquire them, whether or not they have any aptitude. In fact, such overwhelming cultural pressure actually results in an ideological transformation, where people come to believe that skills in literacy or numeracy are actually "biologically" given. Universal literacy is currently a religion, with the dogma that everyone can and must learn to read by the age of 7 to 8 years. Whereas formerly it was believed that slowness in learning a writing system was due to laziness or to poor teaching, now we believe that poor readers have something wrong with their brains.

Examine the logic carefully. It is fashionable today for people who have little knowledge of research to believe that all behavior is culturally conditioned. One constantly hears the terms "conditioning" and "socialization" employed as if they were both causal and factual descriptors of developmental phenomena. No data are ever cited in support of these beliefs, as they are supposed to be self-evident "truths." Yet, when considering early classroom performance, the socialization argument is abruptly abandoned to be replaced by an unstated biological assumption. This biological assumption is implicit in every argument about early learning problems, including the diagnosis of hyperactivity.*

---

*This condition, suffered mainly by young boys (sex ratio of nine to one) is in fact defined entirely by the teachers' or parents' "tolerance for annoying

The reasoning behind this assumption is clear. No one must be to blame. The teacher cannot be blamed for an inability to teach, the parents cannot be blamed for raising unruly children, and the child cannot be blamed for being stupid or lazy. If, however, literacy is a God-given property of the human brain, this means that there must be something wrong with a child's brain if the child remains illiterate. This belief has led to a number of studies purporting to look for brain damage in dyslexic populations. On the other hand, children who are bad at sports and piano lessons are merely reckoned to have little talent for athletics and music. In other words, most of us feel entirely comfortable with the belief that people have different talents and predispositions, but this attitude is rarely applied to skills acquired in the classroom. We never talk about a "talent for reading."

Earlier I reviewed two major studies on genetic factors in "dyslexia." Please bear in mind that a genetic predisposition to dyslexia and the fact that this problem runs in families, especially in males, do not mean that these people have brain damage. Their brain organization may be different, but it is the organization and not pathology that makes them "abnormal." Recall that "abnormal" means simply statistically rare. Dyslexic individuals have more reading problems than most people. Musical talent also runs in families; by the same token, Mozart, Beethoven, and Brahms were also abnormal, because they had more musical talent than most people. Similarly, a lack of musical talent may also run in families, should we care to investigate this. As it is of little consequence to our social organization, we have no programs on the genetic basis of "dysmusia." We would consider such programs utterly nonsensical.

Let me leave you with this thought: It makes no more sense to study the absence of a talent for music than to study the absence of a talent for reading. The distinction depends entirely upon how much music and reading are valued in a particular society.

---

behavior." There is no supportive evidence in over 200 studies on hyperactivity for any motor, attentional, or cognitive difficulty, provided these children are doing something that interests them. The major problem is that the typical classroom organization is neither appropriate for their interests nor for the way they time their behavior.

REFERENCES

Ammons, R. B., S. I. Alprin, and C. H. Ammons. 1955. "Rotary Pursuit Performance as Related to Sex and Age of Pre-Adult Subjects." *Journal of Experimental Psychology*, 49:127-33.

Annett, M. 1970. "The Growth of Manual Preference and Speech." *British Journal of Psychology*, 61:545-58.

Asher, S. R., and R. A Markell. 1974. "Sex Differences in Comprehension of High and Low Interest Reading Material." *Journal of Educational Psychology* , 66:680-87.

Badian, N. A. 1982. "The Prediction of Good and Poor Reading Before Kindergarten Entry: A 4-Year Follow Up." *Journal of Special Education*, 16:309-18.

Benbow, C. P., and J. C. Stanley. 1980. "Sex Differences in Mathematical Ability: Fact or Artifact?" *Science*, 210:1262-64.

Bentley, A. 1968. *Monotones*. London: Novello.

Blachman, B. A. 1982. "Linguistic Variables as Predictors of Kindergarten and First Grade Reading Achievement." Paper presented at the 33rd Annual Conference of the Orton Dyslexia Society, Baltimore, MD.

Brabyn, L. B., and D. McGuinness. 1979. "Gender Differences in Response to Spatial Frequency and Stimulus Orientation." *Perception and Psychophysics*, 26:319-24.

Brandt, E. M., and G. Mitchell. 1973. "Pairing Preadolescents with Infants." *Developmental Psychology*, 8:222-28.

Broadbent, D. E. 1958. *Perception and Communication*. New York: Pergamon Press.

Brownell, W. W. 1973. "The Relationship of Sex, Social Class and Verbal Planning to Dysfluencies Produced by Non-Stuttering Children." *Dissertation Abstracts International*, 34A:888.

Burg, A. 1966. "Visual Acuity as Measured by Dynamic and Static Tests: A Comparative Evaluation." *Journal of Applied Psychology*, 50:460-66.

Burg, A., and S. Hulbert. 1961. "Dynamic Visual Acuity as Related to Age, Sex and Static Acuity." *Journal of Applied Psychology*, 45:111-16.

Calfee, R. C., P. Lindamood, and C. Lindamood. 1973. "Acoustic-Phonetic Skills and Reading. Kindergarten Through Twelfth Grade." *Journal of Educational Psychology*, 64:293-98.

Cameron, J., N. Livson, and N. Bayley. 1967. "Infant Vocalizations and Their Relationship to Mature Intelligence." *Science*, 157:331-32.

Cicirelli, V. G. 1967. "Sibling Constellation, Creativity, I.Q. and Academic Achievement." *Child Development*, 38:481-90.

Cohen, L. B., E. R. Gelber, and M. A. Lazar. 1971. "Infant Habituation and Generalization to Differing Degrees of Stimulus Novelty." *Journal of Experimental Child Psychology*, 11:379-89.

Cornell, E. H., and M. S. Strauss. 1973. "Infants' Responsiveness to Compounds of Habituated Visual Stimuli." *Developmental Psychology*, 9:73-78.

Corso, J. F. 1959. "Age and Sex Differences in Thresholds." *Journal of the Acoustic Society of America*, 31:489-507.

Cotler, S., and R. J. Palmer. 1971. "Social Reinforcement, Individual Difference Factors, and the Reading Performance of Elementary School Children." *Journal of Personality and Social Psychology*, 18:97-104.

Davidson, P. S. 1982. "Neuropsychological Perspective of Mathematics Learning." Paper presented at the 33rd Annual Conference of the Orton Dyslexia Society, Baltimore, MD.

Decker, S. N., and J. C. DeFries. 1980. "Cognitive Abilities in Families with Reading Disabled Children." *Journal of Learning Disabilities*, 13:517-22.

DeFries, J. C., and S. N. Decker. 1982. "Genetic Aspects of Reading Disability: A Family Study." In *Reading Disorders: Varieties and Treatments*, edited by R. N. Malatesha and P. G. Aaron. New York: Academic Press.

Denckla, M. B. 1973. "Development of Speed in Repetitive and Successive Finger Movements in Normal Children." *Developmental Medical Child Neurology*, 15:635-45.

___. 1974. "Development of Motor Co-ordination in Normal Children." *Developmental Medical Child Neurology*, 16:729-41.

Denckla, M. B., and R. G. Rudel. 1976. "Rapid Automatized Naming (RAN): Dyslexia Differentiated from Other Disorders." *Neuropsychologia*, 14:471-79.

Diamond, M. C., G. A. Dowling, and R. E. Johnson. 1981. "Morphological Cerebral Cortical Assymmetry in Male and Female Rats." *Experimental Neurology*, 71:261-68.

Dwyer, C. A. 1979. "The Role of Tests and Their Construction in Producing Sex-Related Differences." In *Sex-Related Differences in Cognitive Functioning*, edited by M. A. Wittig and A. C. Petersen, pp. 335-53. New York: Academic Press.

Eagles, E. L., S. M. Wishik, L. G. Doerfler, W. Malnick, and H. S. Levine. 1963. *Hearing Sensitivity and Related Factors in Children*. Pittsburgh: University of Pittsburgh Press.

Elliott, C. D. 1971. "Noise Tolerance and Extraversion in Children." *British Journal of Psychology*, 62:375-80.

Entwhistle, D. R., and D. P. Baker. 1983. "Gender and Young Children's Expectations for Performance in Arithmetic." *Developmental Psychology*, 19:200-09.

Fagan, J. F. 1972. "Infants' Recognition Memory for Faces." *Journal of Experimental Child Psychology*, 14:453-76.

Farnham-Diggory, S., and L. W. Gregg. 1975. "Short-Term Memory Function in Young Readers." *Journal of Experimental Child Psychology*, 19:279-98.

Fennema, E., and J. Sherman. 1977. "Sex-Related Differences in Mathematics Achievement, Spatial Visualization and Affective Factors." *American Educational Research Journal*, 14:51-71.

Feshbach, N. D., and M. A. Hoffman. 1978. "Sex Differences in Children's Reports of Emotion Arousing Situations." Paper presented at the Western Psychological Association, San Francisco, CA.

Finucci, J. M., and B. Childs. 1981. "Are There Really More Dyslexic Boys than Girls?" In *Sex Differences in Dyslexia*, edited by A. Ansara, N. Geschwind, A. Galaburda, M. Albert, and N. Gartrell, pp. 1-9. Towson, MD: Orton Dyslexia Society.

Fraser, C., and N. Roberts. 1975. "Mother's Speech to Children of Four Different Ages." *Journal of Psycholinguistic Research,* 4:9-16.

Gaddes, W. H., and D. J. Crockett. 1975. "The Spreen-Benton Aphoria Tests, Normative Data as a Measure of Normal Language Development." *Brain and Language,* 2:257-80.

Gaines, R. 1972. "Variables in Color Perception of Young Children." *Journal of Experimental Child Psychology,* 14:196-218.

Gies, F. J., B. C. Leonard, J. B. Madden, and J. Jon. 1973. "Effects of Organizational Climate and Sex on the Language Arts Achievement of Disadvantaged Sixth Graders." *Journal of Educational Research,* 67:177-81.

Goodenough, E. W. 1957. "Interest in Persons as an Aspect of Sex Differences in the Early Years." *Genetic Psychology Monographs,* 55:287-323.

Guilford, J. P. 1967. *The Nature of Human Intelligence.* New York: McGraw-Hill.

Gurucharri, K. A. 1974. "Haptic Performance and First-Grade • Reading Achievement." *Dissertation Abstracts International,* 35A:887-88.

Harlow, H. F., K. A. Schitz, and M. K. Harlow. 1969. "Effects of Social Isolation on Learning Performance of Rhesus Monkeys." In *Proceedings of the Second International Congress of Primatology. I: Behavior,* edited by C. R. Carpenter, pp. 178-85. Basel: Karger.

Harris, L. J. 1976. "Sex Differences in Spatial Ability: Possible Environmental, Genetic and Neurological Factors." In *Hemispheric Asymmetries of Function,* edited by M. Kinsbourne. Cambridge: Cambridge University Press.

Harris, Marvin. 1974. *Cows, Pigs, Wars, and Witches: The Riddle of Culture* . New York: Random House.

Hesselholdt, S., and G. Aggerholm-Madsens. 1974. "Process and Product in the Marble Board Test. The Biosocial Interaction and Reading Ability." *Skolepsykologi,* 11:277-303.

Hoffman, M. L. 1977. "Sex Differences in Empathy and Related Behaviors." *Psychological Bulletin,* 84:712-22.

Hull, F. M., P. W. Mielke, R. J. Timmons, and J. A. Willeford. 1971. "The National Speech and Hearing Survey: Preliminary Results." *ASHA,* 3:501-09.

Ingram, T. T. S. 1975. "Speech Disorders in Childhood." In *Foundations of Language Development,* edited by E. H. Lenneberg and E. Lenneberg. New York: Academic Press.

Jacklin, C., and E. Maccoby. 1978. "Social Behavior at 33 Months in Same and Mixed Sex Dyads." *Child Development,* 49:557-69.

Jackson, M. D., and J. L. McClelland. 1979. "Processing Determinant of Reading Speed." *Journal of Experimental Psychology: General,* 108:151-81.

Jacobs, G. H. 1977. "Visual Sensitivity: Significant Within Species Variations in a Non-Human Primate." *Science,* 197:499-500.

Jahoda, G. 1979. "On the Nature of Difficulties in Spatial-Perceptual Tasks: Ethnic and Sex Differences." *British Journal of Psychology,* 70:351-63.

Jansky, J., and K. de Hirsch. 1972. *Preventing Reading Failure.* New York: Harper and Row.

Jarvis, E. O. 1974. "Auditory Abilities of Primary School Children." *Dissertation Abstracts International,* 35A:890-91.

Johansson, G. 1955. "A Note on Differences in Motion Track Enlargement Between Male and Female Subjects. In *Reports from the Psychological Laboratory, No. 24*. Stockholm: University of Stockholm.

Kagan, J., and M. Lewis. 1965. "Studies of Attention in the Human Infant." *Merrill-Palmer Quarterly*, 11:95-127.

Kershner, J. R. 1978. "Lateralization in Normal 6 Year Olds as Related to Later Reading Disability." *Developmental Psychobiology*, 11:309-19.

Kimura, D. 1977. "Acquisition of a Motor Skill After Left-Hemisphere Damage." *Brain*, 100:527-42.

___. 1983. "Sex Differences in Cerebral Organization for Speech and Praxic Functions." *Canadian Journal of Psychology*, 37:19-35.

Kimura, D., and R. A. Harshman. 1984. "Sex Differences in Brain Organization for Verbal and Nonverbal Functions." In *Progress in Brain Research*, edited by G. J. DeVries et al. Amsterdam: Elsevier.

Kipnis, D. M. 1976. "Intelligence, Occupational Status and Achievement Orientation." In *Exploring Sex Differences*, edited by B. Lloyd and J. Archer, pp. 95-122. London: Academic Press.

Knox, C., and D. Kimura. 1970. "Cerebral Processing of Nonverbal Sounds in Boys and Girls." *Neuropsychologia*, 8:227-37.

Lancaster, J. B. 1979. "Sex and Gender in Evolutionary Perspective." In *Human Sexuality: A Comparative and Developmental Perspective*, edited by H. A. Katchadourian, pp. 51-80. Berkeley: University of California Press.

Lanthier, I. J., and T. E. Deiker. 1974. "Achievement Scores of Emotionally Disturbed Adolescents and Parent Educational Level." *Child Study Journal*, 4:163-68.

Lewis, M. 1969. "Infants' Responses to Facial Stimuli During the First Year of Life." *Developmental Psychology*, 1:75-86.

Lewis, M., J. Kagan, and J. Kalafat. 1966. "Patterns of Fixation in the Young Infant." *Child Development*, 37:331-41.

Lexier, K. A. 1979. "Auditory Discriminability, Blending and Phoneme Segmentation Ability: Exploring Basic Skills in Reading Acquisition." *Dissertation Abstracts International*, 2469A-2470A.

Liberman, I. Y., and V. Mann. 1981. "Should Reading Instruction and Remediation Vary with the Sex of the Child?" In *Sex Differences in Dyslexia*, edited by A. Ansara, N. Geschwind, A. Galaburda, M. Albert, and N. Gartrell, pp. 151-68. Towson, MD: Orton Dyslexia Society.

Lindamood, C. H., and P. C. Lindamood. 1971. *Lindamood Auditory Conceptualization Test*. Boston: Teaching Resources Corporation.

Lomas, J., and D. Kimura. 1976. "Intrahemispheric Interaction Between Speaking and Sequential Manual Activity." *Neuropsychologia*, 14:23-33.

Maccoby, E., and C. N. Jacklin. 1974. *The Psychology of Sex Differences*. Stanford, CA: Stanford University Press.

McCall, R. B., and J. Kagan. 1967. "Attention in the Infant: Effects of Complexity, Contour, Perimeter and Familiarity." *Child Development*, 38:939-52.

___. 1970. "Individual Differences in the Infant's Distribution of Attention to Stimulus Discrepancy." *Developmental Psychology*, 2:90-98.

McGlone, J. 1980. "Sex Differences in Human Brain Asymmetry: A Critical Survey." *Behavioral and Brain Sciences*, 3:215-51.

McCoy, C. 1978. "Experimental Study of Hearing in the Aged as Measured by Pure Tones, Word Discrimination and the SSW." *Dissertation Abstracts International*, 38:4719.

McGrew, W. C. 1972. "Aspects of Social Development in Nursery School Children with Emphasis on Introduction to the Group." In *Ethological Studies of Child Behavior*, edited by E. Blurton-Jones. Cambridge: Cambridge University Press.

McGuinness, D. 1972. "Hearing: Individual Differences in Perceiving." *Perception*, 1:465-73.

____. 1976. "Away from a Unisex Psychology: Individual Differences in Visual Perception." *Perception*, 5:279-94

____. 1976. "Perceptual and Cognitive Differences Between the Sexes." In *Explorations in Sex Differences*, edited by B. Lloyd and J. Archer. New York: Academic Press.

____. 1985. *When Children Don't Learn*. New York: Basic Books, Inc.

McGuinness, D., and T. E. Bartell. 1982. "Lateral Asymmetry: Hard or Simple Minded?" *Neuropsychologia*, 20:629-39.

McGuinness, D., and L. A. Brabyn. 1984. "In Pursuit of Visuo-Spatial Ability. Part I. Visual Systems." *Journal of Mental Imagery*, 8:1-12.

McGuinness, D., and A. Courtney. 1983. "Sex Differences in Visual and Phonetic Search." *Journal of Mental Imagery*, 7:95-104.

McGuinness, D., and I. Lewis. 1976. "Sex Differences in Visual Persistence: Experiments on the Ganzfeld and the After Image." *Perception*, 5:295-301.

McGuinness, D., and K. H. Pribram. 1978. "The Origins of Sensory Bias in the Development of Gender Differences in Perception and Cognition." In *Cognitive Growth and Development: Essays in Memory of Herbert G. Birch* , edited by M. Bortner, pp. 1-56. New York: Brunner/Mazel.

McGuinness, D., and J. Symonds. 1977. "Sex Differences in Choice Behavior: The Object-Person Dimension." *Perception*, 6:691-94.

Majeres, R. L. 1977. "Sex Differences in Clerical Speed. Perceptual Encoding vs. Verbal Encoding." *Memory and Cognition*, 5:468-76.

Mateer, C. A., S. B. Polen, and G. A. Ojemann. 1982. "Sexual Variation in Cortical Location of Naming as Determined by Stimulation Mapping. Commentary on J. McGlone: Sex Differences in Human Brain Asymmetry." *Brain and Behavioral Sciences*, 5:310-11.

Meyers, W. J., and G. N. Cantor. 1967. "Observing and Cardiac Responses of Human Infants to Visual Stimuli." *Journal of Experimental Child Psychology* , 5:16-25.

Miller, G. A., E. Galanter, and K. H. Pribram. 1960. *Plans and the Structure of Behavior*. New York: Henry Holt and Co.

Mirabile, P. J., R. J. Porter, L. F. Hughes, and C. I. Berlin. 1978. "Dichotic Lag Effect in Children 7-15." *Developmental Psychology*, 14:277-85.

Mitchell, G. 1979. *Behavioral Sex Differences in Non-Human Primates*. New York: Van Nostrand Reinhold.

Mittler, P., and J. Ward. 1970. "The Use of the Illinois Test of Psycholinguistic Abilities on British Four-Year-Old Children: A Normative and Factorial Study." *British Journal of Educational Psychology*, 40:43-54.

Monagan, D. 1983. "The Failure of Coed Sports." *Psychology Today*, March.

Montessori, M. 1972. *The Discovery of the Child*. New York: Ballantine Books.

Moore, T. 1967. "Language and Intelligence: A Longitudinal Study of the First 8 Years." *Human Development*, 10:88-106.

Neisser, U. 1967. *Cognitive Psychology*. New York: Appleton-Century-Crofts.

Noble, C. E., B. L. Baker, and T. A. Jones. 1964. "Age and Sex Parameters in Psychomotor Learning." *Perceptual and Motor Skills*, 19:935-45.

Pancratz, C. N., and L. B. Cohen. 1970. "Recovery of Habituation in Infants." *Journal of Experimental Child Psychology*, 9:208-16.

Paynter, E. T., and N. A. Petty. 1974. "Articulatory Sound: Acquisition of Two-Year Old Children." *Perceptual and Motor Skills*, 39:1079-85.

Phillips, J. R. 1973. "Syntax and Vocabulary of Mothers' Speech to Young Children: Age and Sex Comparison." *Child Development*, 44: 182-85.

Pishkin, V., and R. Blanchard. 1964. "Auditory Concept Identification as a Function of Subject Sex and Stimulus Dimensions." *Psychonomic Science*, 1:177-78.

Pishkin, V., and J. T. Shurley. 1965. "Auditory Dimensions and Irrelevant Information in Concept Identification of Males and Females." *Perceptual and Motor Skills*, 20:673-83.

Potsova, M. 1975. "Speech Development in Collectively Reared Preschool Children." *Psychologia a Patopsychologia Dietata*, 10:43-60.

Rae, G. 1977. "Auditory-Visual Integration, Sex and Reading Ability." *Perceptual and Motor Skills*, 45:826.

Roberts, E. 1972. "Poor Pitch Singing." Ph.D. thesis, University of Liverpool, England.

Roberts, J. 1964. *Binocular Visual Acuity of Adults*. Washington, D.C.: U.S. Department of Health, Education, and Welfare.

Ross, J. M., and H. R. Simpson. 1971. "The National Survey of Health and Development: 1. Educational Attainment." *British Journal of Psychology*, 41:49-61.

Ross, H. E., and J. M. Woodhouse. 1979. "Genetic and Environmental Factors in Orientation Anisotrophy: A Field Study in the British Isles." *Perception*, 8:507-21.

Rowell, E. H. 1976. "Do Elementary Students Read Better Orally or Silently?" *Reading Teacher*, 29:367-70.

Scarr, S. 1981. "Comments on Psychology, Genetics and Social Policy from an Anti-Reductionist." In *Psychology's Second Century. Houston Symposium II*, edited by R. A. Kasschau and C. N. Cofer. New York: Praeger.

Shea, J. D. C., and G. Yerua. 1980. "Conservation in Community School Children in Papua, New Guinea." *International Journal of Psychology*, 15:11-25.

Sherman, J. 1967. "The Problem of Sex Differences in Space Perception and Aspects of Intellectual Functioning." *Psychological Review*, 74:290-99.

_____. 1980. "Mathematics, Spatial Visualization, and Related Factors: Changes in Girls and Boys Grades 8-11." *Journal of Educational Psychology*, 72:476-82.

Shephard, A. H., D. S. Abbey, and M. Humphries. 1962. "Age and Sex in Relation to Perceptual-Motor Performance on Several Control-Display Relations on the TCC." *Perceptual and Motor Skills*, 14:103-18.

Shuter, R. 1968. *The Psychology of Music*. London: Methuen.

Smith, P. K., and K. Connolly. 1972. "Patterns of Play and Social Interaction in Pre-School Children." In *Ethological Studies of Child Behavior* , edited by N. Blurton-Jones. Cambridge: Cambridge University Press.

Smith, S. D. 1982. "The Search for a Dominantly Inherited Form of Dyslexia." Presented at the 33rd Annual Conference of the Orton Dyslexia Society, Baltimore, Md.

Smith, S. D., W. J. Kimberling, B. F. Pennington, and H. A. Lubs. 1982. "Specific Reading Disability: Identification of an Inherited Form Through Linkage Analysis." *Science*, 219:1345-47.

Spearman, C. *The Nature of Intelligence and the Principles of Cognition* . London: Macmillan and Co.

Spring, C. 1975. "Naming Speed as a Correlate of Reading Ability and Sex." *Perceptual and Motor Skills*, 4:134.

Spring, C., and C. Capps. 1974. "Encoding Speed, Rehearsal and Probed Recall of Dyslexic Boys." *Journal of Educational Psychology*, 66:780-86.

Stallings, J. A. 1979. "Comparison of Men's and Women's Behaviors in High School Math Classes." Paper presented to the American Psychological Association, New York, NY.

Steeves, J. 1982. "Multi-Sensory Math." Paper presented at the 33rd Annual Meeting of the Orton Dyslexia Society, Baltimore, MD.

Tallal, P., and R. Stark. 1982. "Perceptual/Motor Profiles of Reading Impaired Children with or Without Concomitant Oral Language Deficits." In *Annals of Dyslexia, Vol. 32*, pp. 163-76. Baltimore, MD: Orton Dyslexia Society.

Teuber, H. L. 1974. "Why Two Brains?" In *The Neurosciences: Third Study Program*, edited by F. O. Schmitt and E. G. Worden, pp. 71-74. Cambridge, MA: MIT Press.

Thomas, L. L., A. T. Curtis, and R. Bolton. 1978. "Sex Differences in Elicited Color Lexicon Size." *Perceptual and Motor Skills*, 47:77-78.

West, M. M., and M. J. Konner. 1976. "The Role of the Father: An Anthropological Perspective." In *The Role of the Father in Child Development*, edited by M. C. Lamb.

Witelson, S. F. 1976. "Sex and the Single Hemisphere: Specialization of the Right Hemisphere for Spatial Processing." *Science*, 193:425-27.

Yule, W., and M. Rutter. 1968. "Educational Aspects of Childhood Maladjustment: Some Epidemiological Findings." *British Journal of Psychology*, 38:7-13.

Zaner, A. R., R. F. Levee, and R. R. Guinta. 1968. "The Development of Auditory Perceptual Skills as a Function of Maturation." *Journal of Auditory Research*, 8:313-22.

5

THE QUESTION OF SIZE

Roberta Hall

Discussions of differences between the sexes often start with and return to the question of size. However, the study of size is more complex than it appears. What features are to be measured, and in what age groups? These two factors hold the answers to the question of how the sexes differ in size; yet our common view, where the question often both starts and ends, is that "men are larger than women."

Studies of size differences can be grouped in seven categories according to their perspective: theoretical, technical, using nonhuman animals, using early humans, comparing *Homo sapiens* populations, measuring child growth, and using body composition (see Figure 5.1).

THEORETICAL

Contemporary theory of size differences in men and women originated in Darwin's *The Descent of Man and Selection in Relation to Sex*, originally published in 1871. The clarity of Darwin's thought is no less impressive than the masses of observations of animals of all kinds with which he built his case for evolution. However, in his book on sexual selection, Darwin (1917) was misled by his own society's prejudices and behavior patterns. Variation in male size, as well as the larger size of males in comparison with females, is due to natural selection that follows intense competition for females, Darwin asserted. His description of females, both in human and other animals, coy and without sexual passion, no doubt was a bias introduced by his Victorian

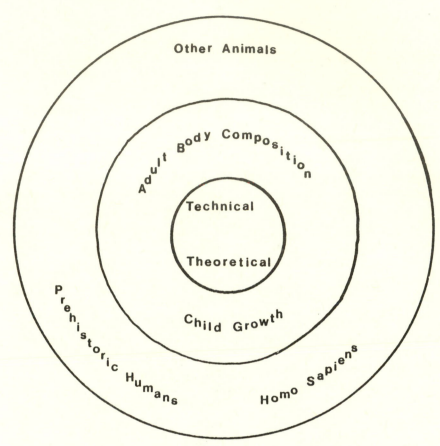

Figure 5.1. Studies of sexual dimorphism: seven perspectives.

upbringing and social mores. Certainly his views of the mental powers of the sexes, by which he meant imagination and courage as well as intelligence, were produced by his own culture's concept of appropriate behavior for men and women:

> As before remarked of bodily strength, although men do not now fight for their wives, and this form of selection has passed away, yet during manhood, they generally undergo a severe struggle in order to maintain themselves and their families, and this will tend to keep up or even increase their mental powers, and, as a consequence, the present inequality between the sexes (Darwin 1917, p. 578).

The most recent addition to the library of theoretical explanations for size differences between males and females is sociobiology (see Hamilton, Chapters 2 and 3), which states that behavior is inherited if it contributes to an individual's ability to leave offspring. Several sociobiologists have done comparative studies with nonhuman primates to test whether competition among males for the sexual possession of females leads to large body size of males. Though Alexander et al. (1979) found some support for this theory in a study of several animal populations, Ralls (1977) found other variables equally important in explaining size variation. Similarly, Leutenegger's studies (1982a, b) with primates found that the sexual selection theory explains only a part of the variation in sexual dimorphism. Ecological factors also conbtribute to variation in size differences. Among polygynous species, body size itself is a factor. The body size factor that Leutenegger identified is a form of positive allometry, the tendency of a feature to increase disproportionately with an increase in another trait. Leutenegger found allometry operating for dimorphism in body weight and in the size of the canine teeth, but only in primates with a polygynous mating pattern. In these, the difference between males and females is much greater in the large than in the small animal groups. By contrast, in species in which animals tend to form permanent pair bonds, sex differences in body weight are directly proportional to the size of the species.

When theoretical arguments turn technical, as in the examples above, their significance can be lost in disputes over data and methodology. What must be remembered is that the question is not just of the size of some animals; the question concerns whether males are "naturally" promiscuous and females are "naturally" uninterested in sexual activity. If males of a species have a greater average body weight than females, can we assume that they normally compete for as many females as they can get? And can we assume it means that females lack choice in the disposition of their own bodies? Female primates, it turns out, play an active role in determining the mating structure (see Chapter 3).

In times when evolution is under attack from fundamentalist religious groups, it is important to reflect that both evolutionary and nonevolutionary rationales have been used to explain the observation that "men are bigger than women." Both rationales have been used to support the dogma that men (should) dominate women. Whereas antievolutionists have asserted that God designed the system of male size and social dominance, some authors have argued that since natural selection produced larger men than women, the survival of the species depends upon male domination of the female sex.

Theory, like technical studies, can lead us astray as well as inform us. In a cross-cultural analysis of male-female relations, Sanday (1981) showed that male dominance is not universal among human cultures. Midgley (1978), in a readable and penetrating analysis, showed the pitfalls and promises that a truly evolutionary, but objective, approach to the study of human and animal nature can provide. Specifically concerned with sex differences, Daly and Wilson (1978) put the evolutionary approach into perspective, offering it not as a rationalization for the status quo, but as a commitment to understand life processes.

TECHNICAL STUDIES

Opposite from theoretical exercises are studies that attempt to more accurately measure sexual dimorphism. Ross et al. (1977) and Ross and Ward (1982) developed a unisex ideal human body named "Phantom" as a standard against which to compare measurements of both males and females. Phantom is a model or ideal in a statistical sense, and its value is descriptive (and hence technical) rather than explanatory. Similarly, Bennett (1981) introduced a measure that takes into account the range of variation within each sex. Most importantly, Bennett's measure demonstrates the extent of overlap betwen the two sexes, which the conventional ratios fail to do. Chakraborty and Majumbder (1982) improved the measure and clarified its mathematical basis. Both projects were technical in that they refined descriptions but did not attempt explanations. In another type of technical study, Glucksmann (1978) presented a review of studies on hormonal and physiological controls for all aspects of mammalian sexual dimorphism, including size.

NONHOMINID STUDIES

The study of sexual dimorphism in animals can tell us a great deal about an animal species and need not be justified by relating it to the perspective of humankind. However, in this book, it is our own species that concerns us, so for us the issue in the study of other mammals is: What does their size sexual dimorphism teach us about our own dimorphism or that of our ancestors?

Commonalities of genetics, anatomy, and behavior bind all animals and prescribe the courses of sexual development (Glucksmann 1978). Particularly in sex differences, we share the largest number of features with the mammals, for among mammals females nourish their unborn young within their bodies. During infancy the young are physically dependent for food on only one of their parents, their mother. For humans the greatest commonalities of genetics, anatomy, and behavior lie with the nonhuman primates, an order of animals that includes prosimian lemurs, lorises, and tarsiers; monkeys; and apes. For this reason, some researchers have sought models of human sexual dimorphism among primates exclusively, though other mammals, chiefly the carnivores, have provided models of human evolution (Hall and Sharp 1978). One rationale for considering other orders lies within evolutionary theory. Adaptive radiation is an important evolutionary process that describes the tendency of closely related species to diversity when they enter a new environment. The result of this process is bioecological experimentation in which new behavioral styles are created along with new species. By adaptive radiation, the primates, an order whose origins lie some 60 million years ago in the tropical forests that once covered much of the northern hemisphere, evolved from shrew-like insect eaters into many distinct groups, including nocturnal tree-dwelling lorises; tree- and ground-dwelling monkeys that are prominent in tropical forests and have penetrated some cold areas such as northern Japan; large, intelligent apes that knuckle-walk and swing through trees in forested and mountainous areas, where few people live; and one bipedal hominid that manufactures tools, builds cities, and alters all the world's climatic zones to suit its needs and whims (see Figure 5.2). The branches of the order benefit by differing from each other ecologically, behaviorally, or anatomically. Hence, our primate relatives may not be the best choice for ecological or behavioral models.

Among other major mammalian orders, similar ranges of diversity have been produced by the continual process of evolutionary experimentation. In the carnivore order, a variety of animals have evolved to occupy all the climates of the world; like primates, carnivores now come in all sizes, to fit the requirements of the available niches. One group, the canids, stands out as the most social and intelligent; the most useful analog for the human, the wolf, is found within that family (Hall and Sharp 1978). Like the human, the wolf's range is vast. Indeed, this animal evolved as the top predator in the northern hemisphere even as the

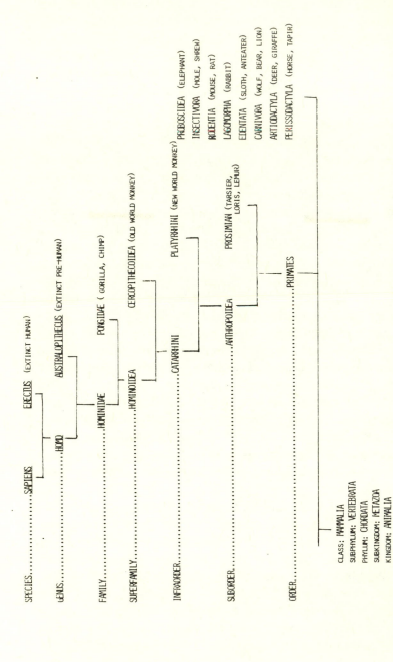

SPECIES..........SAPIENS   ERECTUS (EXTINCT HUMAN)

GENUS............HOMO   AUSTRALOPITHECUS (EXTINCT PRE-HUMAN)

FAMILY...........HOMINIDAE   PONGIDAE (GORILLA, CHIMP)

SUPERFAMILY......HOMINOIDEA   CERCOPITHECOIDEA (OLD WORLD MONKEY)

INFRAORDER.......CATARRHINI   PLATYRRHINI (NEW WORLD MONKEY)

SUBORDER.........ANTHROPOIDEA   PROSIMIAN (TARSIER, LORIS, LEMUR)

ORDER............PRIMATES

PROBOSCIDEA (ELEPHANT)
INSECTIVORA (MOLE, SHREW)
RODENTIA (MOUSE, RAT)
LAGOMORPHA (RABBIT)
EDENTATA (SLOTH, ANTEATER)
CARNIVORA (WOLF, BEAR, LION)
ARTIODACTYLA (DEER, GIRAFFE)
PERISSODACTYLA (HORSE, TAPIR)

CLASS: MAMMALIA
SUBPHYLUM: VERTEBRATA
PHYLUM: CHORDATA
SUBKINGDOM: METAZOA
KINGDOM: ANIMALIA

Figure 5.2. *Homo sapiens* in the Linnean hierarchy. The chart shows categories of the class mammalia. Branches that include the human population are shown in detail on the left; branches that lead to other species appear on the right, with examples in parentheses. Note: Biological taxonomists agree on major features of mammalian classification, but may differ slightly upon specifics. This chart is based on the author's 15 years of experience in research and teaching in biological anthropology.

132

human, after the invention of hunting weapons, emerged as the top predator in the southern hemisphere.

The wolf's division of labor and degree of sexual dimorphism are minimal. Wolves tend to form permanent bonds and to jointly rear their young, and in this way are similar to some primates – notably, the gibbons and many human populations.

In the early 1960s, the "baboon model of human evolution" was fashionable (DeVore and Washburn 1963). It argued that the baboons of Africa provide the best primate model of prehuman life. Baboon females mature much more rapidly than their male counterparts, and males are much larger at maturity. Behavioral patterns of male and female baboons also differ markedly. On the open savanna, the smaller females and their young tend to move across the open lands in the center of a troop that is protected on its periphery by adult and juvenile males. The small size of females was construed as adaptive, on the argument that females would need less food, would mature more rapidly, and could produce offspring sooner. The larger size of males was understood as an adaptation to their role of troop defender. Fewer adult males were found, but fewer were required since a small number of adult males could service the entire female population.

The bioenergetic component of this argument for the small size of females was challenged by Coelho (1974), who suggested that the caloric demands of a small pregnant or lactating female monkey could rival the demands of a large male. Post et al. (1978) analyzed relationships between body weight, the size of the teeth, and the type of diet for 29 species of Old World monkeys. No simple relationships emerged; however, omnivorous monkeys, those species whose diet includes fruits, leaves, and insects, showed more sex differences in their teeth than those primates whose diet was based upon fruits or leaves exclusively. Surprisingly, body weight did not follow this pattern. Like Coelho, Post concluded that in relatively large species, the demand put upon females by reproduction and lactation produces selection for smaller body size, irrespective of any other factors.

It is traditional to use the male as the standard measure of size in a species – and often for behavior as well. In studies of humans, this approach has frequently been taken because males are a more accessible study population, but the practice carries unfortunate symbolic overtones. By contrast, in a study of the expression of skeletal body dimorphism in primates, McCown (1982) opted to take the female as the standard. In this perspective, the standard phenotype became the female body size and shape, with the assumption that its form evolved for the ecological niche that the species occupied. McCown found that the male skull was not merely a larger version of the female, but rather that those parts that supported the animal's aggressive behaviors (both bluffing and fighting) were exaggerated in males.

Innovative studies of sexual dimorphism in nonhuman primates were conducted by Phillips-Conroy and Jolly (1981), who studied hybrid baboons, and Watts (1982), who studied adolescent growth in chimps and rhesus monkeys. The hybrids that Phillips-Conroy and Jolly studied were hamadryas and anubis baboons, which show markedly different degrees of sexual dimorphism in size and pelage, as well as different mating patterns. Most hybrids had a hamadryas father and an anubis mother, owing to the practice among hamadryas males of courting and capturing any available females for their harem. Studies of offspring found that the males most closely resembled the hamadryas, while females resembled the anubis. Inheritance of size and behavior patterns appeared to be sex specific.

In humans and in many other primates, males experience a longer period of growth and their adolescent growth spurt occurs a year or two later than in females (Lieberman 1982). Watts (1982) investigated whether the larger body size of male chimps and rhesus monkeys is due simply to this extended period of growth. However, her longitudinal study found that the two sexes in both species are characterized by distinctly different patterns of growth from birth on, as well as by an extended growth period in males.

In summary, size sexual dimorphism in nonhuman primates is complex. At a minimum, the following factors are involved: size of the species, ecology, and social structure (including the mating pattern). Most importantly, no primate or other mammalian species appears similar enough to humans in morphology, in behavior, or in ecology to be an ideal model for prehuman forebears of *Homo sapiens*. However, the great diversity suggests that the mammalian pattern offers many options.

EARLY HOMINIDS

Carl Linnaeus, the eighteenth-century naturalist who developed the contemporary system for classifying plants and animals, believed that species were created by God and were immutable. Underlying Linnaeus's scheme was the principle of grouping together those species that are most similar in body structure and behavior. Recognizing that humans and apes are similar anatomically, he linked them in his classification. When Darwin's theory of the evolutionary origin of species was accepted in the late nineteenth century, the explanation for similarities between species changed. From an evolutionary perspective, similarities between species are perceived as due to common ancestry.

It will be useful to clarify terms used in the Linnaean system. Figure 5.2 illustrates the principles of the Linnaean hierarchy by showing relationships among primates, the order to which humans, apes, monkeys, and prosimians belong. The Linnaean system is centered on the species in which breeding and reproduction take place. Species are put in the same genus if they are similar in structure and in ecological requirements but do not normally interbreed. The next highest level is the family. Genera (plural of genus) in the same family share many features. Above the family is the superfamily, which is one degree more distinct than the family. Figure 5.2 shows that humans have a genus and species to themselves as well as their own family (hominid); the apes join them at the superfamily (hominoid). The level of the infraorder adds a third important group, the Old World monkeys, and the New World monkeys come in at the suborder Anthropoidea. At the order, all of the prosimians are joined with the humans, apes, and monkeys, and the primate order is one of many that comprise the class Mammalia.

Fossil members of our own hominid family include species that have no ape descendants, though they have ancestors we recognize as apes. Members of the pongid family are apes that share some ancestors with hominids, but do not share descendants. Evolutionary anthropologists have long puzzled over the features of that last common ancestor between human and ape, the "missing link" of popular jargon. Recently, particular interest has been directed toward estimating the time of divergence between the pongid and hominid lines. Several decades ago it was popular to think of the period as 10 to 15 million years ago, but more recently the time estimates have been reduced to from 5 to 8 million years ago. The reasons for this change in scientific consensus involve the following three components:

1. Analysis of biochemical and genetic differences among primates and other mammals has led to the concept of the molecular clock, a means of estimating the time of divergence between groups from studies of their molecular similarities. The basis for this is the principle that the genetic structure of each species changes at

approximately a steady rate – a concept that has proved to be extremely controversial. Most molecular studies of apes and humans have found greater similarities between these two groups than had been anticipated (Goodman and Tashian 1976), and this has suggested that the common ancestor is relatively recent.

2. The punctuated equilibrium concept developed by Eldredge and Gould (1972) proposes that species and communities of species change very little for long periods of time, but stable eras are punctuated by periods of rapid change. This view still requires a great deal of time, as humans normally measure it, for the origin of a new species, but as geologists meaure earth history and the life history of the primates, the time span is relatively short. This model expects a geologically rapid appearance of hominids from an ape stock (Stanley 1975, 1979; Hall and Sharp 1978; Eldredge and Tattersall 1982).

3. The discovery in East Africa of two samples of bipedal hominids who had several features resembling apes, yet were estimated to be less than 4 million years old, suggested that the common ancestor might have lived only a little earlier (Johanson and White 1979).

One of the most publicized aspects of fossil discovery concerns the number of species into which early humans were divided in the early period. For years, anthropologists have debated this point: Were the earliest hominids separated into more than one species, or did they vary among themselves only superficially as modern humans do? It is generally believed that the development of culture, marked by the dependence upon tools and language, replaced biological variation among groups, but at what point in human history this happened is not agreed upon. However, anatomical and size differences were observed in the apelike bipedal hominids found in South Africa in the early twentieth century. These discoveries led to the suggestion that there were several early hominid species, only one of which survived as the ancestor to modern humans. [See Eldredge and Tattersall (1982) for an excellent review of the discovery of hominid fossils, and Winterhalder (1981) and Hall and Sharp (1978, Chapter 8) for a summary of the controversies regarding multiple species in early hominids.]

Thus, when Mary Leakey found several sizes of hominid fossils in beds 3 or more million years of age in Laetolil, Tanzania, and Don Johanson also found several sizes in fossils from the Hadar area of Ethiopia, their initial explanation was that at least two species of hominids were present. Further analysis caused Johanson to change his mind, while Leakey has continued to support the several-species hypothesis. Tim White, Leakey's collaborator at Laetolil, joined with Johanson to argue that the early remains represent one species that shows sexual dimorphism for size that is much greater than that present among modern humans (Johanson and White 1979; Johanson et al. 1982). One basis for rejecting the two-species hypothesis was their conviction that the early hominid males would be much larger than the females (Johanson and Edey 1981). Why did they come to this conclusion only after studying the specimens for several years? And why is the sexual status, as well as the classification, of these early hominids still unresolved?

In a living species, whether it be a carnivore such as the lion or a primate such as the gorilla, the two sexes may differ in behavior, markings, size, or all these. Still, no careful observer can be confused as to the membership of both sexes in the same species. The researcher who is working with samples of the bony skeleton, however, has only indirect access to the animal's behavior. Further, ecological theory and description both tell us that each species is a unique combination of anatomical and behavioral traits. As the degree of difference between the sexes – in size, shape, and behavior – varies enormously among mammals, no rigid guidelines for interpreting these three attributes exist. Therefore, the conclusion to which Johanson and White have come is based on their best judgment at the end of the 1970s. New fossil finds – older, younger, or of the same antiquity – could change their opinions and those of others working in the field.

But what of those who do not agree with Johanson and White? Investigators holding the opinion that the Laetolil and Hadar fossils might represent two or more groups of hominids, and that the genus *Homo* was present alongside bipedal hominids that Johanson includes in the species *Australopithecus afarensis*, are best represented by the Leakey family and its currently most vocal member, Richard Leakey. Unlike Johanson and White, he is uncertain whether the earliest hominids, especially those of our own genus with whom he is most concerned, had a great deal of size sexual dimorphism, but he does not rule it out:

> At the moment there simply aren't enough fossils to judge with any confidence whether sexual dimorphism was substantial or not. . . . In a few years, however, this will become possible. If the difference in size between male and female *Homo habilis* turns out to be substantial this would signify sharp social competition between the males. A substantial dimorphism seems unlikely but the difference between males

and females two to three million years ago is unlikely to have been less than the 20 per cent that exists now. One may ponder on what this degree of human sexual dimorphism implies for the relationship between the sexes in the past – and in the present for that matter. Men may have been 20 per cent bulkier than women for ecological rather than social reasons. But at the moment there is no sound reason for denying the possibility that in our recent past men vied with each other to a limited degree within the framework of a co-operating community, and the more socially and economically successful males may well have commanded greater attention and respect from the females. The competitive edge cannot have been very sharp, however, because of the essentially interdependent nature of the economy. This inescapable biological conflict may have encouraged more subtle cerebral forms of competition rather than overt confrontation (Leakey and Lewin 1978, pp. 236-37).

A close reading of this paragraph reveals what may best be described as hedging – which may be the soundest possible approach, considering the limitations of the data.

Focusing principally on dentition, Brace (1973) and Pilbeam and Zwell (1973) discussed problems of interpreting size variation and separating samples of two species from samples of two sexes. However, the two studies offered opposite viewpoints: Brace viewed the early hominids as one species with a significant degree of sexual variation, while Pilbeam and Zwell saw grounds for recognizing at least two species with less emphasis upon size variation between males and females. In a review paper, Krantz (1982) outlined the technical and philosophical issues that variation in fossils presents. Contributing to variation among specimens are age, species, geography, sex, and purely individual factors. Like Brace, Krantz believes that early hominid males and females showed greater average size differences than do modern humans, and he defined three stages of sexual dimorphism for size in early hominids. The first occurred in the geologic period of the Miocene, 22 to 5.4 million years ago; this was the period of the last common ancestor with the great apes. Krantz believes both tooth and body size differences were great, but sees no adaptive reason for it in those hominoids that were tree dwelling. For the ground-dwelling species, which include the first hominids, he believes the males were selected to be large to offer group protection.

In Krantz's second stage, from about 5 to 1 milllion years ago, the size differences decreased because of the adoption of tools for cutting food and providing defense. The third stage, from 1 million years ago until the current time, is one of minor body size differences with an accentuation of body shape difference. Principal among these, Krantz thinks, is the adaptation of the female pelvis to bearing large-brained infants. In his view, female hominids were selected for increases in body size to accommodate gestation and birth of the large-brained infant.

Brace and Ryan (1980) analyzed variation in the size of teeth in a variety of human populations. Though their emphasis was on dentition, they assumed that the size of the teeth accurately reflects body size. Their paper concluded that hunting groups that employed relatively unsophisticated technology showed more size differences than later human groups that relied more upon the design of tools than upon physical strength in obtaining subsistence. (See Figure 5.3 for a summary of cultural stages in human prehistory.)

Trinkaus (1980) and Smith (1980) analyzed samples of the skeletons (limbs and skulls, respectively) of the European Neanderthal populations of approximately 75,000 to 40,000 years ago. Neanderthal populations are known for highly robust body builds of the cranium and the limbs. Both Smith and Trinkaus found a level of sexual dimorphism in the Neanderthal samples equal to or slightly greater than that of current human populations.

These studies of sexual dimorphism in earlier human populations share one theme: that relatively greater degrees of size dimorphism existed in earlier human populations than in contemporary ones. However, all researchers acknowledge considerable difficulty in separating individual variation, sexual variation, and species variation – that is, difficulty in categorizing the data they analyze. Some ascribe the larger size of males in earlier populations to the greater reliance of males upon strength (rather than technology) in hunting and defense. Krantz (1982) ascribed the reduction in size differences to recent selection for an increase in the body size of females.

COMPARISONS AMONG HUMAN POPULATIONS

By convention, all humans are classified in one genus (*Homo*), one species (*sapiens*), and one subspecies (*sapiens*). It is also generally agreed that evidence for human emergence at least 35,000 years ago can be found in all the continents of the Old World – Europe, Africa, and Asia. *Homo sapiens sapiens* can be distinguished from its best-known

GEOLOGICAL EPOCH	THOUSANDS OF YEARS AGO*	CULTURAL PERIODS AND MAJOR INNOVATIONS	BIOLOGICAL GROUP
H O L O C E N E (OR R E C E N T)		FIRST CITIES AND WRITING	
	10	FARMING VILLAGES: NEOLITHIC	
	12	TRANSITION FROM NOMADISM: MESOLITHIC	
P L E I S T O C E N E			WORLD WIDE HUMAN SPECIES: HOMO SAPIENS
	35	ELABORATE STONE AND BONE TOOLS; ART ON A GRAND SCALE:	
	40	UPPER PALEOLITHIC	
		TRANSITIONAL	
	100	ABILITY TO SURVIVE IN NEAR-GLACIAL COLD; EXTENSIVE USE OF DIVERSE STONE TOOLS: MIDDLE PALEOLITHIC	EUROPEAN POPULATION: HOMO SAPIENS NEANDERTHALENSIS
	125	TRANSITIONAL	
	500	STONE TOOL USE; NOMADIC CULTURES THAT INCLUDE, IN LATER PERIODS, THE CONSTRUCTION OF SHELTERS, BIG-GAME HUNTING, CONTROLLED USE OF FIRE, AND MIGRATION INTO COLD AREAS: LOWER PALEOLITHIC	WORLD WIDE HUMAN SPECIES: HOMO ERECTUS
P L I O C E N E	1800	EARLIEST IDENTIFIABLE STONE TOOLS; ANCESTRAL HUMAN POPULATIONS KNOWN AT MANY SITES IN EASTERN AND SOUTHERN AFRICA	AUSTRALOPITHECUS WITH AT LEAST THREE SPECIES: THE EARLY A. AFARENSIS; AND IN LATER SEQUENCES, A. AFRICANUS AND A. ROBUSTUS
	2200		

* TIME IS NOT TO SCALE.

Figure 5.3. Episodes in the cultural and biological evolution of *Homo sapiens*. (Prehistorians and biological anthropologists agree on the major outlines of human evolution, but differ among themselves on details, particularly of timing. This chart is based on the author's 15 years of experience in research and teaching in anthropology.)

predecessor, the Neanderthal population of Western Europe, chiefly by its distinctive cranium, which approaches a sphere in shape, includes a near-vertical forehead and a chin that juts out to make a vertical plane with the forehead, and is almost perfectly centered on the spinal column. Though all skulls dating within the last 35,000 years approximate this description, variation exists both chronologically and geographically in thickness of the skull wall; width, length, and height; size of the dentition; and general ruggedness.

Though the skeleton that lies below the skull – the spinal column, rib structure, shoulder and pelvic girdles, and the limbs – has been basically modern in shape and form for at least 1 million years, geographic and chronological variation exists in size and ruggedness. Variation in these features includes differences in the degree of sexual dimorphism. Both the size and the ruggedness of the skeleton are controlled by the interaction of the genotype with the environment, and are affected by behavior, for example, in the use of muscles. If used regularly, a muscle develops in size and stimulates deposition of bone in a muscle attachment area. Far from being the dry, lifeless material that many people consider bone to be, the skeleton is highly responsive to an individual's internal and external environment, not only during growth but in adulthood as well. Hence, the bony skeleton serves at least as an indirect record of a person's activities in life.

The trend of the last several centuries toward more delicate bones is usually ascribed to reductions in physical activity that resulted from the growth of technology. Over the last 100 years, the populations of many countries have experienced an increase in average stature. Though most researchers consider diet to be responsible, disagreement exists as to whether increases in the amount of calories or changes in the kinds of food are more important. Several researchers have found that the trend toward increasing stature has been accompanied by an increase in size differences between the sexes. This has led to the concept that males are more affected by nutrition than are females. While some studies have been based upon populations experiencing an increase in food resources (Hall 1982), others have focused upon populations experiencing nutritional stress or famine (Stini 1969, 1972; Tobias 1975). Brauer (1982) showed that the food history of the population, particularly gross conditions such as famine, can affect sexual dimorphism.

Historical and prehistoric samples recovered archaeologically have been studied for sex differences in size. Interest has focused upon relations between the food base (for example, agricultural as opposed to a hunted and gathered food supply) and variation in the quality and quantity of food (Brace and Ryan 1980; Hamilton 1982). Technology and physical efforts required by the food-getting economy have been implicated in these studies too (Frayer 1980). Finkel (1982) found greater size differences in populations that had a greater sexual division of labor and that were experiencing urban development. Similarly, sex differences in size were greater in samples of higher economic classes. Both findings suggest that male variation contributes more to dimorphism than does female variation.

In studies involving large samples of contemporary human societies, Wolfe and Gray (Gray et al. 1980; Wolfe and Gray 1982a, b) analyzed the effect of mating patterns and the subsistence base upon sexual dimorphism for stature. They found statural dimorphism unrelated to mating structure and a greater degree of dimorphism in agriculturalists than in hunter-gatherers, a finding that contradicts that of Brace and Ryan (1980), whose conclusions were based on the assumption that average tooth size differences reflect body size differences. Yet in the last several million years, the human body has increased markedly, but the size of the teeth has decreased. This inverse relationship probably reflects the growth of technology and dependence upon cooking of food. In the last several millenia, the development of agricultural products, including domestic animals (for example, steaks that almost melt in your mouth), have further reduced the role of the teeth in mastication and digestion. Thus, Brace and Ryan (1980) were not measuring the same aspect of body size as Wolfe and Gray (1982a, b).

In summary, studies of the sexual dimorphism of size in contemporary hominids of the species *Homo sapiens sapiens* have identified variables that produce greater dimorphism in some populations than in others. These include greater food resources, an economy and technology requiring great physical labor on the part of the hunter, a social system in which division of labor between the sexes is substantial, and upper-class status in societies with distinguishable social classes. The type of food economy – agricultural versus hunting and gathering, for example – does not seem as crucial as the amount of resources and the behavior patterns required to perform labor.

Problems in interpreting existing studies are many. One concerns the parts of the body measured: Muscle markings on the skeleton tell about robusticity; length of the limbs in skeletal samples tells us about height but not about shape or weight; and the size of the dentition may tell us more about the type of food consumed than about body size. Though modern societies express variation in the way in which mates are chosen, in the degree to which males and females are expected to express their sexuality, and in the amount of time each parent is expected to spend in rearing children, none of these factors have been found to affect sexual dimorphism for size. This is not to deny that the muscularity of males or their ability to conform to cultural norms contributes to their ability to find a mate and to produce offspring – only to say that societies in which males are supposed to compete for as many mates as they can are not those that have produced males who are markedly taller than females. The finding that variations in size differences between the sexes are due more to fluctuations among males than females is still tentative.

CHILD GROWTH

An important issue concerning sex differences in growth is whether the two sexes respond identically to changes, particularly stresses, in their environments. As we have seen, many researchers believe that the female child's growth is more tightly regulated by her genes, while the male child is more likely to be affected by the environment.

A second issue, with a long history in studies of growth and development, concerns the patterns of maturity. Do boys and girls mature, on average, at different rates, but follow the same sequence of growth changes? Are their patterns subject to geographic or environmental variation?

In her review of normal and abnormal patterns of growth in relation to sexual differences, Lieberman (1982) evaluated the cross-sectional and longitudinal approaches. The former type of study looks at a sample at only one pont in time, while in the latter approach one sample of subjects is followed throughout the period of growth. Longitudinal studies are crucial for elucidating the pattern of growth and for suggesting mechanisms that may be responsible for sexual dimorphism, so they will receive greater attention.

Male children at birth, on average, have a larger body size than do females, but early in development females are found to take the lead in maturity. However, the degree of maturity depends in part on how it is defined. In their longitudinal study of the growth of the face and the cranium, Buschang et al. (1983) defined maturity according to the percentage of adult growth achieved, an approach that can be taken only after a longitudinal study is complete. This method focuses on size rather than on markers indicating the completion of growth, which is common to studies of growth in the long bones. Buschang et al. (1983) found that females were consistently more mature (that is, further along in their own pattern of growth) than male children of the same age, but areas of the head and face that experienced rapid growth did not occur in the same sequence for both boys and girls.

This observation suggests that females are smaller primarily because they stop growing sooner. Though both sexes experience a surge known as the "adolescent growth spurt" near the end of their childhood, it usually affects girls several years before it affects boys. As reviewed in the section on nonhominid studies, Watts (1982) examined this generalization in her studies of the linear height of rhesus monkeys and chimpanzees. Yet Watts found that male monkeys in fact were larger at all ages; by contrast, the male chimpanzees were slightly smaller until their adolescent growth spurt. In both primate species, as in humans (Lieberman 1982), the male adolescent growth spurt occurs later than that of females, and the lag allows the chimp males the growth time to catch up. For the monkeys, the delay in the spurt increases the existing male advantage in size. Watts suggested that humans fall between these two groups of primates in linear dimorphism but that the same principle applies: namely, that the tempo of growth during childhood is as important as the length of the growth period in determining the degree of adult sexual dimorphism.

In looking for critical developmental events that determine sex-specific adult dimorphism for size, many researchers have analyzed the adolescent growth spurt, particularly its relationship to female puberty (Valenzuela 1983). Baughan et al. (1980) found in a longitudinal study of French Canadian children that boys showed a consistent relationship between muscular growth and growth in stature, whereas in the female pubertal period complex changes took place between growth in muscle and stature. The muscle development of boys was enhanced compared with tissue growth over a several-year span. For girls, two major peaks in the increase of fat occurred – one before the spurt in stature and one after. Muscle growth peaked after statural development in girls, but in boys the muscle growth proceeded in pace with stature.

These topics anticipate studies of the relationship between fatness and the onset of puberty in girls, which pertains to body composition. Frisch (1974, 1978, 1981) has hypothesized a universal critical percentage of fat that a girl must achieve before the onset of menarche.

Her concept of the critical ratio, which has been debated extensively, has focused interest upon the relationship between the quantity of food resources and the pace of adult development. Too long ignored, this topic has implications for causes of variation in stature and fertility as well as in the age of first menstruation.

Several studies comparing size dimorphism in contemporary human populations concluded that sexual dimorphism is increased in times of surplus calories. For example, Stini (1972) found that malnourishment reduces the muscle mass of boys. However, girls as well as boys are affected by surplus calories. As Newman (1975) reported, studies in both industrial and developing countries have found a relationship between food resources, menarche, and body stature. Greater food supplies tend to produce girls who grow larger younger, and who also experience an earlier menarche. Recent studies by Garn (1980) suggest that the upper limit in this trend may be reached; girls who gain weight early and who experience early menarche have been found to achieve a shorter adult stature than more slowly maturing age mates. It appears that malnourishment affects the soft tissues of the sexes in areas where each sex ideally has the most gains to make. This area is muscle development for adolescent boys, and for adolescent girls it is their reserves of fat.

Even in child growth, in which standard methods have been employed for years and in which a large body of valid data exists, there is room for speculation on degrees of sex differences and the causes for the observed patterns. At the same time, several generalizations can be advanced:

1. Boys and girls differ in the timing of rapid growth in parts of the body.
2. Puberty and the adolescent growth spurt, in particular, differ in patterning, tempo, and effects upon the size of males and females. Size and shape differences between boys and girls are statistically present, but not always obvious before puberty; after puberty, they are hard to miss.
3. The effect upon growth of over- or undersupply of calories or of other nutritional defects is still undetermined. Though growth in both sexes is affected, boys may be more responsive to both environmental extremes. Stini et al. (1980) called attention to the problem of extra nutrition, principally artificial feeding from cow's milk, upon the growth pattern and total stature achieved during childhood. Attention should now be directed to the effects of

overnutrition upon young girls who may respond with obesity or early menarche, both of which may have negative effects upon their health.

BODY COMPOSITION

With the study of body composition we consider function. What is the male body built to do? What activities does the female body do best? How does the behavior of each affect the body's muscle mass, the percentage of fat, and the ability to do work? In this section we will not be talking about the reproductive anatomy, which is covered in many anatomy texts, or about genetic controls of maleness and femaleness, which are covered by Otten in Chapter 6. Rather, this section will review studies of the relative quantities of fat, muscle, and bone and their relationship to human behavior.

As Glucksmann (1978) noted for mammals in general:

The shape of the body is modelled in the first place by four of its constituent parts: the bones, the muscles attached to the skeleton, the subcutaneous fat layer, and the skin with its appendages of hairs, glands and horns. Sex differences in these components individually and in combination account for the differences in appearance. (P. 89)

Body composition studies permit us to consider changes during adulthood as well as childhood, as we can investigate variations in muscle or fat as response to food patterns, exercise, or work.

Bailey (1982), calling attention to the "complex and mutable structure of soft tissue"(p. 363), pointed out the importance of fat in comparing the size and shape of males and females. Fat is particularly important because it can come and go quickly, and the amount of fat at a particular body site varies from person to person and between the sexes. Fat serves as a storehouse of energy, and contains a variety of lipids, cellular solids, and other fluids. It makes up about 27 percent of body weight in a young adult female but only 15 percent of body weight in a young adult male (Bailey 1982). In addition to developing more precise and interpretable measures of body shape and size (Bailey and Katch 1981; Ross and Ward 1982), researchers have recently considered evolutionary and functional explanations for differences between the sexes (Huss-Ashmore 1980; Stini 1982). The interaction between behavior, fat deposition, and developmental stages such as female menarche (Douglas and Miller 1977; Meleski et al. 1982; Malina 1983) has also received serious attention.

Stini (1982) outlined the requirements and hazards that prehistoric humans faced in obtaining enough protein and calories in the feast-to-famine dietary cycles common to hunting and gathering economies. Reviewing the advantages to the infant of having an adequate supply of breast milk he considered the nutritional requirements of lactating females. In his view, the energy requirements of males in the hunting-gathering economy are not as rigidly fixed as are female requirements for calories. The evolutionary response to the different base level of caloric requirements, Stini suggests, has been a greater canalization of development in females and the provision of a larger proportion of body fat stores.

Relationships between fat levels and menarche have been explored extensively (Frisch 1981). A related phenomenon is the tendency of female athletes to undergo periods of amenorrhea when the menstrual cycle does not operate. The possibility of delayed menarche in young female athletes in some sports is also under investigation (Malina 1983). Both the behavioral aspect of intense training and one result, the replacement of fat with muscle tissue, have been implicated in irregular menstrual patterns, though results are by no means conclusive. One of the complicating factors is that athletes are to a large extent selected according to physique for the sports in which they perform. (For example, how many short basketball stars – male or female – can you name?) Further, the process favoring the naturally gifted athlete is especially strong in female athletics. Giftedness may encompass the fat-bone-muscle proportions that comprise physique, yet the ratio of muscle to fat changes dramatically with training.

Several years ago at the Department of Anthropology at Oregon State University, we playfully tested the concept that body size and shape affect an individual's ability to do well at particular sports with a sport series we called the "Primate Olympics." All of the contests involved skills that other primates have both the natural ability and the training to perform: knuckle-walking, quadrupedal running, and hand-over-hand swinging along a rope.

Before the contests started, we measured all student participants for stature, leg length, arm span, and sitting height, and we recorded their age, sex, and weight. In assessing who performed best at these skills, for which none had trained, we found body measures to be highly relevant. For example, a long arm span and relatively low body weight helped students perform well at arm swinging. Sex was not as good a predictor of a skillful performance as were measures of body proportion.

Only in the recent past have talented female athletes been encouraged to develop careers in sports and to undergo the rigorous training needed to succeed. Accordingly, the possibility that behavior can modify the body composition of females is only now becoming susceptible to systematic study. This is especially important since cultural norms in Western culture of the last several centuries have emphasized tasks that do not require strenuous activity. However, a sedentary life-style is not a normal pattern for women in most cultures. Only for the very small percentage of women at the top of the social structure has the ideal of inactivity been fostered. It indicated a family's high economic status and apparently was adopted for that reason by the middle classes of industrial societies.

As in other areas of sex differences, preliminary studies of sex differences in response to rigorous athletic training indicate that differences, though real, are not ones that our cultural stereotypes have led us to expect. One of the findings of studies by Jack Wilmore and colleagues (Brown et al. 1974; Wilmore 1974; Wilmore and Brown 1974; Douglas and Miller 1977) is that with training a sedentary female's oxygen uptake increases to a greater extent than that of a sedentary male. This finding also was made in studies of the effects of training on strength. In 10 weeks of weight training, women students increased their leg strength by 29.5 percent compared with a 26.0 percent increase for men under a similar regimen, but in the arm and shoulder, women's strength increased by 28.6 percent compared with 16.5 percent for the male subjects. The difference between parts of the body was hypothesized to be due to the women's lesser use of the arm and shoulders in their daily routine and a greater sex similarity of activity level in the use of the legs.

Interpretation of these new concepts is at present risky, but there are exciting possibilities if research continues. Some sports physicians believe that the extra fat women's bodies carry may prove advantageous in long-distance sports events such as marathon running; however, research has not confirmed this hypothesis (Wells and Plowman 1983). Studies of female athletes who are pushing their bodies to high levels of performance may be most useful in providing models of the evolutionary function of high levels of fat deposition, which may have supplied energy for long-distance treks as well as for suckling young. With the rising popularity of exercise gyms for women, particularly those involving weight training, it may be possible to explore the potential of behavior to alter body composition. As Wells and Plowman (1983) noted in a review of sex differences in athletic ability:

> Since both highly active men and women tend to be leaner than those who are less active, and since both sexes can lose weight and body fat with a combination of restricted diet and increased exercise, there is apparently a life-style component as well as a biological component to body composition. The relative contribution of these two factors remains to be determined. (Pp. 55-56)

Just as Freud's study on the psychology of women has been criticized because it was conducted with a group of women who not only were self-selected patients but who lived in a culture that provided rigid limitations upon female sexuality, studies of the body composition of young girls in the U.S. culture may be criticized for not representing the general human condition. Body composition studies in times of behavioral change – in this case, when norms concerning activity levels of both males and females are changing – should increase our understanding of the range of actual and potential differences between the sexes in size and in shape.

SUMMARY

Scholars have approached sex differences in size from theoretical and from technical perspectives. They have studied animal models, early humans, comparative *Homo sapiens* populations, child growth, and body composition. Each of these seven perspectives has something important to offer, but none is adequate by itself, for the study of size is not as simple as it appears.

Reviews of mammalian sexual dimorphism show that there are many alternative patterns of size differences. Still unsettled is the question of body size differences in the male and female prehumans who diverged from their ape ancestors, began to use their legs for locomotion and their hands for carrying and manipulating objects, and developed a human ecological niche on the savanna.

Evolutionary approaches to the study of differences in size and body proportion between males and females are illuminating when they focus upon function and the responsiveness of the body. They are not useful if they are interpreted to mean that the body and its behavior are fixed, and are misused if the inference is drawn that females accept male dominance when males are larger.

Average size differences between males and females have changed prehistorically and are fluctuating in contemporary populations. A number of environmental and behavioral forces affect size within the lifetime of an individual, and some affect males and females in different ways. Both nutrition and activities affect the total size achieved during childhood and continue to affect body composition in adults, particularly the relative proportion of fat to muscle. In the case of humans, evolution has produced an organism with the ability to respond rapidly to external and internal changes. The adjustment of body size and composition, in both sexes, is but one of the many intriguing responses available.

ACKNOWLEDGMENTS

The comments of Kenneth A. Bennett and Don Alan Hall were received with appreciation. Responsibility for errors remains my own.

REFERENCES

Alexander, R. D., J. L. Hoogland, R. D. Howard, K. M. Noonan, and P. W. Sherman. 1979. "Sexual Dimorphism and Breeding Systems in Pinnipeds, Ungulates, Primates and Humans." In *Evolutionary Biology and Human Social Behavior: An Anthropological Perspective*, edited by N. A. Chagnon and W. Irons, pp. 402-35. North Scituate, MA: Duxbury Press.

Bailey, S. M. 1982. "Absolute and Relative Sex Differences in Body Composition". In *Sexual Dimorphism in Homo sapiens: A Question of Size*, edited by Roberta L. Hall, pp. 363-90. New York: Praeger.

Bailey, S. M., and V. L. Katch. 1981. "The Effects of Body Size on Sexual Dimorphism in Fatness, Volume and Muscularity." *Human Biology*, 53:337-49.

Baughan, B., M. Brault-Dubuc, A. Demirjian, and G. Gagnon. 1980. "Sexual Dimorphism in Body Composition Changes During the Pubertal Period: As Shown by French-Canadian Children." *American Journal of Physical Anthropology*, 53:85-94.

Bennett, K. A. 1981. "On the Expression of Sex Dimorphism." *American Journal of Physical Anthropology*, 16:31-49.

Brace, C. L. 1973. "Sexual Dimorphism in Human Evolution." *Yearbook of Physical Anthropology*, 16:31-49.

Brace, C. L., and S. Ryan. 1980. "Sexual Dimorphism and Human Tooth Size Differences." *Journal of Human Evolution*, 9:417-35.

Brauer, G. 1982. "Size Sexual Dimorphism and Secular Trend: Indicators of Subclinical Malnutrition?" In *Sexual Dimorphism in Homo sapiens: A Question of Size*, edited by R. L. Hall, pp. 45-49. New York: Praeger.

Brown, C., H. Wilmore, and J. H. Wilmore. 1974. "The Effects of Maximal Resistance Training on the Strength and Body Composition of Women Athletes." *Medicine and Science in Sports*, 6:174-77.

Buschang, P. H., R. M. Baume, and G. G. Nass. 1983. "A Craniofacial Growth Maturity Gradient for Males and Females Between 4 and 16 Years of Age." *American Journal of Physical Anthropology*, 61:373-81.

Chakraborty, R., and P. P. Majumbder. 1982. "On Bennett's Measure of Sex Dimorphism." *American Journal of Physical Anthropology*, 59:295-98.

Coelho, A. M. Jr. 1974. "Socio-Bioenergetics and Sexual Dimorphism in Primates." *Primates*, 15:263-69.

Daly, M., and M. Wilson. 1978. *Sex, Evolution, and Behavior*. North Scituate, MA: Duxbury Press.

Darwin, C. 1917. *The Descent of Man and Selection in Relation to Sex*, 2nd ed. New York: D. Appleton.

DeVore, I., and S. Washburn. 1963. "Baboon Ecology and Human Evolution." In *Viking Fund Publications in Anthropology, No. 36: African Ecology and Human Evolution*, edited by F. C. Howell and F. Bourliere, pp. 335-67. New York: Wenner-Gren Foundation.

Douglas, J. H., and J. A. Miller. 1977. "Record Breaking Women." *Science News*, 112:172-74.

Eldredge, N., and S. J. Gould. 1972. "Punctuated Equilibria: An Alternative to Phyletic Gradualism." In *Models in Paleobiology*, edited by T. J. Schopf, pp. 82-115. San Francisco: Freeman.

Eldredge, N., and I. Tattersall. 1982. *The Myths of Human Evolution*. New York: Columbia University Press.

Finkel, D. 1982. "Sexual Dimorphism and Settlement Pattern in Middle Eastern Skeletal Populations." In *Sexual Dimorphism in Homo sapiens: A Question of Size*, edited by R. L. Hall, pp. 165-85. New York: Praeger.

Frayer, D. W. 1980. "Sexual Dimorphism and Cultural Evolution in the Late Pleistocene and Holocene of Europe." *Journal of Human Evolution*, 9:399-415.

Frisch, R. S. 1974. "A Method of Prediction of Age of Menarche from Height and Weight at Ages 9 Through 13 Years." *Pediatrics*, 53:384-90.

___. 1978. "Menarche and Fatness: Re-examination of the Critical Body Composition Hypothesis." *Science*, 200:1509-13.

___. 1981. "Fatness and Reproduction." *Human Biology*, 53:479.

Garn, S. M. 1980. "Continuities and Change in Maturational Timing." In *Constancy and Change in Human Development*, edited by O. Brim, Jr., and J. Kagan, pp. 113-62. Cambridge, MA: Harvard University Press.

Glucksmann, A. 1978. *Sex Determination and Sexual Dimorphism in Mammals*. London: Wykeham.

Goodman, M., and R. E. Tashian, eds. 1976. *Molecular Anthropology* . New York: Plenum.

Gray, J. P., and L. D. Wolfe. 1980. "Height and Sexual Dimorphism of Stature Among Human Societies." *American Journal of Physical Anthropology*, 53:441-56.

Hall, R. L., ed. 1982. *Sexual Dimorphism in Homo sapiens: A Question of Size*. New York: Praeger.

Hall, R. L., and H. Sharp, eds. 1978. *Wolf and Man: Evolution in Parallel*. New York: Academic Press.

Hamilton, M. 1982. "Sexual Dimorphism in Skeletal Samples." In *Sexual Dimorphism in Homo sapiens: A Question of Size* , edited by R. L. Hall, pp. 107-63. New York: Praeger.

Huss-Ashmore, R. 1980. "Fat and Fertility: Demographic Implications of Differential Fat Storage." *Yearbook of Physical Anthropology*, 23:65-91.

Johanson, D. C., and M. A. Edey. 1981. *Lucy: The Beginnings of Humankind*. New York: Simon and Schuster.

Johanson, D. C., M. Taieb, and Y. Coppens. 1982. "Pliocene Hominids from the Hadar Formation, Ethiopia (1973-1977): Stratigraphic, Chronologic, and Paleoenvironmental Contexts, with Notes on Hominid Morphology and Systematics." *American Journal of Physical Anthropology*, 57:373-402.

Johanson, D. C., and T. D. White. 1979. "A Systematic Assessment of Early African Hominids." *Science*, 203:321-30.

Krantz, G. 1982. "The Fossil Record of Sex." In *Sexual Dimorphism in Homo sapiens: A Question of Size*, edited by R. L. Hall, pp. 85-105. New York: Praeger.

Leakey, R. E., and R. Lewin. 1978. *Peoples of the Lake*. Garden City, NY: Anchor Press/Doubleday.

Leutenegger, W. 1982a. "Scaling of Sexual Dimorphism in Body Weight and Canine Size in Primates." *Folia Primatologica*, 37:163-76.

___. 1982b. "Sexual Dimorphism in Nonhuman Primates." In *Sexual Dimorphism in Homo sapiens: A Question of Size* , edited by R. L. Hall, pp. 11-36. New York: Praeger.

Lieberman, L. S. 1982. "Normal and Abnormal Sexual Dimorphism Patterns of Growth and Development." In *Sexual Dimorphism in Homo sapiens: A Question of Size*, edited by R. L. Hall, pp. 263-316. New York: Praeger.

Malina, R. M. 1983. "Menarche in Athletes: A Synthesis and Hypothesis." *Annals of Human Biology*, 10:1-24.

McCown, E. R. 1982. "Sex Differences: The Female as Baseline for Species Description." In *Sexual Dimorphism in Homo sapiens: A Question of Size*, edited by R. L. Hall, pp. 37-83. New York: Praeger.

Meleski, B. W., R. F. Shoup, and R. M. Malina. 1982. "Size, Physique, and Body Composition of Competitive Female Swimmers Through 20 Years of Age." *American Journal of Physical Anthropology*, 54:609-25.

Midgley, M. 1978. *Beast and Man: The Roots of Human Nature*. Ithaca, NY: Cornell University Press.

Newman, M. T. 1975. "Nutritional Adaptation in Man." In *Physiological Anthropology*, edited by A. Damon, pp. 210-59. New York: Oxford.

Phillips-Conroy, J. E., and C. J. Jolly. 1981. "Sexual Dimorphism in Two Subspecies of Ethiopian Baboons (*Papio hamadryas*) and Their Hybrids." *American Journal of Physical Anthropology*, 56:115-29.

Pilbeam, D. R., and M. Zwell. 1973. "The Single Species Hypothesis, Sexual Dimorphism, and Variability in Early Hominids." *Yearbook of Physical Anthropology*, 16:69-79.

Post, D., S. Goldstein, and D. Melnick. 1978. "An Analysis of Cercopithecoid Odontometrics II. Relations Between Dental Dimorphism, Body Size Dimorphism and Diet." *American Journal of Physical Anthropology* , 49:533-44.

Ralls, K. 1977. "Sexual Dimorphism in Mammals: Avian Models and Unanswered Questions." *American Naturalist*, 111:917-38.

Ross, W. D., J. E. L. Carter, K. Roth, and K. Willimczik. 1977. "Sexual Dimorphism in Sport by a Somatotype I-Index." *Symposia Biologica Hungarica*, 20:365-76.

Ross, W. D., and R. Ward. 1982. "Human Proportionality and Sexual Dimorphism." In *Sexual Dimorphism in Homo sapiens: A Question of Size*, edited by R. L. Hall, pp. 317-61. New York: Praeger.

Sanday, P. R. 1981. *Female Power and Male Dominance*. New York: Cambridge University Press.

Smith, F. H. 1980. "Sexual Differences in European Neanderthal Crania with Special Reference to the Krapina Remains." *Journal of Human Evolution*, 9:359-75.

Stanley, S. M. 1975. "A Theory of Evolution Above the Species Level." *Science*, 72:646-50.

___. 1979. *Macroevolution. Pattern and Process*. San Francisco: Freeman.

Stini, W. A. 1969. "Nutritional Stress and Growth: Sex Differences in Adaptive Response." *American Journal of Physical Anthropology*, 31:417-26.

___. 1972. "Reduced Sexual Dimorphism in Upper Arm Muscle Circumference Associated with Protein-Deficient Diet in a South American Population." *American Journal of Physical Anthropology*, 36:341-52.

___. 1982. "Sexual Dimorphism and Nutrient Reserves." In *Sexual Dimorphism in Homo sapiens: A Question of Size* , edited by R. L. Hall, pp. 391-419. New York: Praeger.

Stini, W. A., C. W. Weber, S. R. Kemberling, and L. A. Vaughan. 1980. "Bioavailability of Nutrients in Human Breast Milk as Compared to Formula." *Studies in Physical Anthropology*, 6:3-22.

Tobias, P. V. 1975. "Anthropometry Among Disadvantaged Peoples; Studies in Southern Africa." In *Biosocial Interrelations in Populational Adaptation*, edit ed by E. S. Watts, F. E. Johnston, and G. W. Lasker, pp. 287-305. The Hague: Mouton.

Trinkaus, E. 1980. "Sexual Differences in Neanderthal Limb Bones." *Journal of Human Evolution*, 9:377-97.

Valenzuela, C. Y. 1983. "Pubertal Origin of the Larger Sex Dimorphism for Adult Stature of a Chilean Population." *American Journal of Physical Anthropology*, 60:53-60.

Watts, E. S. 1982. "Adolescent Growth and Sexual Dimorphism in Chimpanzees and Rhesus Monkeys [Abstract]. *American Journal of Physical Anthropology*, 57:240.

Wells, C. L., and S. A. Plowman. 1983. "Sexual Differences in Athletic Performance: Biological or Cultural?" *Physician and Sports Medicine*, 11:52-63.

Wilmore, J. H. 1974. "Alterations in Strength, Body Composition and Anthropometric Measures Consequent to a 10-Week Weight Training Program." *Medicine and Science in Sports*, 6:133-38.

Wilmore, J. H., and C. Harmon Brown. 1974. "Physiological Profiles of Women Distance Runners." *Medicine and Science in Sports*, 6:178-81.

Winterhalder, B. 1981. "Hominid Paleoecology and Competitive Exclusion: Limits to Similarity, Niche Differentiation, and the Effects of Cultural Behavior." *Yearbook of Physical Anthropology*, 24:101-21.

Wittig, M., and P. F. Secord. 1983. *Too Many Women? The Sex Ratio Question.* Beverly Hills, CA: Sage.

Wolfe, L. D., and J. P. Gray. 1982a. "Subsistence Practices and Human Sexual Dimorphism of Stature." *Journal of Human Evolution*, 11:575-80.

____. 1982b. "A Cross-Cultural Investigation into the Sexual Dimorphism of Stature." In *Sexual Dimorphism in Homo sapiens: A Question of Size*, edited by R. L. Hall, pp. 197-230. New York: Praeger.

6

GENETIC EFFECTS ON MALE AND FEMALE DEVELOPMENT AND ON THE SEX RATIO

Charlotte M. Otten

Sex differences, like other heritable traits, are determined by the interaction of genetic-hormonal and environmental factors. In part they have evolved through the pressures of sexual selection, that aspect of natural selection relating to mating behavior and reproduction (see Chapter 3). Sexual selection derives from Darwin, but its implications have been ignored for decades.

We are now aware that mammalian mating is seldom random. Consequences of nonrandom mating strategies may be reflected in the relative number of male and female offspring born in a population, their physical condition, and their own eventual fertility. Conversely, imbalance in the adult sex ratio has consequences for culturally proscribed interactions between the sexes (see Chapter 7).

This chapter presents a summary account of the genetics and endocrinology of sex determination, the early development of sex differences, the genesis and implications of sex ratios, and hypotheses and observations concerning sex differences in morbidity and mortality.

CHROMOSOMES AND GENES

All mammals, humans included, carry a comparable number of genetic determinants, or genes, which are organized into darkly staining bodies called "chromosomes," present in the nuclei of all cells. Although the total amount of genetic material, deoxyribonucleic acid (DNA), is relatively equal between species, even closely related forms may vary

155

remarkably as to chromosome count. For instance, certain Old World monkeys, the guenons, have as many as 72, while the spider monkeys of the New World carry but 34. These apparently contradictory findings are resolved when we understand that the functional hereditary material is erratically distributed among chromosomes, being more widely scattered in some species, as in guenons, and more concentrated in others. Further, a large proportion of DNA, as much as 90 percent, may be useless or what is known as "junk DNA." Humans, with their 46 chromosomes, differ little in chromosome count from their close relatives the chimpanzees and gorillas, both of which carry 48.

Chromosome count has nothing to do with the number of traits characterizing a species or with their complexity. Apparently the splitting and fusion of chromosomes and the loss of nonfunctional chromosomal material have been common occurrences throughout evolutionary history. They contribute to species formation, an important consequence of which is the prevention of fertility between species, that is, the creation of reproductive isolation. The identification, function, and evolutionary interpretation of apparently inert chromosomal material constitute an important area of current genetic research. The proposed presence of parasitic genes, silent genes, introns, and pseudogenes give some hint of the complexity of this field of study. These points are stressed to prevent the placing of a value judgment on the relative smallness and inertness of the male Y chromosome in contrast to the larger and genetically more active X chromosome, which females possess in double dose and males in single dose.

At the time of either simple cell replication by mitosis or the production of reproductive cells by meiosis, chromosomes appear to coalesce out of the amorphous or granular darkly staining material that characterizes cell nuclei. They are most satisfactorily studied in white blood cells, or leukocytes, which can be gathered from the surface of defibrinated blood samples, where they collect in a visible layer. After the cells are removed and allowed to proliferate in nutrient broth for several days, they are chemically fixed in the process of chromosomal division, then spread on slides in a thin film and appropriately stained. Some nuclei will exhibit their chromosomes nicely scattered, transfixed in their characteristic X-shaped metaphase stage. At this time, the four arms of the dividing chromosome are still held together at the centromere, a more or less centrally located point.

Individual chromosomes are distinguished by their size, the relative length of their "arms," and their characteristic patterns of staining. With the routine techniques in use before 1969, only numbers 1, 2, 3, and 16 and Y could be identified with certainty. Since the innovation of new staining techniques and the discovery of distinct patterns of banding, however, chromosomes can be characterized individually, and abnormalities in their morphologies and numbers accurately described. This microscopic examination of chromosome structure and number is known as "karyotyping."

Numbers of Chromosomes, Base Pairs, and Genes

In thinking about the relative quantity of genetic material, we must keep several sets of figures straight:

1. Chromosome numbers (just discussed).
2. Base pairs: Mammals may have, in each cell nucleus, as many as 1 billion base pairs, the so-called rungs of the DNA ladder. These are arranged in three-pair codons, or triplets, each of which organizes a specific amino acid link in the construction of a protein.
3. Genes: Codons are assembled into genes, which are functional DNA segments, each of which produces a specific protein (polypeptide) product. For example, the hemoglobin molecule is composed of 572 amino acid links, arranged in four chains. Counting the ribonucleic acid (RNA) involved, as many as 5,000 base pairs must be involved in this complex gene.

A gene, then, is a sequence of codons (or triplets) that produces a single protein. We refer here to single-gene traits such as enzymes, serum protein types (for example, haptoglobins), blood types, and tissue and cell components – direct expressions of the DNA-RNA code that follow Mendelian laws and are amenable to genetic analysis. By contrast, several genes often function in concert to determine or influence polygenic, or multifactorial, traits, for example, stature and skin color, which vary along a continuum. Such traits may be modified by environmental influences, such as climate and nutrition.* By contrast,

---

*The long-accepted relationship between stature and nutritional adequacy has greater complexity than was formerly assumed. Evidence presented by Stini (1969), Beilicki and Charzewski (1977), Tobias (1975), and Greulich (1951) indicates that males respond more sensitively to nutritional adequacy or

single-gene traits are unchanged from generation to generation, except by the accident of genetic mutation. Regulatory genes represent still another category in that they do not produce proteins or collaborate in trait expression, but regulate the structural or manufacturing genes by turning them on and off as their products are required.

Ohno (1979, p. 18) and Hartl (1977, p. 64) both estimate that an individual genome, the total genetic endowment of an individual, carries at most about 100,000 genes. This number is considerably smaller than past estimates such as the 2.5 million estimated by Bodmer and Cavalli-Sforza (1976, p. 132) on the basis of biochemical data. The former, more conservative number has been the more widely accepted, but the lack of certainty reflects the newness of the field of gene counting and the indeterminate state of much of the basic data. Much of this uncertainty arises from the present lack of knowledge concerning the proportion of genetic material that is functional and that that is nonfunctional or represents duplicate genes.

At least one-third of human genes exist in a number of variant forms; technically, we express this by saying genes have alternative expressions at the same locus (the Latin word for place). It is by its chromosomal location and expression that we recognize a single gene. A trait that has several genetic alternatives is called "polymorphic"; the family or set of genes is a polymorphism, implying several (poly) options with regard to the same trait.

The A, B, and O blood group-determining genes, the dozens of known hemoglobin variants, and the yellow-green and tall-short alternatives of Mendel's peas are all examples of polymorphisms. Since chromosomes are present in pairs (one donated by the father, one by the mother) in all sexually reproducing forms, genes are also present in pairs. An individual who has inherited similar alleles from both parents is designated as "homozygous" for that trait; conversely, if his/her two genes code for different proteins because he/she has inherited different alleles from each parent, we call the individual "heterozygous." Thus, the carrier of two blood type-A genes (AA) is homozygous; AO or AB persons are heterozygous. Because of polymorphic forms, the number of

---

deprivation than do females, the latter having some physiological protection. Other scholars find the stature of both sexes relatively resistant to environmental modification. Sociobiologists would relate the degree of sexual dimorphism for many physical features, including stature, to marriage and kinship patterns and competition between males for mates. For further discussion see Hall (1982).

genetic variants present in a population is always far larger than the number of genes carried by any individual.

In spite of the tremendous potential for variability and the large number of units involved, the sexes differ in only a very few genes. Only the *tfm* and the H-Y genes are firmly established as sex specific, and three or four others await confirmatory evidence. The fact that genetic differences between the sexes are minor suggests that these few loci exert considerable influence over the developmental processes resulting in male-female distinctions.

Y Chromosome

Along with numbers 21 and 22, the Y is the smallest of the human chromosomes. It is characterized by a long arm (yq) and a very short arm (yp) as measured from the centromere.

Y chromosomes are heterogeneous in both size and morphology throughout the primate order, and even vary within the human species, as do some other chromosomes. Two percent of males demonstrate somewhat larger Y chromosomes than average (Hartl 1977, p. 69). The size and arm length of the Y apparently are inherited. Variation in the length of the long arm appears to characterize some ethnic groups. Since the Y is largely inert genetically, and most of the long arm appears to be dispensable, these variations have no functional significance. Twenty percent of the normal newborns in a New Haven study showed atypical morphologies (Hartl 1977, p. 59).

Of the several thousand known hereditary traits, only one is known to be transmitted exclusively from father to son: the determination of maleness itself. The only other locus that may be carried on the Y is that of the gene that gives rise to the condition known as hairy ears, a trait of no known biological significance. Common in India but uncommon elsewhere, this trait is described as a stiff tuft of hair 2 or more centimeters in length, growing on the external rim of the ear near the canal opening. The gene has incomplete penetrance, meaning that not all persons who carry the gene manifest the condition.

The H-Y gene, which is located on the short arm of the Y near the centromere, codes for production of a male-specific tissue antigen. The gene exists in multiple copies. H-Y was discovered when scientists observed that highly inbred female mice reject grafts from male littermates, although they accept them from female siblings (Eichenwald and Silmser 1955). This component, foreign to females, but characterizing male tissues, causes the immune reaction of rejection in females. It is this H-Y substance that sets in motion the developmental sequence by which the undifferentiated embryonic gonad is caused to develop into a testis. The newly formed testis soon begins to secrete the hormone testosterone, which induces the initial development of the male urogenital system and later the external male genitalia.

In the absence of H-Y and testosterone, the primordial gonads progress in a female direction and become ovaries. No one has yet isolated a gonadal organizing substance necessary for female differentiation, but since the embryo devlops in the maternal environment, such a substance probably would be difficult to detect. However, Wachtel and Ohno (1979, p. 133) and Ohno (1979) postulated the existence of an ovary-inducing antigen that competes with H-Y antigen for anchorage sites on the cells of the ambiguous gonad. This hypothesis is based on the observation that in XX-XY chimeras, persons who have both male and female organs, an ovotestis is formed and H-Y is present in the testicular, but not the ovarian, portion of the composite organ.

H-Y antigen has been found in every vertebrate species tested, affirming its universal indispensable function – the determination and organization of sexual differentiation. It is apparently a tremendously ancient, uniform, and stable character (Wachtel et al. 1975).

H-Y's testis-organizing role was firmly established when genetically female gonadal tissues from embryonic calves were cultured in the presence of H-Y antigen. After 5 days, the precocious formation of testicular seminiferous tubules and accessory male structures was observed (Ohno 1979, p. 66). However, reports of aberrant XY "females" with normal Y genes but variable expressions of H-Y secretions, as well as XX females who aberrantly show a secretion of H-Y, and other discordances between H-Y and testicular development all indicate that the simple picture of masculinization by H-Y falls short as an overall explanatory model. Wachtel (1978) concluded that testicular development involves not only H-Y genes, but the *tfm* X-linked gene that activates the Y. Further, testicular development involves another autosomal gene that determines the structure of an "H-Y carrier," which disseminates the antigen from one cell to another. Mutations and chromosomal translocations may also complicate findings. The situation is immensely complex (Gordon and Ruddle 1981), and here we can deal only with well-established expressions and consequences of H-Y secretion.

In spite of these uncertainties, the H-Y antigen correlates with maleness so well that it is used along with karyotyping as a clinical test for sex determination in infants born with indeterminate genitalia. Such conditions of indeterminacy arise from prenatal hormone imbalances in the mother, from hormone therapies that inadvertently masculinize female fetuses, or from genetic mutations or abnormal chromosomal complements, to be discussed in detail later in this chapter. The under-development of the male external genitalia and the overdevelopment of the female clitoris are conditions that are well known to all delivery-room personnel.

X Chromosome

The normal mammalian female carries two X chromosomes, the male a single X. The X is one of the largest and genetically most active of the 46 and is also the best known. More than 100 gene loci have been iden-tified as "X linked" or sex linked through their distinctive pattern of inheritance. These genes determine a miscellaneous assortment of traits, only one of which (*tfm*) has anything to do with sex determination per se.

So well is the chromosome known that a map showing the relative position of a number of gene loci on the chromosome has been constructed. New staining techniques have revolutionized the identification of individual chromosomes as well as the discrimination of detailed morphological characters by specific patterns of banding. Changes in phenotypic expressions resulting from the loss of chromosomal fragments or areas can also give us clues to the location of genetic determinants. These several procedures have been used to determine chromosomal areas controlling and influencing sex differentiation and development, as well as other traits.

Examples of fruitful studies include the identification of the Y centromere region as the loci of genes controlling the expression of H-Y antigen. In females, initial ovarian differentiation may require an analogous determinant. In support of this theory, phenotypic correlations with specific karyotypes indicate that sites on both the X and Y arms are necessary for oocyte (potential egg cell) maintenance. Normal autosomal genes also contribute to successful oogenesis (Simpson and LeBeau 1981). With two X chromosomes, females can be heterozygous or homozygous for X-linked alleles. If a deleterious recessive gene appears on one of the X chromosomes, females usually carry a normal dominant allele on the other X that will override the effects of the recessive gene. These women are called "carriers" of recessive, unexpressed genes. Men, having only one X, a condition called "hemizygosity," have no normal allele to mask the effects of the recessive gene, and so express the trait. The "royal hemophilia" was introduced into several of the royal families of Europe in this way by a sex-linked recessive gene carried by Queen Victoria and passed to two daughters before being expressed in several of their sons and grandsons.

X chromosomes are far more genetically active than the almost inert Y's, but this unequal endowment is somewhat equalized by the inactivation of one of the female X chromosomes, an event that occurs very early in embryonic life. Which of the two X chromosomes is initially turned off is believed to be a random occurrence, but upon chromosomal duplication and cell division, any particular cell lineage continues to inactivate the same X. In cases where only one X carries a dominant gene for an abnormal tissue enzyme or other marker trait, the adult will express a condition termed "mosaicism," which is expressed as a patchwork distribution of normal and abnormal areas.

The inactivated X chromosome can be observed microscopically in many cells as a darkly staining body lying against the membranous wall of the cell nucleus. This is known as a "Barr body," after the reports of Murry Barr, who first described the structures (Barr and Bertram 1949). Their compensatory function was first accurately interpreted by Lyon (1961, 1962). In the abnormal condition in which an individual has three X chromosomes, two Barr bodies are present – a useful phenomenon for diagnostic purposes.

Some cells with complex segmented nuclei, such as white blood cells, show Barr bodies that take the form of nuclear extrusions that, because of their shape, are called "drumsticks." An experienced observer can accurately sex a blood smear by noting their presence.

Inactivation of the X must be incomplete, however, since individuals who carry only a single X (XO), known as "Turner's syndrome," demonstrate sterility and other abnormal characters. It thus appears that both X chromosomes are necessary for normal ovarian development and fertility. One arm of the X especially seems to escape inactivation. The Xg^a blood group gene, located on the X, shows a dosage effect; this means that a more effective antigen is formed in XX females who carry the gene in double dose than in XY males with only a single gene. The glucose-6-phosphate dehydrogenase (G6PD) X-linked gene, which codes for a red blood cell enzyme, occurs in a number of variant forms. Males never have more than one form of G6PD but females can be heterozygous, carrying a mixture of enzyme traits.

Why, we may ask, does the X chromosome so little resemble the Y that an individual can survive with a single X but never a single Y? According to a hypothesis of Lyon (1962), primordial mammals probably had a pair of homomorphic (structurally similar) sex chromosomes. She proposed that the bulk of genetic material of the original Y was accidentally transferred to the X, an event that effectively duplicated the X gene. In support of this theory are several redundancies on the X, for example, two genes for antihemophilic factors and several for different expressions of color vision. This virtual doubling of the sex chromosome in female mammals, Lyon holds, necessitated the dosage compensation mechanism (inactivation). Alternatively, Lucchisi (1978) proposed that the evolution of marked differences in the X and Y was gradual and occurred as the result of dosage compensation. Both theories are plausible, but neither is susceptible to testing. At present, the questions of the origin and detailed function of sex chromosome inactivation are still open, although Lyon's interpretation is the more widely accepted.

ENDOCRINE SYSTEM

Endocrinology is that branch of physiology concerned with the ductless glands, their secretions (hormones), and the organs, tissues, and target glands at which the hormones are directed. Hormones are released directly into the bloodstream for rapid transport and reaction. The endocrine system is closely linked to the nervous system; together they comprise a communication and regulatory unit that coordinates the functions of complex organisms. This collaboration is necessary both for long-term (organizational) programming and for immediate short-term (activational) responses. Constant minor adjustments make possible homeostasis, or the delicate functional equilibrium of an organism in its particular environment. Determination of sex is one of their prime long-term functions.

Hormonal peptides and steroidlike molecules, formerly thought to be specific to vertebrates, are found to be secreted by invertebrates such as sponges and even unicellular organisms. Still, the phylogenetic history of the close relationship of the nervous system to the endocrine system remains unclear. The general belief has been that the nervous system is older than the endocrine system and is its probable progenitor. Alternatively, Roth et al. (1982) suggested that both systems were derived from a common ancestral system. They hypothesized that many compounds involved in intercellular communication, including hormones and neurotransmitters, began as local tissue factors acting on secretory cells.

A remnant of the evolutionary divergence of endocrine and exocrine systems is seen in the diversity of sources of some hormones: For example, human chorionic gonadotropin (hCG) appears in placental tumors, in urine, and in the tissues of people with neither tumors nor placentas; androgens and estrogens are also synthesized at many sites. Apparently these conservative compounds of inter- and intracellular communication arose early in evolution, while the differentiation and specialization of secretory and target cells evolved later.

The intimate connection of the central nervous system with the endocrine system is demonstrated by the association of precocious puberty with brain lesions, the effects of population density on mating and parenting behavior and on ovulation in many species, the coordination of courtship signals with ovulation in birds and amphibians, and the effects of hypothalamic brain stimulation on experimental animals.

Hormones and Sexual Processes

In primates, either prenatally or shortly after birth, hormones organize the brain as male or female. For effective integration of sex-specific reproductive behavior, the maximum exposure to hormones must be accurately timed, even to the day. Effects of inaccurate timing may not be evident at the time of exposure but may appear years later, at puberty. Once established, the organization is permanent and usually irreversible, or only partially reversible by the administration of antagonistic or other-sex hormones.

Our understanding of endocrine function is derived mainly from three sources: (1) the observed effects of natural upsurges and diminutions of hormone levels throughout the life cycle, which are especially marked at puberty and throughout the menstrual cycle, pregnancy, menopause, and old age; (2) abnormal conditions such as hyperplasias, which produce hypersecretion of certain hormones, mutations that by blocking enzyme production interrupt metabolic or feedback sequences as well as hormone formation or regulation, and abnormal chromosomal numbers (aneuploidies); and (3) observations on experimental animals following the removal of endocrine glands or after artificial alteration of hormone levels.

Figure 6.1 illustrates hormonal activities in the hypothalamus of the brain, the anterior lobe of the pituitary, the adrenal cortex, and the sex glands, or gonads. Most of these glands synthesize not one but several hormones, each of which stimulates or depresses the activity of other glands and/or target organs. Some secretions (for example, progesterone) are precursors in the biosynthesis of others; the same steroid hormone may function interchangeably as an androgen or as an estrogen, or one may be transformed into the other within the cells of a target organ. Further, hormones are effective only where specific receptors incorporate them and effect their transfer to the DNA of the cell nuclei. As some hormones function in concert, they cannot be accurately described in isolation. Thus, the gonadotropins luteinizing hormone (LH) and follicle-stimulating hormone (FSH) are closely interrelated and complementary in their ovarian action: stimulating the maturation of the follicle, the preparation and release of the ovum, the secretion of testrogenic hormone, and the transformation of the empty follicle into the corpus luteum, or yellow body. These complexities tend to defeat our intent to simplify the system by summarizing discrete hormonal roles in the diagram!

Hormones may be designated as polypeptides, that is, molecules composed of long chains of amino acid units; glycoproteins, protein chains compounded with a carbohydrate group; or steroids, fattylike substances derived from a cholesterol base.

The Hypothalamus

Consideration of the mammalian endocrine system begins with the hypothalamus, the cerebral integration center. This small area functions as both a nerve structure and an endocrine gland. Situated in the ventral floor of the forebrain, it can be stimulated by messages originating in the central nervous system, or arriving via connections with more peripheral autonomic nerve centers, or by chemical feedback of information from the bloodstream. It thus responds to nervous stimuli, secretions, or both. Specialized hypothalamic nerve cells, the neurosecretory cells, possess

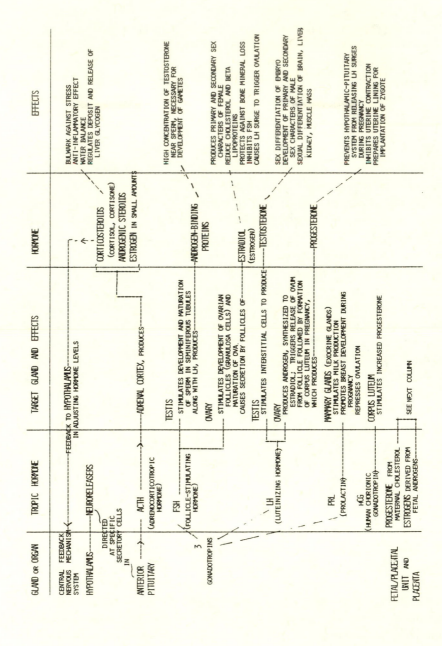

Figure 6.1. Glands and hormones involved in sex differentiation and reproduction.

glandular activity. They elaborate and secrete chemical messengers, specific releasing factors that signal the anterior pituitary to secrete a specific hormone or hormones. Neurosecretory cells combine the speed of neural response with the specificity and sustained activity of hormonal function.

The pituitary, a two-part gland with functionally distinct anterior and posterior lobes, hangs like a small berry on a short stalk from the hypothalamus. A network of capillaries traverses the stalk, leading from the neurosecretory cells to the main body of the pituitary. As the hypothalamic cells elaborate their releasing substances, they are picked up by the network or plexus of vessels and carried to the pituitary, which responds by secreting the specified hormone.

The hypothalamus is organized prenatally as male or female by the secretion of testosterone or its lack, respectively. If testosterone is present, the potential for the monthly menstrual cycle is canceled, and the steady-state male pattern is established. Lacking testosterone, the hypothalamus is organized as female, and the cyclic secretory pattern of estrogen and progesterone develops.

Although extremely important in a number of physiological processes, the posterior lobe will not be discussed further. Nor will we pursue the several functions of the anterior lobe, which include bodily growth, temperature control, and metabolic rate, although sex differences are known to characterize these traits.

Anterior Pituitary Lobe

Adrenocorticotropic hormone (ACTH) normally regulates the secretion of corticosteroids and some androgens and estrogens from the adrenal cortex. The cortex is the barklike outer layer of the adrenal glands, which perch on top of the kidneys. The inter portion, or medulla, constitutes another endocrine gland, the secretions of which are in some ways antagonistic but in other ways complementary to corticoid action. In any case, they do not have a direct influence on sex differences. The origins and structure of the two adrenal components are independent and largely unrelated, in spite of their intimate structural association.

Important to our topic are the three gonadotropins, or reproductive regulating hormones, FSH, LH, and prolactin (PRL). FSH incites the development of ovarian follicles. Responding to FSH, immature egg cells move into the body of the ovary from the outside germinal epithelium where thousands of potential ova are stored from birth, although only 350 to 400 are released in a lifetime. Ova mature physiologically and genetically in little globular sacs of fluid surrounded by cells. These follicles and their contents enlarge until, stimulated by a monthly surge of LH, normally, one ruptures the ovary wall and escapes. (The simultaneous escape of two may result in fraternal twins.) FSH also stimulates spermatozoon formation in the seminiferous tubules, which are coiled in the testes. As sperm are transformed from immature (Sertoli) cells lying against the outer wall of the tubules to mature, haploid spermatozoa, they move inward to the central lumen, or duct, down which they pass when ready for fertilization. FSH also collaborates with LH in causing the elaboration of the estrogen estradiol by the ovarian follicles.

After the ovum is released by the action of LH, cells fill in the empty follicle, creating a corpus luteum, or yellow body. The secretion of the corpus luteum (progesterone) prepares the uterine lining for implantation of the zygote and maintains it, inhibiting menstruation and uterine contractions before birth.

Human chorionic gonadotropic (hCG), which is secreted by the embryo in its earliest stages, functions much as does LH, preventing the corpora lutea from degenerating, inhibiting uterine contractions, and stimulating the further production of progesterone. In the last trimester of pregnancy, the placenta itself becomes an endocrine organ as it secretes progesterone.

In males, pituitary LH causes the interstitial (Leydig) cells of the testis, which form little islands between the seminiferous tubules, to secrete the male hormone testosterone.

PRL (prolactin or lactogenic hormone) collaborates with ovarian steroids to stimulate mammary gland development and growth during pregnancy, with subsequent production of milk. Apparently the effects of prolactin are variable, depending upon the species. Administration of the hormone has led to marked behavioral effects in fish, birds, and small laboratory mammals. These effects include nest building and spawning migration in fish; premigratory restlessness, broodiness, and feeding of young in birds; and retrieval of young in rats. Behavioral reactions to PRL factors in humans have never been demonstrated but are suspected by some observers.

PRL represses ovulation; in societies where nursing periods are necessarily prolonged, the arrival of a sibling is thus normally delayed (see Chapter 7). Shortening nursing periods, or substituting bottle feeding, has reduced periods between conceptions and has contributed to excessive population growth in many developing countries and among aboriginal peoples.

Adrenal Cortex

Although not important in sex differentiation and function, corticosteroids are crucial in periods of stress when stored sugars are released from the liver for instant energy. Other functions are noted in Figure 6.1.

The androgens secreted by the adrenal cortex are much less potent than testicular androgens. However, when large amounts are involved as the result of prolonged ACTH stimulation or adrenal cortical enlargement, females may show the effects of masculinization. Adrenal androgens stimulate increases in facial hair in both sexes, receding hairlines, and acne or skin eruptions, especially on the face. Growth and patterning of pubic and chest hair are influenced by these androgens, which also act as sexual stimulants to both sexes; in contrast, estrogens stimulate female but inhibit male sexual activity.

Hormones and the Brain

In addressing the function of hormones in differentiating the sexes, we have not discussed the development of sex differences in the brain, since virtually all observations on neuron fine structure and the pattern of distribution in males and females have been made on rodents and birds. In 1971, using electron microscopy, Raisman and Field observed quantitative sex differences in the preoptic neurons of rat brains. These are situated in a deeply embedded region near the floor of the cerebrum. All nerve cells are polarized with regard to the impulse-carrying function; dendrites are the afferent processes that carry stimuli to the main body of the cell. Male and female preoptic neurons were found to carry different numbers of dendritic shafts or spines, and thus of synaptic connections, with females having the larger number of relationships formed by the dendritic terminals. Greenough et al. (1977) made similar observations in the hamster. By prenatally masculinizing female rats with hormones or by castrating newborn males, researchers have modified these synaptic patterns to resemble those of the other sex.

By 1978 Gorski and his colleagues reported that male and female rat brains sectioned through the preoptic area could be sorted grossly by the varying size and positioning of a densely staining aggregate of nerve cells, which he called the "sexual dimorphic nucleus." The male aggregate he observed to be strikingly larger than the female configuration. Again, prenatal treatment of female rat fetuses with testosterone enlarged their nuclear volume, while castration diminished the size in males. As these procedures effected only a modification of the structure, other mechanisms must be involved as well. More recently, Bleier and her colleagues (1982) extended Gorski et al.'s sexually dimorphic nucleus into a larger preoptic and hypothalamic region of the rodent brain, using rat, guinea pig, hamster, and mouse sections. Apparently the difference in sex patterns continues through an extensive area including most of the hypothalamus. Surprisingly, in all species except the mouse, they found the preoptic aggregate to be larger and more densely cellular in females than in males, the enlargement being most marked in the guinea pig.

The significance of this dimorphism is unknown. However, the responses of rodents to experimental lesions and electrical stimulation of the site have led some workers to propose its function to be related to the organization of reproductive behavior. The immense complexity of the human brain has defeated the attempts of workers to identify analogs with certainty; thus we have no information on sex differences in the human brain with regard to these structures or their possible significance.

Concerning sex differences in cerebral hemispheric asymmetry, we find another area of controversy. By lateralization, brain capacity has been progressively increased in higher primates and is most highly developed in humans. A number of researchers have attempted to investigate the timing of lateralization development in males and females (Wittelson 1976; Waber 1979).

In most right-handed persons, the left hemisphere is specialized for verbal processing, and the right for a variety of nonverbal functions, including spatial perception and the interpretation of patterns, although both hemispheres function in concert in most cognitive operations. Studies on impairment of brain function and recovery after injury have expanded our recognition of sex differences in brain lateralization, with men showing greater impairment of verbal performance after left-sided lesions and impaired spatial abilities following right-sided injuries. Women with left brain lesions tend to demonstrate fewer language deficits, including a lesser frequency of aphasia than men show. Impaired spatial performance may result from injury to either side of the brain.

Psychologists have devised a legion of tests for assessing the development and divergence of the hemispheres throughout childhood and for estimating the relative proficiency of each in processing various kinds of data. However, not all investigators agree as to the timing and nature of lateralization differences between the sexes (see Chapter 4).

MALE AND FEMALE DEVELOPMENTAL STAGES

Mammalian embryos of both sexes develop morphologically in an identical fashion during the first days of gestation. However, as early as the 8- to 16-cell stage, after three or four mitotic divisions, males can be differentiated from females both microscopically and immunologically. By this time, one of the X chromosomes has been inactivated in female cells, forming a Barr body in each. Anti-H-Y antibody applied to nonhuman blastulas (early cell clusters) has been shown to kill approximately half of them. The killed blastulas are believed to be males that carry the H-Y antigen on their cell surfaces, and it is assumed that human blastulas would react similarly. Subtle sex differences, then, are apparently manifested very early.

Male Development

In his pioneering works, Jost (1953, 1961) set forth a concept of male sexual differentiation as an ordered process established at conception. For Jost, male gonadal sex development is initiated by the hormonelike antigen we now know as H-Y. Gonadal sex, in turn, regulates the development of male phenotypic sex. Sexual development depends on a sequence of interactions between genetic determinants, hormonal regulatory factors, and specific cellular receptors. The details of these complex interactions are still being researched and debated.

About 3 weeks after fertilization, the precursors of spermatozoa and ova, the primordial germ cells that eventually form the germinal epithelium of the ovary and the germinal lining of the seminiferous testicular tubules, appear. They are first located in the yolk sac, an atavistic organ more useful to egg-laying forebears than to placental mammals. From the yolk sac, the germ cells migrate amoebalike to the genital ridges of the embryo. For some weeks, the early reproductive-excretory systems of males and females develop in identical fashion. These early systems have three components: the developing gonads themselves, two genital duct systems (the Müllerian and Wolffian ducts), and a common duct opening into the urinary tract.

The embryonic testis, which develops in response to H-Y antigen, performs two early secretory functions. The first is the synthesis of testosterone in the interstitial cells that lie between the convoluted germinal tubules of the testes. Testosterone is the main agent transforming gonadal to phenotypic sex; its essential role is the virilization of the male urogenital tract. The second secretion is a hormone known as the "Müllerian regression hormone," a substance produced in the seminiferous tubules themselves. This hormone causes the atrophy of the Müllerian duct, while the Wolffian duct persists and develops into the internal accessory organs of the male genital system. During the last trimester, the descent of the testes into the scrotal sac and the growth of the internal genitalia are completed.

In females, the opposite process takes place, with the atrophy of the Wolffian duct and the transformation of the Müllerian duct system into the fallopian tubes, uterus, and a part of the vagina. This internal differentiation is completed by the end of the second month of gestation; the external genitalia undergo little differentiation compared with male development. Male mammalian embryos that are experimentally castrated retain the Müllerian duct; when testosterone subsequently is administered, the embryos develop both male and female reproductive tracts.

The normal stages of growth are characterized by the brief appearance of structures, followed by their resorption or transformation, seemingly pointless and inefficient arrangements and rearrangements. These comprise some of the irreducible developmental steps traversed by all higher vertebrates, a complex of largely invariant processes inherited from remote forebears. Although not all phylogenetic ancestors are vestigially represented, a minimum residue of stages has been preserved, each necessary to the initiation of the next developmental step.

The interaction here between somatic cells, genetically programmed secretions, and the early germinal cells and tissues normally results in a functional gonad, assuming the hormonal and genetic sex coincide. However, hormones and chromosome complements sometimes differ. A classic example is the freemartin, wherein twin calves, sheep, or goats of different genetic sex share a common placenta and common circulating hormones. Female freemartin animals undergo partial sex reversal and are sterile. A similar situation in humans has been known to result from placental interactions between male and female dizygotic twins, with maternal-fetal placental exchange. However, hormones alone will not change an ovary into a testis, or vice versa. Males are less affected than females, since the male gonads are protected against maternal hormones by specific cellular androgen receptors, as detailed below.

Estrogens

Estrogens, like androgens, are steroids, a class of lipid compounds derived from a cholesterol base. Although a number of abnormalities result from gene mutations leading to testosterone deficiency or hypersecretion or to cellular resistance to its action, no mutations are known that result in estrogen hypersecretion or hyposecretion or in resistance to estrogenic effects. Early estrogen synthesis is crucial to both male and female embryos; apparently the presence of the hormone is necessary for successful implantation in the uterine wall. In contrast, androgen action is not necessary to embryonic survival. Estrogen apparently exerts its early effects locally where produced, its action depending on the distribution of estrogen receptors. Even before histological differentiation of the ovary occurs, estradiol formation begins. Not all of its effects are clear, however, because numerous maternal and fetal hormones are present at the same time. Estrogen probably functions in the growth and development of the female internal genitalia during the latter period of gestation. Its most striking effects appear at puberty with the establishment of secondary sex characters: the growth of breasts, uterine and vaginal epithelium, female hair distribution and body configuration, and the establishment of the menstrual cycle and ovulation.

The importance of estrogen to males in mediating the action of androgen on the brain has been established only recently. Estrogens also function in controlling the effects of testosterone both by synergistic and antagonistic action.

Gene Mutations Affecting Hormone Level and Phenotypic Sex (Pseudohermaphroditism)

Mutation of the *tfm* gene results in androgen insensitivity or testicular feminization. The *tfm* gene, which surprisingly is located on the X chromosome, is normally responsible for the development of androgen receptors in fetal target tissues, notably those of the internal and external genitals and secondary sex characters. It is the only genetic locus on the X chromosome known to relate to sex differentiation per se, and is either a structural gene or a regulatory gene controlling structural genes. Both males and females carry androgen receptors that give them the capacity of responding to male hormones, but sex differences in the amount of sex hormones produced cause males to develop in one direction and females in another.

If female embryos are subjected to increased amounts of androgen, for instance, through maternal or fetal tumors or hormone therapy administered to the mother, they will be masculinized to a degree consistent with the amount and timing of the male hormone introduced. Experimental sex changes in monkeys have been effected repeatedly by prenatal hormone injections. From these experiments, the relationship between the amount of androgen and the critical time for exposure to the hormone, to the degree of masculinization has been ascertained.

Well-documented although fairly rare cases of sex transformation caused by a recessive mutant *tfm* gene have provided some insights into the effects of androgen and estrogens. As in hemophiliacs, the mutant gene is transmitted by an unaffected female to approximately half her children; male offspring (with only one X chromosome) express the trait. The mutation renders sex-specific tissues androgen resistant, so that male hormones cannot reach the cell nuclei and interact with DNA and RNA. No matter how high the level of circulating androgen from the fetal testes, internal and external genitalia fail to become masculinized. The resulting XY pseudohermaphrodites develop as phenotypic females in response to adrenal estrogens unopposed by androgens. Often tall and willowy, with fashionably narrow hips and female breast development and hair distribution, they make ideal models. Such persons may carry palpable but undescended testicles in the groin or in the abdomen or labia, blind-end vaginas, and vestigial or missing uteri. Failure to menstruate and conceive most often sends them to their doctors. Psychosexually they identify as females without ambivalence, and may marry successfully.

Some *tfm* transformations may be less complete than the extreme example described above; varying degrees of feminization, which reflect differing degrees of tissue responsiveness to androgens, have been observed. The Reifenstein syndrome is characterized by decreased virilization and often intermediate phallic development. It is probably caused by partial androgen insensitivity due to a less effective expression of the X-linked mutant with inadequate androgen influence during development. These aberrations provide classic demonstrations of the transforming potential of hormones and also show that hormone levels alone cannot achieve selective effects on organs and tissues. Equally necessary are the specific cytoplasmic receptors that render the cells susceptible to hormonal effects. The *tfm* defect is especially useful in demonstrating the extent to which hormones can influence sex differences in extragenital phenotypes.

Adrenal Cortical Hyperplasia
(Adrenogenital Female Hermaphroditism)

Adrenal cortical hyperplasia is the most common masculinizing aberration, another phenotypic deviation that arises from a homozygous autosomal recessive mutation. This gene combination blocks the manufacture of an enzyme (21-hydroxylase) responsible for synthesizing the steroid hormone cortisol of the adrenal cortex. Normally, the output of cortisol is controlled by ACTH secreted by the anterior lobe of the pituitary gland. When the amount of cortisol in the bloodstream falls too low, the pituitary, via the hypothalamus, is alerted to increase ACTH production. As the required amount is attained, ACTH secretion is normally shut off. Since the enzyme defect in the mutant condition prevents the formation of cortisol, the feedback inhibitor fails to function, and ACTH continues to flow unabated. Elevated ACTH leads to increased steroid precursors, from which androgens are converted. The uninterrupted secretory activity also causes hyperplasia (excessive development) of the adrenal cortical tissue, a condition known as "hyperplasia," which increases the androgen flow. The weight of the adrenals may be increased excessively in severe cases. Continued androgen secretion after birth leads to rapid somatic growth. As a result, the height is well ahead of that normal for chronological age until ages 8 to 12 years when the growth spurt is exhausted. Body build tends to be masculine, with strong musculature and undeveloped breasts. The external genitalia are especially affected, with clitoral enlargement to the extent of apparent sex reversal in newborns, or may present an indeterminant condition. The several variant forms of enzyme deficiency causing masculinization are discussed by Simpson (1982). The disease is unique among sex-reversal conditions in that it is largely amenable to treatment with corticoids, which can reverse masculine development if started early enough (Lev-Ran 1977). Infant boys carrying the homozygous mutation may demonstrate what is known as the "infant Hercules syndrome," developing precocious characters of puberty when only a few months or years old.

According to Money and Ehrhardt (1972), masculinization by adrenal androgens has a profound psychological effect on females, and results in what they call "tomboyism," characterized by career rather than domestic ambitions, masculine clothes preference, high energy level with a keen liking for competitive sports and boys' toys and games, and a general disinterest in maternal and domestic play. Reinisch and colleagues (1979) find these traits predictable in view of the behavior of female monkeys who were prenatally masculinized in studies reported by Goy (1968) and Phoenix (1974). The animals demonstrated more activity, competitiveness, aggressiveness, chasing play, threat, and initiation of games than nontreated females.

Conversely, Baker and Ehrhardt (1974) tested a number of androgenitally affected boys and girls along with their normal peers, but found no significant differences in those cognitive traits in which males and females are reported to differ, namely, verbal performance and spatial perception (Maccoby and Jacklin 1974). The evaluation of personality traits such as career ambitions, interest in sports, and assertiveness as the province of males is itself a cultural rather than a biological perspective, and one that is increasingly outmoded. Thus, the personality profiles, claimed for persons with such aberrations have elicited criticism, especially from social scientists.

Experimental Masculinization and Feminization

In two highly intriguing papers, Ward (1972, 1980) described the feminization of male experimental rats *in utero* by stressing their pregnant mothers. As adults, the offspring demonstrated reversed copulatory patterns and disturbed mate choice, effects first interpreted as resulting from maternal oversecretion of adrenal cortical hormone. Stress causes central nervous system activation of the anterior pituitary via the hypothalamus, which in turn effects increased ACTH secretion in order to elevate the blood level of cortisol. Adrenal corticoids free glycogen stored in the liver for energy and increase the responsiveness of the autonomic nervous system. The level of adrenal androgens is also increased by the elevated output. In Ward's research, the overabundant adrenal androgen, a less effective masculinizing agent than testosterone, was thought to be picked up preferentially by fetal androgen receptors, resulting in feminization of males and possibly some masculinization of females as well.

In the second paper, Ward extended her explanation to include the timing of the elaboration of testosterone by the testes. During specific periods of normal male development, testosterone exerts permanent effects on the organization of the brain, determining in nonhuman animals the appropriate sexual behavior of the species in adulthood. In Ward's stressed rats, the short period most critical for the influence of testosterone on brain development failed to synchronize with the highest concentration of hormone. The result was that the hormone reached the level prematurely and fell dramatically, instead of peaking on the crucial day.

Although it has not been explored in humans, one might question whether the stresses of contemporary life, involving illegitimacy, insecurities, and overcrowding, might function as fertility regulators through the hormone-timing mechanism. Do the trend toward "unisex," the changing socal roles of women, and the growing acceptance of the homosexual life-style reflect such a psychobiological effect? In making such speculations, it is important to remember that human beings as both biological and as culturally-conditioned creatures have experienced, and survived, many radical alterations over the last millenia. Though people are capable of adapting to almost any set of stresses, including radical changes in ideas about normative sexual behavior, each transition is hazardous and each new equilibrium, though it may permit survival, offers new circumstances for deviation as its price.

Aneuploidies

Now we turn to abnormalities arising from errors in the number of sex chromosomes, rather than from genetic mutations or environmental stresses.

Sexual differentiation, being basically dependent upon XX or XY directives, is critically affected by abnormalities in sex chromosome numbers, or aneuploidies. Chromosomes and genes exert their influences in concert on the developmental process, so that alterations affect the overall organization of growth and differentiation. Approximately half of the spontaneous abortions during the first trimester carry chromosome abnormalities (Boué et al. 1975).

The four best-known clinical syndromes in which chromosomes deviate from 46 XX and 46 XY are the 45 XO, known as "Turner's syndrome"; the 47 XXX and its supernumerary variations, for example, 48 XXXX; 47 XXY, known as "Klinefelter's syndrome"; and the 47 XYY, the so-called "aggression complement." Supernumerary combinations such as 48 XXYY, and 48 XXXY occur very rarely.

These conditions are most often the result of errors in chromosome duplication and separation in meiosis, the process that reduces the chromosome number of the sperm and egg cells to exactly half. Normally, one chromosome of each pair is distributed to each developing gamete; thus in XY males, half the gametes receive the Y, the other half, the X. Discrepancies occur if newly duplicated X's or Y'x fail to pull apart – an error called "nondisjunction." If one of the chromosomes is left behind, in the mischance known as "anaphase lag," it becomes incorporated with its duplicate in one gamete or daughter cell. This results in one gamete or cell lineage with a missing chromosome, while the other carries double the normal number.

Excess or insufficient autosomal chromosomes in most cases result in fetal death. In fact, aberrant numbers of sex chromosomes seem less detrimental to individual development than aberrant numbers of any other chromosomes. However, the YO condition, in which no X is present, appears to be lethal in the early embryonic stage, for no YO subjects have been described.

Most chromosomal aberrations involve one extra or one missing chromosome, but occasionally several or even many extra chromosomes are present. Such an aberration may result if an ovum is fertilized by two different sperm (dispermy). In this condition, double or half again as many chromosomes as are normal can be included in an individual. A similar effect may occur if the developing ovum fails to lose its excess chromosomes in a polar body after penetration by a sperm. Delayed fertilization seems to be the most common cause of dispermy and polar body retention. Even greater numbers of chromosomes are found in the rare cases of triploidy and tetraploidy, where extra chromosomal divisions occur spontaneously within cells and produce tripling or quadrupling of chromosome numbers. These accidents are common in plants but lethal in higher forms.

45 XO – Turner's Syndrome

In Turner's syndrome, the most common aneuploidy, the individual's karyotype reveals only a single X, and Barr bodies are missing. Twenty percent of spontaneous abortions due to chromosome anomalies are XO aneuploidies, and 70 percent of liveborn XO individuals have lost a paternal sex chromosome. The typical XO individual is described as a short female having a relatively short neck with lateral webbing and a broad shield-shaped chest with widely spaced, undeveloped breasts. She may also demonstrate low-set ears, osteoporosis, epicanthic folds, and forearms that angle sharply away from the body. Without estrogen replacement therapy, such individuals do not experience puberty and their ovaries are represented only by dysgenic streaks. The risk of other organ defects is increased, although not all persons show them. Shaffer (1962) first administered tests for cognitive functioning to a large number of females with Turner's syndrome. He concluded that on full-scale intelligence quotient (IQ) they averaged within the range of normal population variation, and on verbal IQ significantly above the average. However, performance IQ was significantly below average. Money's continuing work substantiated these findings. In 1966, Money and Alexander reported space-factor scores notably below normal levels, and the IQs of most were defective when the task involved visual memory and the drawing of geometric shapes.

47 XXX – Aneuploidy

The 47 XXX aneuploidy is easily diagnosed by the presence of two Barr bodies. These individuals have normal female constitutions, but often have diminished fertility and may fail to menstruate. Mental retardation is not uncommon, but otherwise no distinguishing features are known.

47 XXY – Klinefelter's Syndrome

Klinefelter's complement appears in about 1 in 700 liveborn males (Polani 1972). It usually arises as a result of meiotic nondisjunction in maternal or paternal meiosis. (The source may be determined by *Xg* blood group and G6PD enzyme studies, in cases where maternal and paternal alleles differ, or by studies of individual banding patterns. As in the case of Down's syndrome, a maternal age effect has been recognized in the formation of these aneuploidies.) The XXY individuals are masculine in body type, with disproportionately long arms and legs. Their external genitals are often relatively small, with characteristically degenerate testes and underdeveloped penis, since the androgen level is usually diminished. The histological picture of testicular tissue reveals severe abnormalities of the germinal tubules, with few sperm cells.

A number of workers have reported that the proportion of XXY persons in mental or penal institutions is far higher than that found in the general population. In this, they resemble XYY persons, and accordingly the disorder has been claimed to constitute a psychopathological risk (Jacobs et al. 1974). However, Witkin et al. (1976), using statistical adjustments for background influences, parental socioeconomic status, and Army cognitive level scores, determined that persons with the XXY aneuploidy do not differ significantly in criminality from XY persons of similar background, opportunities, and intelligence. Money and Ehrhardt (1972) reported that they display an increased number of gender-identity anomalies, such as transvestism, transsexualism, and homosexuality, and are characterized by instability of mental functioning. Reinisch et al. (1979) reported that the syndrome is not incompatible with normal intelligence, although affected individuals display mental deficiency more often than unaffected persons. Performance, verbal, and perceptual IQs were found within normal range, according to Money (1964). However, Nielsen (1969) reported lower verbal and performance IQs than in hypo-gonadal subject controls. Several workers agree on the marked distractability that characterizes many XXY subjects. However, these personality profiles do not apply to all individuals with the chromosome abnormality, and are open to criticism from social scientists and psychologists.

47 XYY – Aneuploidy

During the late 1960s and early 1970s, the presumed association of the XYY syndrome with increased aggressive tendencies and criminality was widely and acrimoniously debated. Controversies regarding the implications of these studies for the presumed association with aggressive behavior and the male hormones have been largely political in nature, pitting a conservative view of biological predetermination against a more liberal conviction of human plasticity. One result of these arguments was a cessation of some types of research on the question. Specifically, the attempt of scientists to investigate the genetic basis for antisocial behavior by conducting longitudinal studies of XYY individuals drew fire as unethical from a number of critics. They argued that the study could create problems in the affected individual, at worst making the syndrome a self-fulfilling prophecy in effect, and at best occasioning personal distress if findings were shared with subjects and their families, either intentionally or by mischance. Accordingly, longitudinal aneuploidy studies were discontinued (Culliton 1974; Kopelman 1978).

The XYY controversy was initiated in 1965 when Jacobs et al. first reported an association of that karyotype with deviant behavior. They found that 3.5 percent of patients in a maximum security hospital in Carstairs carried the abnormality but found no persons with XYY in a control sample of 2,040 adult males. Another mental and penal institution in Scotland also yielded rates considerably higher than expectation. Further, a few individuals with the XXYY chromosome constitution were found to be institutionalized, a distribution 100 times more frequent than among normal newborns (Jacobs 1975).

Since the original studies, workers have come to a general agreement that persons with the XYY syndrome tend to be taller than average; accordingly, many researchers limit their investigations of the syndrome to tall subjects. Of the 35 subsequent studies of mental and penal inmates, Hook (1973) concluded that in 60 percent of them the occurrence rates of XYY significantly exceeded expectations derived from comparisons with the general population. Hook considered this an underestimation, suggesting that in some cases persons who suspected they carried the trait or demonstrated some of its characteristics did not agree to be research subjects. A mean estimate of 2 percent XYY-afflicted prison inmates was judged by Hook, on the basis of pooled data, to be a reasonable figure. This is five times the maximum background rate that Hook gave as 0.4 percent, and is 20 times the newborn rate of 0.1 percent.

Prevalence of the XYY combination has been reported as significantly higher in white than black persons. This finding may indicate differential reporting and studies, a valid difference in the rate of aberrancy, or it may be due to differential survival of embryos and fetuses in the two social groups.

Testosterone levels in XYY individuals have not been found to be abnormally elevated; in fact, spermatogenesis in adults may be reduced, even to the point of sterility. Other anomalies may or may not be present. The conclusion is inescapable that the prevalence of the XYY syndrome is higher among inmates of mental and penal institutions than predictable from the background rate. However, because of the lack of more rigorous studies of general distribution and of reliable tests for aggression level, not to mention an operational definition of the term, causal connections between the anomaly and deviant, criminal, or aggressive behavior cannot be firmly established. Although some XYY individuals demonstrate a variety of endocrinological, neurological, and psychological abnormalities that appear related to their constitution, others show no such characteristics. Aggressive tendencies in many cases may be no more marked than those, say, of hockey or football players, whose ebullience finds a socially acceptable outlet and is modified by normal intelligence.

Witkin et al. (1976) exhaustively reviewed all relevant studies and added detailed information on 4,139 tall males from Copenhagen. Of the 4,139, 12 proved to carry the XYY syndrome and 16 the XXY syndrome. Five of the 12 XYY individuals had been convicted of one or more criminal offenses. By contrast, the Klinefelter (XXY) rate of 3 percent convictions was not statistically significant nor were their offenses serious (only one case involved aggression against another person and the 3 percent rate is comparable with that for normal XY males). Witkin and colleagues concluded that the high incidence of XYY persons with convictions was related to their low intellectual potential and the general lack of educational and socializing influences that characterize low socioeconomic households, rather than to their genetic complement per se. Their low intelligence and social inadequacies were held to increase the likelihood of their being apprehended and convicted in situations where the more mentally and socially competent might escape detection and detention.

Mosaicism

All aneuploidies can occur as mosaics, or partial aberrancies that occur in only some cells of the body. In total aneuploidy conditions, such as those surveyed above, the chromosome irregularity originates in the process of gametogenesis or in the fertilized zygote, and all cells of the new individual carry the abnormal chromosome complement. In mosaics, the chromosomal error arises later, during the blastula or gastrula stage, that is, when the early embryo consists of a cluster of dividing cells. At that time, if one of the cells undergoes an irregular chromosomal division, the cell lineages, areas, and organs that are derived from that original cell will carry the aneuploid condition, while other areas will be normal. The presence of the normal derivatives modifies the effects of the abnormal tissues. For instance, XO/XX Turner's syndrome mosaics may be fertile and may experience a normal puberty. As 11 percent of all individuals with Turner's syndrome have been found to be mosaics, the condition can be considered relatively common.

XX/XY Chimerism (True Hermaphroditism)

A true simultaneous hermaphrodite or chimera is a rare individual who carries both male (XY) and female (XX) cell types from different sources. An ovary and a rudimentary uterus may be present on one side, and a testis and internal male genitalia on the other, or one or both gonads may be a combination ovotestis. External genitalia are known to vary from feminine to masculine types; most often they are ambiguous, with clitoral hyperplasia, labial-scrotal swelling, and often a single orifice at the base of the phallus. Although a few gametes may be formed, no functionally reproducing hermaphrodite has been known. Histologically, Barr bodies may or may not be visible.

Chimeras are classified as whole body or partial, according to their mode of origin. Whole-body chimeras arise from the early fusion of male and female zygotes, from the fertilization of both an ovum and its polar body by two different sperms, or from the fusion of a full-complement sperm with a female zygote or with a diploid ovum. Partial chimeras can be effected by placental interactions between dizygotic twins, with maternal-fetal transplacental exchange transfusions, or from cellular graftings that fuse. Although the hermaphroditic condition characterizes many invertebrates, it is so rare among humans that the discovery of an XX/XY person always elicits a detailed scientific paper.

Abnormalities Due to Partial Chromosome Loss

Simpson (1982) discussed a number of abnormalities in sex characters associated with chromosomal arm deletions of varying size: For example, (1) A deletion of the X short arm may cause gonadal dysgenesis and other Turner-like characters. (2) Loss of a certain chromosomal band on the short arm results in primary amenorrhea (loss of the menstrual cycle). (3) Several short-arm deletions on the Y chromosome have been reported; affected individuals are female in appearance and have bilateral streak gonads. This finding has served to locate the H-Y genes on the short Y arm near the centromere.

Phenotypic-karyotypic associations of partial chromosome loss are gradually being worked out. Although the field is still in its infancy, it promises a better understanding of sex and sex-associated chromosomal gene loci and function.

Male and Female Developmental Stages

Because of the complexity of the human system and indeed of the biological systems of all higher plants and animals, it is easier to describe what goes wrong, that is, mechanisms which interfere with development, than it is to map out all of the interactions that must take place to ensure normal development. Owing to appropriate ethical constraints, we must learn about human development by reasoning back from the end process, by studying early abortions and miscarriages and investigating the early stages of other primates. Biological systems, of which human bodies are our most interesting examples, generate their own strategies to achieve functional goals.

Sexual development provides a classic example of these generalizations. Humans can survive, and some can even reproduce, with marked abnormalities, and the range of the normal is so broad we have not yet been able to map it. However, we have achieved some understanding of the mechanisms that act as triggers in distinguishing the developing organism as male or female.

THE SEX RATIO

Evolutionary Models

The number of offspring born to mammalian females is limited by the duration and physiological demands of their gestation and nursing periods. Males, on the other hand, can theoretically sire an almost limitless number of descendants. The question naturally arises, then: Would it not be biologically more economical and thus selectively advantageous for a species to produce more females than males? Why has this not occurred?

Fisher (1958) pointed out that in a hypothetical population in which females greatly outnumber males, each male will necessarily leave more offspring than each female. Since each male produces more offspring, any genotype favoring the production of males over females will have a selective advantage, and such an advantage will raise the proportion of males – assuming, of course, that the male-female ratio, or the factors influencing that ratio, have a hereditary basis. Natural selection, then, is expected to increase the number of the rarer sex, and to maintain the approximate 50:50 ratio that we observe. This ratio maximizes the chance of male and female encounters at maturity and provides for optimum genetic variability. It also minimizes genetic drift (which may counter the selective process) and inbreeding effects.

Fisher held that it is not the number of each sex produced that tends to be equalized, but rather the ratio at reproductive maturity. Relative parental effort expended in the conception, birth, and nurturance of offspring, as well as sex differences in the probability of survival, thus affect the ratio. Human males are more vulnerable embryologically, fetally, and postnatally than are females. When males are aborted or die in infancy, the parental investment is diminished. Thus, Fisher's model predicts that males will be produced in larger numbers, a prediction that is fulfilled in almost all human populations. Colombo (1975) calculated a world average sex ratio of 105, that is, 105 males per 100 females. In U.S. citizens of European descent, 106 males are born to every 100 females, but owing to greater male mortality, by the age of reproduction the sex ratio approaches equality.

Trivers and Willard (1973) hypothesized that natural selection adjusts the sex ratio according to which parent's physical condition enhances his/her ability to invest in offspring. In their model, a male in good condition at maturity will outreproduce a sister in poor condition; if both are physiologically depleted, the female will, on average, prove more fertile and will leave more surviving grandchildren. An adult female in good condition who produces a robust son will leave more descendants than one who produces a daughter.

Data from a number of mammalian species support this prediction. Studies on dogs, sheep, mink, and pigs correlate increased litter size (which implies less attention to any one offspring) inversely with the sex ratio. Humans fulfill the prediction by the tendency of females to marry males of higher socioeconomic status, thereby increasing the individual investment possible in offspring and – if the model is correct – also raising the sex ratio. Trivers and Willard qualify their model by saying that its application to humans is complicated by the tendency of males to invest heavily in their young and by the importance of kin interactions in human families.

Hamilton (1967) argued that Fisher's predictions also are modified if competition for mates exists between related males. When sib- and kin-related males compete, the sex ratio should be biased in favor of females. Taylor and Bulmer (1980) agree that the sex ratio is skewed by the extent of sib and kin competition for a genetic share in the next generation.

According to these evolutionary models, skewing is achieved by physiological controls that permit the sex ratio to vary according to parental investment and the relative probability of effective breeding of each sex. Sociobiologists have been particularly interested in this topic (see Chapter 3). Any particular sex ratio not only is affected by the social and environmental system, but may have major effects upon the system too. Guttentag and Secord in their provocative book *Too Many Women* (1983) give their interpretation of the historical effects of skewed sex ratios. They suggest that the sex that is in short supply commands the more desirable mating choices, has higher expectations for lasting relationships, and claims an elevated status in society. Their application to the United States is, in brief, as follows:

In the country's early history, selective migrations produced a largely male society. Women were valued as wives and mothers and were protected accordingly; their sexuality was closely circumscribed and their relationships were confined by ideals of purity and chastity. But by 1970, in spite of a birth ratio of 106, the sex ratio was only 82 in the young adult age group. Accordingly, women, particularly those over age 25, faced a serious shortage of mates. Guttentag and Secord attribute to this imbalance the devaluation of women, sexual libertarianism with brief liaisons, general lack of commitment in relationships, and, as a result, the women's movement of the 1970s, which demanded political redress. Whether or not these hypotheses will be confirmed remains to be seen. But it is important to note the suggestion that the sex ratio may effect social consequences as well as being itself influenced by social concepts and conditions.

Sex ratios are calculated at different stages of life: a primary sex ratio at the time of conception, a secondary sex ratio at birth, a tertiary sex ratio at the time of maturity, and a quaternary ratio that considers all the adults in a population and thus provides a profile of differential mortality.

Primary Sex Ratio

It is difficult to establish the sex ratio at conception since many zygotes fail to become implanted in the uterine wall and since embryos are often aborted spontaneously too early for recovery or detection. Recent advances in chromosome identification on deliberately aborted fetuses promise more reliable figures. Research on other mammalian species suggests a primary sex ratio higher than that found at birth, but because humans may not show as great a deviation as other mammals, it is prudent to use animal studies for comparative purposes rather than as models.

Whether the initial deviance from a 50:50 ratio is the result of the production of more Y- than X-bearing germ cells or gametes, a phenomenon known as "segregation distortion," or results from an advantage of Y-bearing sperm in motility or penetrance is uncertain. According to Shettles (1964), electron microscopy has revealed two distinct human spermatozoon types: a smaller, lighter male with a round head and a larger female with an elongated head, with the former outnumbering the latter by two to one. The male gamete has been observed to outdistance the X-bearing sperm in its progress through the viscous cervical mucus, which is especially heavy at the time of ovulation (Goodall and Roberts 1976). Possibly segregation distortion, differential gametic motility, and differential mortality all influence the primary sex ratio.

Cultural habits appear to influence profoundly the primary sex ratio through the timing and frequency of coitus. Cyclic changes in the pH and viscosity of cervical mucus and sperm count following the enforcement of sexual abstinence by religious or other prohibition together provide an advantage for Y-bearing sperm. The result can be an exceptionally high primary sex ratio (Guttentag and Secord 1983).

Cavalli-Sforza and Bodmer (1971, p. 654), however, find reports of high primary sex ratios spurious and judge them either artifactual or derived from inadequate samples. They quote the large series of Carr (1965, 1975) and McKeown and Lowe (1951) in support of their argument for a more balanced sex ratio. Chromosome analyses of Moore and Hyrniuk (1969), as well as those of a number of Japanese workers on several series of embryos that were aborted after less than 2 months of gestation, also suggest a sex ratio not far from equality. At the other extreme, Makino (1968) found an early fetal sex ratio of 63.6. The primary sex ratio, then, may either be nearer 100 than was formerly believed, or it may be characterized by erratic fluctuations.

Authorities also disagree radically concerning the sex ratio of the approximately 15 percent of fetuses lost by spontaneous abortion during the second trimester. Glucksmann (1978, p. 60), while emphasizing the unreliability of sexing by anatomical, that is, genital, differences at this stage, cites reports of striking excesses of males, with sex ratios from 228 to over 400. Even workers who use current cytological techniques for sex determination differ widely in their figures, some claiming a preponderance of males and some of females. Again, Cavalli-Sforza and Bodmer (1971) consider the ratio of normal, *in utero* fetuses to be not far from 50:50. During the last trimester, stillbirths are relatively rare, occurring in only 2 to 3 percent of all pregnancies. Stillbirth sex ratios varying from 119 to 324 have been recorded (Glucksmann 1978, p. 60). It is difficult to reconcile these figures with those of McKeown and Lowe (1951) who reported only a 5 to 10 percent excess of males in stillbirths when two disorders, spina bifida and anencephalus, were excluded. (Spina bifida is a defect in the dorsal closure of the spinal canal, which exposes the spinal cord; anencephalus is the absence of the cranial vault, in which cerebral hemispheres are vestigial or missing.) Both conditions are three times as frequent in females as in males at 7 months, and are over twice as frequent at 9 months. There is no known explanation for this distribution, which must be sex influenced.

Some authors who accept male excesses in spontaneous abortions and stillbirths postulate the expression of recessive lethal mutations on the X chromosome as a cause. This perspective has been reinforced by the experimental irradiation of mice, which increases male losses and so decreases the sex ratio. X-linked recessive traits are suppressed in the heterozygous female condition, but expressed in the hemizygous condition in males. Since these genes are exposed to selection in males as if they were dominants, they are under strong selective pressures and, except under special circumstances, should appear at low frequencies. Accordingly their effects on the sex ratio are smaller than might be assumed. Meyer et al. (1968, p. 123) reported a sex ratio of 92.3 in their sample of 488 individuals in which human ovaries were exposed to X-rays.

After World War II, Neel and Schull (1956) and Neel (1967) carried out extensive genetic investigations on the survivors of Hiroshima and

Nagasaki and on their children. They examined the frequencies of stillbirths, spontaneous abortions, and genetic defects, and looked for expected changes in the sex ratio as indicators of mutational damage. Although an apparent relationship between exposure to radiation and a decrease in male births was at first noted in exposed mothers, further studies failed to yield evidence of detectable changes. Possibly the small initial effect had disappeared as the study was not launched until several years after the bombing. Firm data were difficult to obtain because of the frequency of consanguinous marriages and the fact that spontaneous abortions and stillbirths, which frequently occur at home, may go unreported. Bayley (1966) found that in growth retardation and persistence the effects of the Hiroshima bombing were more severe in boys than in girls.

Evidence from a number of sources suggests immunological involvement in the selective loss of gametes and zygotes. In such reactions, an antigen (usually a protein specific to a species, lineage, or individual) is introduced into the living system of an individual who lacks it. This foreign protein causes the host to produce antibodies that incapacitate or destroy the antigen by an interaction process. The same phenomenon takes place in therapeutic immunization against pathogenic bacteria and viruses.

The molecular configurations of some bacterial antigens are so similar to those of blood group substances that their respective antigens and antibodies may cross-react; that is, antibodies against specific bacteria may react with blood group A or B antigens, and conversely blood group anti-A or anti-B antibodies may inhibit the growth of certain bacteria.

Antibacterial antibodies known as immunoglobulin (Ig)A, which are produced locally, protect the portals of entry to the body: the mouth, respiratory tract, and urogenital tract. These antibodies in the mother's uterus may inadvertently react against spermatozoa carrying a specific blood group character. The antigenic character of gametes may be adsorbed on their surfaces from secretions in the spermatic fluid, or may be intrinsic to the cell membranes of the zygote or embryo. Since males are more vulnerable than females, theoretically they may suffer more damage from maternal-fetal ABO incompatibility than females.

In support of this thesis, Sanghvi (1951) and Allen (1975) found an association of ABO blood type with the secondary sex ratio. As the theory predicts, type-AB mothes, who carry neither anti-A nor anti-B antibodies in their secretions, had a higher ratio of male births than mothers of other blood types. Jackson and colleagues (1969) reported an association of sex ratio with the Xg^a blood group reaction, the ratio being raised significantly when the father was Xg^a positive and the mother negative.

Further evidence of immunological involvement was found by Drew and colleagues (1978) in studying the hepatitis B virus and its surface antigen (called the Australia antigen). The sex ratio is significantly raised when parents are chronically infected with the virus. If there is a cross-reactivity of the Australia antigen with a male-associated antigen (that is, H-Y), the male immunological system will interpret the viral antigen as self and fail to react against it. Owing to the lack of specific antibodies, the virus will be maintained in a carrier state rather than be destroyed (Goodman et al. 1971). Predictably, the presence of Australia antibodies in mothers has been associated with a lowered sex ratio.

The finding that the sex ratio is higher in consanguinous marriages, wherein antigenic similarities are likely to be greater than among unrelated couples, further reinforces the hypothesis of an immune involvement in the secondary sex ratio. Darlington (1960, p. 297) reported a sex ratio of 122.2 in consanguinous marriages, and a high male preponderance was also noted in studies on first-cousin marriages (Glucksmann 1978, p. 62).

A decline in the sex ratio with each succeeding birth in large families is also consistent with this interpretation. If a mother is intolerant of an antigen of her male fetus, the incompatibility should become more marked with each succeeding male conception, for she will progressively add antibodies that can migrate transplacentally and attack the embryo or fetus. This process is best known in Rh incompatibility, but the principle is the same in repeated exposure to other foreign antigens inherited from the father. The finding of a decreased sex ratio among secondborn in women whose firstborn was male supports this hypothesis.

That seasonal differences in the sex ratio have been reported, with a higher ratio observable between July and August, may be supported by my research finding that the secretion of peripheral IgA antibodies falls dramatically in spring and rises to its higher winter levels during the autumn months (Otten 1967). Although this work was carried out on salivary secretions, it may prove valid for all localized antibodies.

Not all human geneticists agree that antigen-antibody reactions are involved in the primary sex ratio. For example, Cavalli-Sforza and Bodmer (1971) discredit immunological involvement in sex ratio determination, finding "no experimental evidence for the phenomenon" (p. 662).

In conclusion, the secondary sex ratio can be explained equally well by a high primary sex ratio with a high rate of male zygotic and embryonic mortality or by a primary ratio near equality with little sex-differential mortality. But if the primary sex ratio is in fact high, there must be substantial male losses during early pregnancy to produce the observed secondary sex ratio. Thus, studies of the sex of very young embryos may provide answers in the near future.

Secondary Sex Ratio

It is with some relief that we turn to the more secure data on the secondary sex ratio, which usually refers to full-term livebirths and excludes stillbirths as well as spontaneous abortions. In all population studies, the sex ratio at birth normally is above 100, although a few unusual conditions have skewed the figures dramatically.

Throughout history, innumerable speculations as to factors influencing the sex ratio have been advanced. However bizarre, they hardly seem more far-fetched than some of the variables researched recently. Among suggested agencies we find hard water, cigarette smoking, high-altitude flying, coffee drinking, various drugs, season of the year, blood type, birth control devices and medications, stage of menstrual cycle at which conception occurred, geography, toxemia of pregnancy, illegitimacy, occupation of father, urban versus rural home, IQ, schizophrenia and other mental abnormalities, and father's baldness. Perhaps the most strikingly aberrant ratios have been reported with toxemia of pregnancy, wherein the most severe cases resulted in a sex ratio of 171 (Toivanen and Hirvonen 1970, p. 187); high-altitude flying, which reportedly lowered the ratio to 59.3 in offspring of 236 pilots, contrasted with a figure of 151.4 for children fathered by off-duty pilots (Snyder 1961); and schizophrenic women who conceived within 1 month of the onset of psychosis and produced all female offspring, while the children of women who became psychotic after delivery had a sex ratio of 550, or 22 males to 1 female (Taylor 1969, p. 223).

However, only three associations – birth order, population, and socioeconomic status – have consistently survived scrutiny.

Birth Order

Formerly researchers believed that youthfulness of one or both parents was associated with a high sex ratio. However, Novitski and Kimball (1958) showed by multiple regression analysis that birth order, rather than age, is the significant variable. Teitelbaum (1972, p. 100) also demonstrated a significant birth order effect accounting for a 2.6 percent shift in the relative odds of a male birth. As birth order increases, the sex ratio declines. On this basis, Teitelbaum eliminated parental age per se as a significant variable. An increase in male births during and immediately following wars has been documented in England, Belgium, Italy, France, and Germany (Bernstein 1958) during World War I and in the United States and Germany during World War II (James 1976, p. 550; Damon 1977, p. 165). Although the rise may be accounted for by the increased number of firstborns, resulting from the many sexual unions formed during the stresses of warfare, MacMahon and Pugh (1954) doubted that the small rise in sex ratio that they found, from 105.8 to 106.1, was due to the relatively large number of firstborns. Bernstein reported that Germans marrying between 1900 and 1918 produced firstborns with a sex ratio of 124 if born within the first 18 months of marriage; those born later had a ratio of 85. He proposed that wartime conditions, requiring long absences of fathers, favor the early reproducers and result in high sex ratios. The closer the birth to the marriage date, then, the greater the likelihood of a male offspring. This finding has been supported by data from Australia and Finland (Damon 1977, p. 166).

A related theory by James (1976, 1977) holds that the rate of male conceptions is related to the frequency of intercourse, and thereby to the earlier days of marriage, especially in wartime. According to his theory, some days of the menstrual cycle provide more favorable conditions for male sperm survival and mobility than others. The more frequent the intercourse, the greater the probability of providing conditions optimum for a male conception. As will be discussed in considering the high sex ratio of Orthodox Jews, cultural habits can in this way influence profoundly the primary and secondary sex ratios owing to the religious regulation of sexual abstinence and indulgence. Cyclic changes in the character of cervical mucus, together with increased sperm count following periods of abstinence, foster fertilization by Y-bearing sperm and result in a heightened sex ratio (Guttentag and Secord 1983).

Some workers have suggested that a cultural preference for children of one sex or the other might influence the overall sex ratio of a population (see Chapter 7). According to Edwards (1966), parents whose first two children are of the same sex are more likely to continue having children than parents whose first two are of unlike sex. However, Cavalli-Sforza and Bodmer (1971, p. 661) state that as long as the sex of each birth is independently determined by chance, no amount of family planning can change the population's secondary sex ratio. The tendency of families to limit the number of offspring according to the sexes of children already born has proved a handicap to studies attempting to demonstrate a heritable factor in the sex ratio. The small size of many contemporary families also means that between-family variability will be confounded with the much greater statistical variability consequent upon sampling variation.

Edwards (1961) devised a statistical method to overcome the influences of family limitation and birth order in studying the sex ratio. After analyzing several large bodies of data, he found a remarkable absence of variability in the sex ratio that might be genetically controlled and concluded (1966) that "either any such variability would be disadvantageous under natural selection, or the sex ratio, being the consequence of a simple Mendelian segregation, is not susceptible to evolutionary forces" (p. 59).

Population

In discussing differences in sex ratio according to population – a concept often popularly confused with "race" or sometimes identified as "ethnic group" – we are plagued by problems both of definition and of population structure. No human group is completely isolated from all others, and most that we choose to define are characterized by both biological and cultural elements. Though no human population remains constant, writers for almost half a century have claimed a significant sex ratio discrepancy between U.S. "black" and "white" births. Since none of these workers appear to have ascertained the amount of European admixture carried by so-called "black" populations, or the African, Indian, and Asian admixture of so-called "white" or European samples, the general agreement of the findings is all the more remarkable.*

---

*Reed (1969), using a number of genetic markers (for example, blood group systems, hemoglobins, and other monogenic polymorphic traits) with known African and European frequency distributions, calculated the present proportions of European genes carried by persons designated as U.S. blacks. Depending upon the

Teitelbaum (1970, 1972), whose work has become a standard source on population differences, used data from the U.S. Office of Vital Statistics, and hence used categories of the common folk taxonomy, with its inherent limitations. He corrected for birth order and socioeconomic effects and ascertained that the relative odds of a male birth were 3 percent lower for blacks than for whites. This figure is found throughout the literature. Since black status is associated in the United States with greater probability of stress, disease, and malnutrition owing to economic and social discrimination, and a depressed sex ratio is associated with these conditions as well, it is likely that the phenomena are linked. Interestingly, Ayeni (1975), who surveyed 548,558 livebirths of the Nigerian Yorubas, reported a sex ratio close to that of North American whites.

Lyster (1968) studied the livebirth sex ratio in the United States and in Fiji and, like Teitelbaum, used data from the Office of Vital Statistics as well as from the annual reports of the Medical Department and Registrar General's Department, Government of Fiji. Native Fijians, whose births were studied over a 12-year period, showed a high average sex ratio of 110.8, while that of "unmixed" East Indians averaged 103.2, a discrepancy of 7.6 points for which no obvious explanation could be found. Neither group practices infanticide and Indian mothers tend to marry at a slightly earlier age than Fijian mothers. Lyster also calculated a consistent gap of 3 percent between sex ratios of white and nonwhite populations in the United States, an estimate consistent with Teitelbaum's findings.

The most strikingly elevated sex ratios have been found in Koreans, some Central and South American Indian populations, and Orthodox Jews. Lerner and Libby (1976, p. 153) reported a fourth locus in Greeks, who have a ratio of 113.

Kang and Cho (1962) derived from delivery records of 11,131 livebirths in the hospitals of five major Korean cities a mean sex ratio of over 115. The effect of birth order was evident, as the first to third

---

marker used, the areas of African origin, and present U.S. habitation, his frequencies of European-derived genes ranged from slightly under 0.20 to 0.40 with a few instances over 0.40. As Hall (1982, p. 192) pointed out, the system commonly used in the United States involves classifying a person as "black" if he/she has one or more African ancestors who have contributed particular phenotypic traits, principally, a darkly pigmented skin and tightly curled hair. This classification system, which is a folk taxonomy, has a few characteristics in common with biological classification, but principally serves to affix social labels.

offspring had a ratio of 117.4, the fourth to sixth had one of 116.1, and for the seventh and later offspring it was 113 – still a very high ratio.

Cowgill and Hutchinson (1963), using government census records, found an average birth ratio for Tabascan Indians of 119. Figures given for Chiapas and Veracruz Indians – 111.3 for both groups – are also elevated. However, the secondary sex ratios for inhabitants of Peten, Guatemala, give an overall average of 103.6 for the Indian population and 104.5 for the Ladinos, figures that differ little from worldwide averages. Only the Tabasco, Chiapas, and Veracruz data show a notable excess of male births.

In studies of the sex ratio of Indian children in the 0 to 5 age group around Lake Peten, Cowgill and Hutchinson recorded 86 for Ladino families of mixed background and a extraordinarily high ratio of 178 for all Indians. The effect for Indians persisted, in whatever way their populations were classified – by occupation, rural or urban residence, ethnic unit, or other socioeconomic criteria. The authors accounted for the wide discrepancy between the birth and cohort ratios as the consequence of preferential treatment of sons who are nursed longer and receive consistently better nutrition and a generally higher quality of care than daughters. This gives sons some protection from the ordinary debilitating diseases of poverty, such as dysentery. Indians in this area are known to place a greater importance on sex differences and sex roles in small children than do their Ladino neighbors. However, one might question whether the difference in treatment in itself can account for so high a sex ratio.

Chagnon and his colleagues (1979) determined sex ratios of Yanomamo Indians in five Amazon Basin villages that they studied from 1964 to 1975. Obtaining reliable data was unusually difficult because of the lack of written records, disinterest in accurate counts, and cultural restrictions against discussing dead kin. Further, infant deaths tended to be quickly forgotten. By repeated questioning of villagers, however, Chagnon et al. estimated an average sex ratio at birth of 129, with 143 for firstborns. Previously the observed high sex ratio had been believed to be the result of female infanticide, rather than the sex differential at birth. Although infanticide is a common solution in cases of weak or defective offspring, disputed paternity or the presence of another sibling who still is nursing, Chagnon et al. found that children are not necessarily marked for infanticide by their sex. Rather, the arduous domestic duties of Yanomamo women, duties that involve long-range gathering and extensive traveling, leave little time or energy for the care of ailing or unwanted infants. Many die of systematic neglect, but as many as half of the women were found to have destroyed at least one child.

Although the Yanomamo take more interest in male children, daughters are needed for marriage exchange in acquiring wives for sons and for the drudgery of daily domestic work. Therefore, they are a strategic resource and are recognized as such. Men have a higher death rate owing to warfare and more men than women die from wounds, infections, accidents, and snakebite. The result is that the sex ratio in children of 14 years and younger is 132, but for the adult population in general it falls to 118.

Rejection of the selective infanticide hypothesis for the high secondary sex ratio of the Yanomamo has promoted a search for other explanations. One possible explanation was sought in Trivers and Willard's hypothesis (1973) that higher-status families produce more male offspring than lower-status families. In testing this theory, Chagnon et al. (1979) compared the sex ratio of headmen lineages with those of other families but found no trend with regard to family status or rank. Since all members of this economically egalitarian society appeared in excellent physical condition, with no nutritional or child care disparities between headmen and other families, the lack of sex ratio differences was hardly surprising. The continual exchange of kinswomen among a closely related group of males may also contribute a genetic homogeneity not characteristic of stratified societies. The high sex ratio appears to be shared by the entire group, but the mechanism for it remains unknown. Comparably high sex ratios of other Amazon tribes (for example, the Xavante with 124 and the Cashinahua with 148) probably reflect biocultural situations analogous to those of the Yanomamo and are similarly perplexing.

By contrast, Netsilik Eskimo childhood ratios of 200 have been observed to result from the practice of female infanticide (Riches 1974). The sex ratio in middle-aged members of the population is approximately equality; the killing of girl babies compensates for heavy male mortality from hunting accidents, drowning, and suicide. Another social strategy used to equalize the ratio, if too many women and too few men survive, is polygyny, a practice that is adopted by proficient male hunters who can provide for additional wives.

Demographic and historical literature has for centuries referred to the high sex ratio of Orthodox Jews. Although neither classical nor biblical references offer reliable figures, the phenomenon has been so marked as to command repeated attention. Rafalovick [quoted in Guttentag and Secord (1983, p. 84)] found in an investigation of medical statistics for Odessa that in 1842, 345 Jewish males and 154 females were born – a sex ratio of 224. Russian censuses for 1867 through 1884, which provide separate data by religious group, report Jewish ratios with an average of 137 and include one sample with a sex ratio of 146. Even Charles Darwin (1874) noted:

> It is a singular fact that with Jews the proportion of male births is decidedly larger than with Christians, thus in Prussia, the proportion is as 113, in Breslau as 114, and in Livonia as 120 to 100; the Christian births in these countries being the same as usual, for instance, in Livonia as 104 to 100. (P. 275)

The secondary sex ratio for 3,300 Jews in the Grodno Province in 1840 was reported at 156. In Vilna, during the interval from 1897 to 1916, the state Rabbi's books showed 112 boys per 100 girls, a figure closer to credibility. Chocem inhabitants produced a sex ratio of 140 in one generation. Guttentag and Secord (1983, pp. 85-89) have assembled further examples. From these, two generalizations have emerged: (1) The high sex ratio continues into adulthood in Orthodox Jewish populations. (2) In modern secular society, the ratio falls to between 105 and 106.

Why are the ratios so high only under Orthodox practices? Since neither infanticide nor failure to register the birth of girls nor genetic factors are supported by the data, Guttentag and Secord concluded that the cultural and sexual practices of Judaism must hold the answer. Because male embryos and infants seem at especially high risk, one part of the answer could lie in the high quality of care ordained in Orthodox Jewish families. Family stability and relative lack of stress, along with the commitment of both parents to the welfare of infants and children of both sexes, could lessen the possibility of high prenatal and infant male losses. Pregnant and nursing mothers, under Orthodox practices, receive exceptional care and protection from overexertion, and their diets, like those of infants and children, are carefully monitored.

Another part of the answer may lie in sex practices unique to Orthodox Jews. Sexual intercourse is considered a duty for the husband and a right of the wife; because of restrictions on infidelity and mastur-bation, coital rates are believed to be high. Husbands are required to have intercourse at least twice a week when permitted by canon and in some cases more often. However, sexual unions are forbidden during menstruation and for 7 days thereafter. This enforces male abstinence, which is known to increase seminal volume. After this period, the husband is advised to have intercourse twice in succession if sons are desired. The combination of abstinence for 12 days plus coitus just before ovulation is believed to raise the probability of a male embryo. Supporting this interpretation is a study carried out by Seguy (1975) on 100 couples with normal fertility. Intercourse was permitted only at the time of ovulation, as determined by thermal shift. The resulting pregnancies produced 77 boys and 23 girls, a sex ratio of 335. Another study by the same investigator resulted in the births of 61 males and 39 females.

Socioeconomic Status

Trivers and Willard (1973, p. 91) predicted that sex ratios at birth correlate positively with socioeconomic status, insofar as the tendency holds for females to marry males with higher status than their own. This predicts that, on average, a male high in the social scale will outreproduce his sister; a female at the lower end will exceed her brother's reproductive success.

Both the tendency of females to marry males who are socially and economically their superior and the predicted increase in sex ratio with increased male social status have been verified by a number of researchers (Teitelbaum 1972). In Scotland, Stott (1966) found that in economically deprived families, there were 22.6 percent more girls than boys. A sharp upswing is noted as one moves from low to moderate social score (for example, in England it was found to vary from 103.4 at the lower end to 106 at the higher), but no further increases occur in going from moderate to higher social levels (Teitelbaum 1972). Overall, children born in the lowest social category have an approximate 8 to 9 percent lower probability of being male than those born to families in middle or higher levels. We may speculate on the vulnerability of males to maternal stresses – social, emotional, nutritional, hormonal, or immunological – any of which might reduce the chance of normal embryonic and fetal development. An answer to the question of why the sex ratio is higher among legitimate than illegitimate births may also be found here. Even in healthy mothers, emotional stress can stimulate hypersecretion of both the adrenal cortex and medulla, which in turn may retard the process of normal development. Experimental stressing of pregnant pigs and rodents has markedly modified the sex ratio of litters (Trivers and Willard 1973, p. 91).

Tertiary and Quaternary Sex Ratios

The tertiary sex ratio is set imprecisely at the age of maturity, when equality of the sexes is predicted. Eighteen has been used commonly, but recent assessments have advanced by 10 or more years the age at which equal representation of the sexes occurs. Higher probabilities for survival of young males have contributed to this change. This section considers genetic, physiologic, and behavioral aspects of adult male-female susceptibilities.

The sex differential in mortality has widened strikingly during the last half-century in the United States. In 1920 the life expectancy for women was only 56. By 1970 women's expectancy was 75, almost 8 years longer than men's, and the male death rate in the 55 to 65 age group exceeded the female rate by 110 percent. Recently, however, the mortality gap in that age group has begun to narrow (Wingard 1984). Though these generalizations apply to some modern societies, they do not reflect the situation in all countries and populations, especially where childbirth is still a life-threatening experience or where men claim traditional privileges, for example, in nutrition (see Chapter 7).

The striking sex differential in morbidity and mortality in humans as they age has been accounted for by three variables: (1) the direct genetic effects of the unguarded male X chromosome; (2) the physiological consequences of sex differences in hormones, tissue hormone receptor distribution, and immunologic competency; and (3) differing behavioral patterns of males and females or in society's treatment of them.

Genetic Explanations

As Trivers (1972, p. 152) points out, simple genetic explanations fail to account for the observation that in some homogametic species, for example, in fish, where the X and Y differences described in the first section of the chapter do not apply, males still suffer higher mortality. Thus, possession of two different sex chromosomes is not consistently related to mortality risk.

Hamilton and Mestler (1969) observed a sample of castrated men who markedly outsurvived a control group of intact men living under similar conditions. The castrated group had an average life span of 64, while the normal controls averaged 56 years at death. Madigan (1957) found the sex differential in mortality rates between Roman Catholic Brothers and Sisters comparable with that of the population at large in spite of the two orders' similar roles, life-styles, and environmental influences – a further indication of a persistent biological factor. The fact that the Brothers were allowed minor indulgences in smoking and moderate wine drinking, which the Sisters eschewed, may have contributed to their average reduced longevity, however.

Hormones and Cancer

The effects of sex hormones on morbidity and mortality are undergoing vigorous investigation. Changes in levels of hormone secretion and their differential effects on the sexes apparently contribute substantially to the most important ills that plague the aging members of civilized populations. Environmental pollution may also be a factor in the epidemic proportions of cancer. The reduction of deaths from infectious disease, trauma, and childbirth has led to an increased proportion of pathologies common to people of middle- and advanced-age, and may have provided an opportunity for innate sex differences related to hormone level to express themselves in morbidity and mortality.

According to many investigators, exposure to the female hormone estradiol, both during and after the reproductive period, increases susceptibility to cancer of the breast and uterus. These consequences are most marked after menopause when the effects of estrogen are not counteracted by the action of progesterone. Obese women are more susceptible to breast cancer than are thinner women, presumably because they begin menstruating earlier and cease later and have shorter menstrual cycles. This exposes them to increased amounts of estrogen, especially since adipose (fat) tissue, like adrenal cortical tissue, continues to produce estrogens throughout life.

Aging men do not undergo the dramatic changes in hormone production that characterize women at menopause. Some investigators have found a decrease in testosterone production after age 50; others, as in the Baltimore Longitudinal Study, have found concentrations in aging men comparable with those of younger men (Harman 1979). However, the subjects in the Baltimore study were relatively well educated, prosperous, and healthier than average, and potential subjects with cardiovascular symptoms, obesity, and alcoholism were eliminated. Other hormonal changes typically occur as men age. For example, younger men produce more pituitary gonadotropins as well as more estrogens, which may function in the slow decline in sexual activity that most men experience.

Hormones and Cardiovascular Disease

Aging affects the cardiac function of men and women differently, with morbidity and mortality rates for cardiovascular disease far higher for the former than for the latter. This sex difference is especially marked in those countries that are most affluent and highly industrialized, while in some underdeveloped countries the differences shrink to insignificant numbers.

Shortly after 1920, a steady rise in the sex ratio of cardiovascular disease was recorded in the United States, Canada, and England (Anderson 1983). However, men have six times as great an incidence if compared with premenopausal women but only double that of postmenopausal women. For this reason, attention has focused on estrogen, the levels of which differ substantially between the sexes, especially before menopause. It has been suggested that estrogen exerts its protective function through regulation and suppression of lipoprotein and serum cholesterol levels (Gordon et al. 1978; Dawber 1980). Estrogens in general decrease serum cholesterol and beta-lipoproteins (low-density lipoproteins) and increase serum triglycerides and pre-beta-lipoproteins (very-low-density lipoproteins). Conversely, androgens cause an increase in beta-lipoproteins and a decrease in serum trigylcerides and pre-beta-lipoproteins, but have variable effects on cholesterol levels. However, androgen levels in men apparently bear no relationship to susceptibility to cardiac heart disease, and castrated men do not exhibit a reduced incidence.

Though several studies have noted that in young women the removal of ovaries, the main source of estrogen, is associated with increased risk of heart disease, inconsistent findings remain. Women with only their uteri removed but with ovaries intact appear to be equally prone to atherosclerotic heart disease as are women who lose both organs (Ritterband et al. 1963). This finding has caused speculation as to whether the uterus may have an unrecognized hormonal function, perhaps prostaglandin secretion, which prevents atherosclerosis in premenopausal women (Centerwall 1981). However, no specific mechanisms relating uterine hormones to heart disease have been proposed. Attempts to administer estrogens therapeutically to men with myocardial infarct, which involves damage to the heart muscle due to the occlusion of local circulation, have been unsuccessful and have resulted only in an increase in death from pulmonary embolism and phlebitis. Estradiol and progesterone, including those given as oral contraceptives, are reported to increase coagulation factors and vascular lesions in women, although they do not influence mortality rates in substantial numbers. Thus, the advantages of estrogen administration and therapy are somewhat offset by other, less desirable effects.

Cook et al. (1976) hypothesized that an overload of stored iron may have deleterious, toxic effects on males. Sullivan (1983) cited supportive evidence for the association of heart disease with iron overloads and held that estrogen influence does not adequately explain the low incidence of cardiac disease in menstruating women. An increase in stored iron occurs in women in later life, especially after menopause. High red blood cell concentrations, most often characterizing males, may also predispose them to atherosclerosis, according to Sullivan.

Work with several primate species on the etiology of heart disease has revealed that male and female hearts show striking contrasts not only in heart muscle mass, but also in the distribution of sex hormone receptors on myocardial (heart muscle) cells. Atrial and especially ventricular cells, that is, the cells surrounding the main cavities of the heart, carry androgen receptors in both sexes (McGill et al. 1980). This suggests that circulating androgens must directly affect the heart and indicates an androgen role in cardiac growth.

Target cells for estradiol, like those found in uterine muscle, are identified in the atria but not in the ventricles of the heart (Stumpf et al. 1977). This indicates a sexually selective concentration of estrogen in female hearts, with a specific effect on the auricular muscle through which a protective reaction may be mediated. Estrogen also affects the smooth muscle of the arteries, the capillaries, and the adrenal cortex, and, like androgens, can influence cardiac function through its action on the brain. Though these findings suggest ways in which both hormonal factors and anatomical features account for sex differences in heart disease, there remain many questions. Still to be explained are such facts as the greater incidence of angina pectoris among women, the relatively small sex differential for cardiac disease among nonwhites, and the observation that women register a lower systolic blood pressure than men before middle life while in later life nonsmoking men may show lower pressures.

Osteoporosis and Hormones

Osteoporosis, or bone mineral loss, predisposes the aged, especially women, to fractures, most often of the hip and vertebrae. The debilitating effects of these breaks constitute a common precipitating cause of death, with almost a half million cases of osteoporotic fractures reported annually. In aging, bone is increasingly robbed of minerals in order to maintain homeostatic blood calcium levels. Both men and women are afflicted, but the loss is more severe in women, since they carry a smaller initial bone mass. Although demineralization begins in middle age, the most drastic remodeling begins with menopause, with estrogen-deprived women exhibiting rates of bone loss 15 to 20 percent greater than premenopausal women. In women, resorption exceeds bone formation by an amount sufficient to account for observed sex differences (Heaney 1979).

High protein and high phosphorus intake have been found to exacerbate the process by increasing calcium excretion. The daily calcium requirement slowly rises from 800 to 1,500 milligrams. Other factors (lack of exercise, poor general nutrition including vitamin deficiencies, and the action of other hormones) also contribute to demineralization. Apparently the risk of fractures can be minimized by calcium supplements in the diet or by estrogen therapy. A quart of skim milk per day plus swimming and vigorous walking are common recommendations for protection, as an alternative to the carcinogenic hazards of postmenopausal estradiol therapy.

Hormones and Sex Differences in Other Organs

Other sex differences that involve extragenital androgen influence have been reported in liver, kidney, and brain, where multiple hormones from several sources act in concert with androgens and estrogens (Bardin and Catterall 1981).

Sexual dimorphism in kidney structure, reported in a number of mammalian species, characterizes humans as well. Androgens acting on the developing kidney effect the enlargement of gross size as well as the size of proximal tubules and Bowman's capsules by an increase in cell size. This does not involve an increase in cell number, as in the enlargement of the male reproductive tract. In castrated animals, kidney size may regress to that of females. By contrast, estrogens have no effect on size.

Other hormones (for example, pituitary secretions, PRL, adrenal cortical hormone constituents) modulate, amplify, and sometimes mimic androgenic action. Thus, progestins (synandrogenic steroids) can masculinize the female kidney as well as the external genitalia (as when female fetuses are masculinized by the therapeutic administration of progestin to pregnant women). Testosterone and associated hormones thus establish at puberty sex-specific kidney function, which results in different protein constituents of male and female urine.

Sex differences in liver physiology have also been investigated (Bardin and Catterall 1981). Because liver enzymes are involved in the metabolism of many drugs, steroids, and toxins, the importance of sex-differentiated liver function to this chapter is evident. These sex differences are established with prenatal exposure to both androgens and estrogens, which together determine liver dimorphism by the regulation of microsomal enzymes, but other hormones may act as modifiers. Some sex differences in liver function (for example, higher female reductase activity) may be the result of stimulation by estrogens rather than androgens and may provide further indications of the differential distribution of specific hormone receptors.

Androgens function in the complex metabolic pathways that regulate hepatic proteins (Bardin and Catterall 1981); they also influence hemoglobin synthesis in hematopoietic tissues such as red marrow. Males normally have a higher hemoglobin concentration and larger number of erythrocytes than females.

Sex Differences in Disease Susceptibility

Direct genetic factors, specifically X-linked immunoregulatory genes, are implicated in the clear advantage shown by women in resisting infectious diseases. Surveys of serum antibody levels show that healthy women carry characteristically higher concentrations of immunoglobulins than men (Butterworth et al. 1967; Purtilo and Sullivan 1979). Rhodes et al. (1969), in studying 28 XXX aneuploid women, determined that they produce still higher levels. Michaels and Rogers (1971) assayed the sera of 120 infants hospitalized for *Escherichia coli* infections; levels for females proved significantly higher than those of males at the ages of 6 to 9 months and at 12 months. They also found the female antibody response to rubella vaccine to exceed the male response in each of ten field trials in Costa Rica, which involved a total of over 15,000 children. Purtilo and Sullivan (1979, p. 1252) offer a number of further examples.

Five immunoglobulin deficiency diseases, including total agammaglobulinemia (the inability to produce antibodies), occur solely in males, indicating that the disorder probably arises from mutant genes on the exposed X chromosome. Where transmitted, they follow the characteristic pattern of X-linked inheritance discussed earlier in this chapter.

Although women benefit from their vigorous antibody response to infectious agents, they also have increased susceptibility to autoimmune disorders, which involve the formation of antibodies against the tissues of one's own body. Nine times as many women as men contract systemic lupus erythematosis; more also suffer from rheumatoid arthritis. An increased antibody production reported in castrated males reinforces a hormonal explanation. Testosterone appears to offer protection against autoimmunity, but reduces antibody response to infection. Talal (1976) finds that the equilibrium between helper and suppressor T-cells may also be modulated by sex hormones, with androgens favoring suppression. These specialized lymphoid cells act as a major defense mechanism against viral infections, foreign tissues (for example, transplants and parasites), and probably some cancer cells and autoimmunity. They also collaborate with B-cells in regulating normal immune response. The superior competence of women in combating infectious agents is probably the result of long selective pressures in adapting to the conditions of aboriginal childbirth, as well as the advantage afforded by two X chromosomes.

In addition to their greater susceptibility to cardiovascular and immunodeficiency diseases, men are also more likely to develop all neoplasms except for the sex-limited cancers of the breast and female reproductive tract. Lymphomas and leukemias especially are associated with low antibody production. Their reduced globulin levels may account for the high male incidence of infections, including osteomyelitis, respiratory infections such as pneumonia and bronchitis, gastroenteritis, poliomyelitis, and mononucleosis. Because of immune incompetence, males are more prone to develop carrier states in which they harbor living pathogens (Goodman et al. 1971).

Male metabolism of purines, which at puberty produces elevated blood uric acid levels, predisposes men to gout, a disease caused by the deposition of uric acid crystals in joints. They are also more prone to ulcers of the digestive tract, cirrhosis of the liver, and proteinuria, by virtue of structural and physiological differences. All of these diseases are also profoundly influenced by life-style and health habits.

Females are less susceptible to most serious ailments, with the exceptions of the autoimmune and sex-limited conditions indicated above. Of 64 specific causes of death listed in the U.S. census, 57 show lower rates among women (Lerner and Libby 1976, p. 153). Related to the female reproductive anatomy and physiology are the tendencies to iron deficiency, including pernicious anemia from periodic blood loss, and susceptibility to cystitis and kidney infections. Women also develop diseases of the thyroid gland, diabetes, and phlebitis more often than men.

As they age, women wage a harder battle against obesity, which is linked to a diminution of estrogen; those who succumb to excess calories are more likely to curtail their life span. The incidences of gall bladder diseases (cholelithiasis and cholecystitis), pancreatic malfunction, and the development of tumors all increase with weight gain, especially after menopause (Sherman et al. 1979). Wingard (1984, p. 453) holds that women experience more minor ailments than men, despite their advantage in mortality. This finding may be more apparent than real, as women have a greater willingness to admit and report illnesses.

Biocultural Aspects of Male-Female Differences in Mortality

The importance of biocultural factors in effecting recent shifts in male-female mortality ratios can hardly be overemphasized. Since the advent of antibiotics, the high mortality figures for young males in industrial nations are due almost entirely to violent and accidental deaths: homicide, impairment by drugs and alcohol, suicide, automobile accident, gang warfare, and occupational hazards account for two-thirds of male deaths in the age group of 15 to 24 years (Potts 1970). Where such life-threatening situations do not exist, male death rates are substantially reduced. In fact, in societies where childbirth complications have not been eliminated, we may find a higher female than male mortality before middle age.

U.S. men who are married have substantially lower death rates at middle age than unmarried men, but this association holds less strongly for women. Men, it seems, derive more advantages from marriage than women, at least in respect to health. The excess of mortality in divorced and widowed men usually comes from cirrhosis, malnutrition, lung cancer, and other conditions in which health care is crucial. Widowers have a death rate 40 percent above that of married men of the same age (Murray Parkes et al. 1969).

Medical advances in the control of infectious disease have increased the relative incidence of cancer, cardiovascular diseases, and other degenerative conditions associated with old age. Most important in the etiology of respiratory diseases (such as emphysema and lung cancer) and cardiovascular disease has been cigarette smoking. Death from lung cancer in men has been calculated as 6.5 times higher than in women, and emphysema 5 times higher, but if men and women who have never smoked are compared, the male differential shrinks to 1.5 times as high for lung cancer, 3.5 times as high for cardiovascular disease, and 3 times as high for emphysema. Smoking thus adds a 300 percent increase in male over female deaths from coronary heart disease alone (Waldron 1976).

A considerable body of evidence also links higher male death rates from coronary heart disease to the stresses of jobs demanding competitive and aggressive behavior, in contrast to the more supportive, less competitive roles that women traditionally have occupied. Several studies indicate that the risk of male cardiovascular disease is greatest among men who work long hours overtime or who moonlight with a second job. This has led to the concept of a "type-A," or coronary-prone, behavior pattern of work-oriented, aggressive, ambitious, impatient individuals, preoccupied with job status and deadlines. "Type-B" individuals are described as more relaxed, less aggressive, and less driving in personality. Type-A persons are roughly twice as likely to develop cardiovascular disease at an early age as type-B persons. The extent to which genetic and hormonal factors contribute to the determination of such personality differences is uncertain, but surely the influences of ambitious parents and schools that push children unduly to excel constitute enormous social pressures toward type-A behavior, especially for men.

Cross-cultural studies reinforce the conclusion that a substantial part of the higher rate of male mortality is related to smoking, drinking alcohol, and the higher levels of stress in the U.S. marketplace. In many countries, the sex differential is considerably smaller; for instance, in 1960 the male mortality rate for heart disease was only 30 percent higher than the female rate in Greece and Hungary. The fact that a residual sex differential remains suggests contributory biological factors.

The large numbers of women who have recently filled occupational niches that were formerly the province of men have led to predictions of their increased rates of the so-called "executive diseases," including cirrhosis, hypertension and cardiovascular disease, ulcers, lung cancer, and emphysema. To some extent, these predictions have been borne out. In both the United States and Britain, cardiac disease and lung cancer have been on the increase among women since the 1950s. The surgeon general's report of 1980 forecast that, owing to increased smoking especially among teenagers, lung cancer soon would overtake breast cancer as the number one cancer killer of women. According to the State Department of Health Services of California, lung cancer mortality in women has indeed swept past breast cancer deaths; while breast cancer rates have remained steady since 1970, deaths from lung cancer have doubled. Health officials in the state of Washington said that lung cancer overtook breast cancer in 1980 (Anderson 1983). Since 1970 deaths from coronary heart disease have also been on the rise among middle-aged females, while male mortality appears to be leveling off. However, analyses of the occupations of women reporting executive diseases reveal the surprising fact that it is not executive women who account for the increased rates, but rather women in the lower economic ranks in routine clerical jobs and especially those burdened further with children. Wingerson (1981) found that homemakers had more chronic illnesses (cancer, diabetes, cardiac heart disease, allergies, and ulcers) than women in positions of responsibility. According to a recent Metropolitan Life Insurance Study, their best risks lie in highly educated women with prestigious jobs; these women appear freer of chronic illnesses and are longer lived than women in any other category. Whether only women in excellent health have the energy to compete successfully with men in these demanding roles, or whether such occupations allow them the self-expression compatible with their need for creativity, is an open question; possibly both factors are present.

The finding that women traditionally verbalize their ailments, stresses, and dissatisfactions, while the male role has demanded a stoic silence, probably contributes another factor. Additionally studies indicate that women more often seek medical advice than men, and are less likely to neglect physical symptoms.

SUMMARY

The literature dealing with the genetic effects of sex differentiation and the sex ratio indicates the tentative, controversial, and even contradictory nature of many of the data and the formidable amount of work still to be undertaken. The clearest understandings have come where simple genetic anomalies are involved. We are much less certain about the genetic and environmental factors involved in the development of normal individuals, nor do we fully understand the range of ordinary variation in sexual features or the interaction of sex and behavior upon health and disease.

Though it appears that sex differences are not the simple, obvious ones that our culture (and many others) have proclaimed self-evident, the genetic effects of sex are real. This review has suggested some areas of interaction between genetics and behavior that should be explored further. Of particular interest are relations between sex and predisposition to disease and between sex ratio and its biosocial components.

Societies integrate biological and social factors in various ways. For example, societies have evolved a variety of mating strategies and patterns of infant care, parenting, and sexual expressiveness, and they inculcate a wide range of ideals regarding the expression of masculinity and femininity. Our culture has been characterized by a more rigorous sex typing of males than of females – female "tomboys" suffer less harassment, for example, than do male "sissies." Other societies demonstrate different levels of anxiety over the failure of individuals to live up to cultural ideals with regard to either or both sex roles. All represent different molds into which the biological substrate is forced.

Though we know that populations differ both at the genetic level and phenotypically, we have virtually no information on comparative hormone levels. In spite of the fact that an overwhelming number of studies characterize males as aggressive and implicate their testosterone level, this relationship has not been pursued cross-culturally. Ember (1981) observed male aggression to be the most consistent sex difference in behavior cited in anthropological literature; Rohner (1976) found mention of a sex difference in aggressive behavior in 71 of 101 societies studied ethnographically. Accordingly the relative average levels of plasma androgen in, say, !Kung Bushman hunters and Yanomamo tribesmen would be of interest – and might offer some surprises. Since hormone levels vary from day to day, and even from hour to hour, such an undertaking would involve batteries of repeated tests. Without the studies, it is an issue of faith rather than observation that hormonal levels and behavior are related causally, based to a large extent upon studies of monkeys. The pitfalls involved in the extrapolation to humans of observations on nonhuman models responding experimentally to the administration of hormones or to other factors have been pointed out repeatedly by thoughtful writers. As Baker (1980, p. 83) reminds us, gender identity and gender role traditions serve to complicate human sexual behavior. These involve not only cultural notions of appropriate gender responses, but a psychology of self-awareness and self-identity, concepts that are only foreshadowed in nonhuman anthropoid primates, if present at all.

The biosocial perspective of the 1980s provides new vistas for exploration and new concepts to test. But it seems highly unlikely to this writer that *Homo sapiens*, the symbolling and value-laden animal, behaves in genetically determined predictable ways. It seems far more likely that cultural imperatives from without overwhelm or at least obscure whatever "whisperings within" may be present.

REFERENCES

Allen, T. M. 1975. "ABO Blood Groups and Human Sex Ratio at Birth," *Journal of Reproduction and Fertility*, 43:209.

Anderson, I. 1983. "Smokers Line Up in California Graveyards." *New Scientist*, 100:169.

Ayeni, O. 1975. "Sex Ratio of Live Births in Southwestern Nigeria." *Annals of Human Biology*, 2:137-41.

Baker, S. W. 1980. "Biological Influences on Human Sex and Gender." *Signs*, 6:80-96.

Baker, S. W., and A. A. Ehrhardt. 1974. "Prenatal Androgen, Intelligence, and Cognitive Sex Differences." In *Sex Differences in Behavior*, edited by R. C. Friedman, R. M. Richart, and R. L. Vande Wiele, pp. 53-77. New York: Wiley.

Bardin, C. W., and J. F. Catterall. 1981. "Testosterone: A Major Determinant of Extragenital Sexual Dimorphism." *Science*, 211:1285-93.

Barr, M. L., and E. G. Bertram. 1949. "A Morphological Distinction Between Neurones of the Male and Female, and the Behaviour of the Nucleolar Satellite During Accelerated Nucleoprotein Synthesis." *Nature*, 163:676-77.

Bayley, N. 1966. "Developmental Problems of the Mentally Retarded Child." In *Prevention and Treatment of Mental Retardation*, edited by I. Philips, pp. 85-110. New York: Basic Books.

Bernstein, M. 1958. "Studies in the Human Sex Ratio: A Genetic Explanation of the Wartime Increase in the Secondary Sex Ratio." *American Journal of Human Genetics*, 10:68-70.

Bielicki, T., and J. Charzewski. 1977. "Sex Differences in the Magnitude of Statural Gains of Offspring over Parents." *Human Biology*, 49:265-77.

Bleier, R., W. Byne, and I. Siggelkow. 1982. "Cytoarchitectonic Sexual Dimorphisms of the Medial Preoptic and Anterior Hypothalamic Area in Guinea Pig, Rat, Hamster, and Mouse." *Journal of Comparative Neurology*, 212:118-30.

Bodmer, W. F., and F. F. Cavalli-Sforza. 1976. *Genetics, Evolution, and Man*. San Francisco: W. H. Freeman.

Boué, J., A. Boué, and P. Lazar. 1975. "Retrospective and Prospective Epidemiological Studies of 1500 Karyotyped Spontaneous Human Abortions." *Teratology*, 12:11-26.

Butterworth, M., B. McClellan, and M. Allansmith. 1967. "Influence of Sex on Immunoglobulin Levels." *Nature*, 214:1224-25.

Carr, D. H. 1965. "Chromosome Studies in Spontaneous Abortions." *Obstetrics and Gynecology*, 26:308-26.

___. 1975. "Chromosome Anomalies as a Cause of Spontaneous Abortions." *American Journal of Obstetrics and Gynecology*, 139:58-61.

Cavalli-Sforza, L. L., and W. F. Bodmer. 1971. *The Genetics of Human Populations*. San Francisco: W. H. Freeman.

Centerwall, B. S. 1981. "Premenopausal Hysterectomy and Cardiovascular Disease." *American Journal of Obstetrics and Gynecology*, 139:58-61.

Chagnon, N., M. V. Flinn, and R. F. Melancon. 1979. "Sex Ratio Variation Among Yanomamo Indians." In *Evolutionary Biology and Human Social Behavior*, edited by N. Chagnon and W. Irons, pp. 290-320. North Scituate, MA: Duxbury Press.

Colombo, B. 1975. "On the Sex Ratio in Man." *Cold Spring Harbor Symposia of Quantitative Biology*, 22:195-202.

Cook, J. D., C. A. Finch, and N. J. Smith. 1976. "Evaluation of the Iron Status of a Population." *Blood*, 48:449-55.

Cowgill, U., and G. E. Hutchinson. 1963. "Sex-Ratio in Childhood and the Depopulation of Peten, Guatamala." *Human Biology*, 35:90-103.

Culliton, B. J. 1974. "Patients' Rights: Harvard Is Site of Battle over X and Y Chromosomes." *Science*, 186:715-17.

___. 1975. "XYY: Harvard Researcher Under Fire Stops Newborn Screening." *Science*, 188:1284-85.

Damon, A. 1977. *Human Biology and Ecology*. New York: W. W. Norton.

Darlington, C. D. 1960. "Cousin Marriage and the Evolution of the Breeding System in Man." *Heredity*, 14:297.

Darwin, C. 1874. *The Descent of Man and Selection in Relation to Sex*. New York: A. L. Burt.

Dawber, T. R. 1980. *The Framingham Study: The Epidemiology of Atherosclerotic Disease*. Cambridge, MA: Harvard University Press.

Drew, J. S., W. T. London, E. D. Lustbader, J. E. Hesser, and B. S. Blumberg. 1978. "Hepatitis B Virus and the Sex Ratio of Offspring." *Science*, 201:687-92.

Edwards, A. W. F. 1961. "A Factorial Analysis of Sex-Ratio Data." *Annals of Human Genetics*, 25:117-21.

___. 1966. "Sex Ratio Data Analyzed Independently of Family Limitation." *Annals of Human Genetics*, 29:337-46.

___. 1970. "The Search for Genetic Variability of the Sex Ratio." *Journal of Biosocial Science*, (Suppl. 2):55-60.

Edwards, R. G. 1982. "Disease and Changes in Sex Ratio." *Research in Reproduction*, 14:1.

Eichenwald, E. J., and C. R. Silmser. 1955. "Communication." *Transplantation Bulletin*, 2:148-49.

Ember, C. R. 1981. "A Cross-Cultural Perspective on Sex Differences." In *Handbook of Cross-Cultural Human Development*, edited by R. H. Munroe, R. L. Munroe, and B. B. Whiting, pp. 531-80. New York: Garland.

Fisher, R. A. 1958. *The Genetical Theory of Natural Selection*, 2nd ed. New York: Dover.

Glucksmann, A. 1978. *Sex Determination and Sexual Dimorphism in Mammals*. London: Wykeham.

Goodall, H., and A. M. Roberts. 1976. "Differences in Motility of Human X- and Y-Bearing Spermatozoa." *Journal of Reproduction and Fertility*, 48:433-36.

Goodman, M., R. L. Wainwright, H. F. Weir, and J. C. Gall, Jr. 1971. "A Sex Difference in the Carrier State of Australia (Hepatitis-Associated) Antigen." *Pediatrics*, 48:907-13.

Gordon, J. W., and F. H. Ruddle. 1981. "Mammalian Gonadal Determination and Gametogenesis." *Science*, 211:1265-71.

Gordon, T., W. B. Kannel, M. C. Hjortland, and P. M. McNamara. 1978. "Menopause and Coronary Disease: The Framingham Study." *Annals of Internal Medicine*, 89:157-61.

Gorski, R. A., J. H. Gordon, J. E. Shryne, and A. M. Southam. 1978. "Evidence for a Morphological Sex Difference Within the Medial Preoptic Area of the Rat Brain." *Brain Research*, 148:333-46.

Goy, R. W. 1968. "Organizing Effects of Androgen on the Behavior of Rhesus Monkeys." In *Endocrinology and Human Behavior*, edited by R. P. Michael, pp. 12-31. London: Oxford University Press.

Greenough, W. T., C. S. Carter, and C. Steerman. 1977. "Sex Differences in Dendritic Patterns in Hamster Preoptic Area." Brain Research, 126:63-72.

Greulich, W. W. 1951. "The Growth and Developmental Status of Guamanian School Children in 1947." *American Journal of Physical Anthropology*, 9:44-53.

Guttentag, M., and P. Secord. 1983. *Too Many Women: The Sex Ratio Question*. Beverly Hills, CA: Sage.

Hall, R. L. 1982. "Sexual Dimorphism for Size in Seven Nineteenth-Century Northwest Coast Populations." In *Sexual Dimorphism in Homo sapiens: A Question of Size*, edited by R. L. Hall, pp. 231-43. New York: Praeger.

Hamilton, J. B., and G. E. Mestler. 1969. "Mortality and Survival: Comparison of Eunuchs with Intact Men and Women in a Mentally Retarded Population." *Journal of Gerontology*, 24:395-411.

Hamilton, W. D. 1967. "Extraordinary Sex Ratios." *Science*, 156:477-88.

Harman, S. M. 1979. "Gonadotrophins, Sex Steroids, and Sexual Activity in the Healthy Aging Male." In *Proceedings of Conference on the Endocrine Aspects of Aging*, edited by S. G. Korenman. Bethesda, MD: NIA and Veterans Administration.

Hartl, D. L. 1977. *Our Uncertain Heritage: Genetics and Human Diversity*. Philadelphia: J. B. Lippincott.

Haseltine, F. P., and S. Ohno. 1981. "Mechanisms of Gonadal Differentiation." *Science*, 211:1272-78.

Heaney, R. 1979. "Age-Related Changes in Calcium Metabolism in Perimenopausal Women and Their Relation to Osteoporosis." In *Proceedings of Conference on Endocrine Aspects of Aging,* edited by S. G. Korenman. Bethesda, MD: NIA and Veterans Administration.

Higano, N., R. W. Robinson, and W. D. Cohen. 1963. "Increased Incidence of Cardiovascular Disease in Castrated Women." *New England Journal of Medicine,* 2168:1123-25.

Hook, E. B. 1973. "Behavioral Implications of the Human XYY Genotype." *Science,* 179:139-50.

Jackson, C. E., J. D. Mann, and W. J. Schull. 1969. "Xg^a Blood Group System and the Sex Ratio in Man." *Nature,* 222:445-46.

Jacobs, P. A. 1975. "XYY Genotype: Letter." *Science,* 189:1044.

Jacobs, P. A., M. Brunton, M. M. Melville, R. P. Brittain, and W. F. McClemont. 1965. "Aggressive Behaviour, Mental Subnormality, and the XYY Male." *Nature,* 208:1351-52.

Jacobs, P. A., M. M. Melville, S. Ratcliffe, A. J. Keay, and J. Syme. 1974. "A Cytogenetic Survey of 11,680 Newborn Infants." *Annals of Human Genetics,* 37:359-76.

James, W. H. 1976. "Timing of Fertility and Sex Ratio of Offspring: A Review." *Annals of Human Biology,* 3:549-56.

___. 1977. "Coital Rate, Cycle Day of Insemination, and Sex Ratio." *Journal of Biosocial Science,* 9:183-89.

Jost, A. 1953. "Problems of Fetal Endocrinology: The Gonadal and Hypophyseal Hormones." *Record of Progress in Hormone Research,* 8:379-418.

___. 1961. "The Role of Fetal Hormones in Prenatal Development." *Harvey Lectures,* 55:201-26.

Kopelman, L. 1978. "Ethical Controversies in Medical Research: The Case of XYY Screening." *Perspectives in Biology and Medicine,* 21:196-204.

Lerner, I. M., and W. J. Libby. 1976. *Heredity, Evolution, and Society.* San Francisco: W. H. Freeman.

Lev-Ran, A. 1977. "Sex Reversal as Related to Clinical Syndromes in Human Beings." In *Handbook of Sexology,* edited by J. Money and H. Musaph, pp. 157-73. New York: Elsevier/North Holland.

Lucchesi, J. C. 1978. "Gene Dosage Compensation and the Evolution of Sex Chromosomes." *Science,* 202:711-16.

Lyon, M. F. 1961. "Gene Action in the X-Chromosome of the Mouse (*Mus musculus L.*)." *Nature,* 190:372-73.

___. 1962. "Sex Chromatin and Gene Action in Mammalian X-Chromosome." *American Journal of Human Genetics,* 14:135-48.

Lyster, W. R. 1968. "The Sex Ratio of Live Births in Integrated but Racially Different Populations, U.S.A. and Figi." *Human Biology,* 40:63-68.

Maccoby, E. E., and C. N. Jacklin. 1974. *The Psychology of Sex Differences.* Stanford, CA: Stanford University Press.

MacLusky, N. J., and F. Naftolin. 1981. "Sexual Differentiation of the Central Nervous System." *Science,* 211:1294-302.

MacMahon, B., and T. F. Pugh. 1954. "Sex Ratio and White Births in the United States During the Second World War." *American Journal of Human Genetics,* 6:284-92.

Madigan, F. C. 1957. "Are Sex Mortality Differentials Biologically Caused?" *Milbank Memorial Fund Quarterly*, 35:202-23.

Makino, S. 1968. "Chromosome Data and Sex Ratio in Induced Abortion." *Mammalian Chromosomes Newsletter*, 9:93.

McGill, H. C., Jr., V. C. Anselmo, J. M. Buchanan, and P. J. Sheridan. 1980. "The Heart Is a Target Organ for Androgen." *Science*, 207:775-77.

McKeown, T., and C. R. Lowe. 1951. "The Sex Ratio of Stillbirths Related to Cause and Duration of Gestation." *Human Biology*, 23:41-60.

Meyer, M. R., E. L. Diamond, and T. Merz. 1968. "Sex Ratio of Children Born to Mothers Who Had Been Exposed to X-Ray *In Utero*." *Johns Hopkins Medical Journal*, 123:123-27.

Michaels, R. H., and K. D. Rogers. 1971. "A Sex Difference in Immunologic Responsiveness." *Pediatrics*, 47:120-22.

Money, J. 1964. "Two Cytogenetic Syndromes: Psychologic Comparisons 1. Intelligence and Specific-Factor Quotients." *Journal of Psychiatric Research*, 2:223-31.

Money, J., and D. Alexander. 1966. "Turner's Syndrome: Further Demonstration of the Presence of Specific Cognitional Deficiencies." *Journal of Medical Genetics*, 3:47-48.

Money, J., and A. Ehrhardt. 1972. *Man and Woman: Boy and Girl*. Baltimore, MD: Johns Hopkins University Press.

Moore, K. L., and W. Hyrniuk. 1969. "Sex Diagnosis of Early Human Abortions by the Chromatin Method." *Anatomical Record*, 136:274.

Morton, N. E., C. S. Chung, and M. P. Mi. 1967. *Genetics of Interracial Crosses in Hawaii*. New York: S. Karger.

Murray Parkes, C., B. Benjamin, and R. G. Fitzgerald. 1969. "Broken Heart: A Statistical Study of Increased Mortality Among Widowers." *British Medical Journal*, 1:740-43.

Neel, J. V. 1967. "Atomic Bombs, Inbreeding, and Japanese Genes." *Michigan Quarterly Review*, 6:202-09.

Neel, J. V., and W. J. Schull. 1956. "The Effect of Exposure to the Atomic Bombs on Pregnancy Termination in Hiroshima and Nagasaki." National Research Council Publication. Washington, D.C.: National Academy of Sciences.

Nielson, J. 1969. "Klinefelter's Syndrome and the XYY Syndrome: A Genetical, Endocrinological, and Psychiatric-Psychologic Study of 33 Severely Hypogonadal Patients and Two Patients with Karyotype 47XYY." *Acta Psychiatrica Scandinavica*, 45 (Suppl. 209).

Novitski, E., and A. W. Kimball. 1958. "Birth Order, Parental Ages, and Sex of Offspring." *American Journal of Human Genetics*, 10:268-75.

Ohno, S. 1967. *Sex Chromosomes and Sex-Linked Genes*. Berlin: Springer-Verlag.

___. 1979. *Monographs on Endocrinology, Vol. II: Major Sex-Determining Genes*. Berlin: Springer-Verlag.

Otten, C. M. 1967. "On Pestilence, Diet, Natural Selection, and the Distribution of Microbial and Human Blood Group Antigens and Antibodies." *Current Anthropology*, 8:209-26.

Phoenix, C. H. 1974. "Prenatal Testosterone in the Nonhuman Primate and Its Consequences for Behavior." In Sex Differences in Behavior, edited by R. C.

Friedman, R. M. Richart, and R. L. Vande Wiele, pp. 19-32. New York: Wiley.

Polani, P. E. 1972. "Errors of Sex Determination and Sex Chromosome Anomalies." In *Gender Differences: Their Ontogeny and Significance*, edited by C. Ounsted and D. C. Taylor, pp. 13-39. London: Churchill Livingstone.

Potts, D. M. 1970. "Which Is the Weaker Sex?" *Journal of Biosocial Science*, (Suppl. 2):147-57.

Purtilo, D. T., and J. L. Sullivan. 1979. "Immunological Bases for Superior Survival of Females." *American Journal of Diseases of Children*, 133:1251-53.

Raisman, G., and P. M. Field. 1971. "Sexual Dimorphism in the Preoptic Area of the Rat." *Science*, 173:731-33.

Reed, T. E. 1969. "Caucasian Genes in American Negroes." *Science*, 165:762-68.

Reinisch, J. M., R. Gandelman, and F. S. Spiegel. 1979. "Prenatal Influences on Cognitive Abilities: Data from Experimental Animals and Human Genetic and Endocrine Syndromes." In *Sex-Related Differences in Cognitive Functioning: Developmental Issues*, edited by M. A. Wittig and A. C. Petersen, pp. 215-40. New York: Academic Press.

Rhodes, K., R. L. Markham, P. M. Maxwell, and M. E. Monk-Jones. 1969. "Immunoglobulins and the X Chromosome." *British Medical Journal*, 2:439-41.

Riches, D. 1974. "The Netsilik Eskimos: A Special Case of Selective Female Infanticide." *Ethnology*, 13:351-61.

Ritterband, A. B., L. A. Jaffe, P. M. Densen et al. 1963. "Gonadal Function and the Development of Coronary Heart Disease." *Circulation*, 27:237-51.

Roberts, A. M. 1978. "The Origins of Fluctuations in the Human Secondary Sex Ratio." *Journal of Biosocial Science*, 10:169-82.

Rohner, R. P. 1976. "Sex Differences in Aggression: Phylogenetic and Enculturation Perspectives." *Ethos*, 4:57-72.

Roth, J., D. LeRoith, J. Shiloach, J. L. Rosenzweig, M. A. Lesniak, and J. Havrankova. 1982. "The Evolutionary Origins of Hormones, Neurotransmitters, and Other Extracellular Chemical Messengers." *New England Journal of Medicine*, 306:523-27.

Sanghvi, L. D. 1951. "ABO Blood Groups and Sex Ratio at Birth in Man." *Nature*, 168:1077.

Sasaki, M., S. Makino, J. I. Muramoto, T. Ikeuchi, and H. Shimba. 1967. "A Chromosome Survey of Induced Abortions in a Japanese Population." *Chromosoma*, 20:267-83.

Seguy, B. 1975. "La selection volontaire du sexe: point actuel de nos connaissances." *Journal de gynécologie obstétrique et biologie de la reproduction*, 4:29-36.

Shaffer, J. W. A. 1962. "A Specific Cognitive Deficit Observed in Gonadal Aplasia (Turner's Syndrome)." *Journal of Clinical Research*, 18:403-06.

Shaw, R. F., and J. D. Mohler. 1953. "The Selective Significance of the Sex Ratio." *American Naturalist*, 87:337-42.

Sherman, B. M., R. B. Wallace, and A. E. Treloar. 1979. "Pathogenic Implications of Menstrual and Hormonal Patterns." In *Proceedings of*

Conference on Endocrine Aspects of Aging, edited by S. G. Korenman. Bethesda, MD: NIA and Veterans Administration.

Shettles, L. B. 1961. "Conception and Birth Sex Ratios." *Obstetrics and Gynecology,* 18:122-30.

___. 1964. "The Great Preponderance of Human Males Conceived." *American Journal of Obstetrics and Gynecology,* 89:130-33.

Simpson, J. L. 1982. "Abnormal Sexual Differentiation in Humans." *Annual Review of Genetics,* 16:193-224.

Simpson, J. L., and M. M. LeBeau. 1981. "Gonadal and Statural Determinants on the X Chromosome and Their Relationship to In Vitro Studies of Prolonged Cell Cycles in 45X; 46X, del(X)(p11); 46X, del(X)(q13); and 46X, del(X)(q22) Fibroblasts." *American Journal of Obstetrics and Gynecology,* 141:830-40.

Snyder, R. G. 1961. "The Sex Ratio of Offspring of Pilots of High Performance Military Aircraft." *Human Biology,* 33:1-10.

Stini, W. A. 1969. "Nutritional Stress and Growth." *American Journal of Physical Anthropology,* 31:417-26.

Stott, D. H. 1966. *Studies of Troublesome Children.* London: Tavistock.

Stumpf, W. E., M. Sar, and G. Aumüller. 1977. "The Heart: A Target Organ for Estradiol." *Science,* 196:319-20.

Sullivan, J. L. 1983. "The Sex Difference in Ischemic Heart Disease." *Perspectives in Biology and Medicine,* 26:657-71.

Talal, N. 1976. "Disordered Immunologic Regulation and Autoimmunity." *Transplantation Review,* 31:240-63.

Taylor, M. A. 1969. "Sex Ratios of Newborns Associated with Prepartum and Postpartum Schizophrenia." *Science,* 164:723-24.

Taylor, P. D., and M. G. Bulmer. 1980. "Local Male Competition and the Sex Ratio." *Journal of Theoretical Biology,* 86:409-19.

Teitelbaum, M. S. 1970. "Factors Affecting the Sex Ratio in Large Populations." *Journal of Biosocial Science,* (Suppl. 2):61-71.

___. 1972. "Factors Associated with Sex Ratio in Human Populations." In *The Structure of Human Populations,* edited by G. A. Harrison and A. J. Boyce, pp. 90-109. Oxford: Oxford University Press.

Tobias, P. V. 1975. "Anthropometry Among Disadvantaged Peoples: Studies in Southern Africa." In *Biosocial Interrelations in Population Adaptation* , edited by E. S. Watts, F. E. Johnston, and G. W. Lasker, pp. 287-305. The Hague: Mouton.

Toivanen, P., and T. Hirvonen. 1970. "Sex Ratio of Newborns: Preponderance of Males in Toxemia of Pregnancy." *Science,* 170:187-88.

Trivers, R. L. 1972. "Parental Investment and Sexual Selection." In *Sexual Selection and the Descent of Man,* edited by B. Campbell, pp. 136-79. Chicago: Aldine.

Trivers, R. L., and D. E. Willard. 1973. "Natural Selection of Parental Ability to Vary the Sex Ratio of Offspring." *Science,* 179:90-92.

Waber, D. P. 1979. "Cognitive Abilities and Sex-Related Variations in the Maturation of Cerebral Cortical Functions." In *Sex-Related Differences in Cognitive Functioning: Developmental Issues,* edited by M. A. Wittig and A. C. Petersen, pp. 161-68. New York: Academic Press.

Wachtel, S. S. 1978. "Genes and Gender." *The Sciences*, 18:16-32.

Wachtel, S. S., G. C. Koo, and E. A. Boyse. 1975. "Evolutionary Conservation of H-Y ('Male') Antigen." *Nature*, 254:270-72.

Wachtel, S. S., and S. Ohno. 1979. "The Immunogenetics of Sexual Development." In *Progress in Medical Genetics, Vol. III*, edited by A. G. Steinberg, A. G. Bearn, A. G. Motulsky, and B. B. Childs, pp. 109-42. Philadelphia: W. B. Saunders.

Waldron, I. 1976. "Why Do Women Live Longer than Men?" *Journal of Human Stress*, 2:2-13.

Ward, I. L. 1972. "Prenatal Stress Feminizes and Demasculinizes the Behavior of Males." *Science*, 175:82-84.

___. 1980. "Maternal Stress Alters Plasma Testosterone in Fetal Males." *Science*, 207:328-29.

Weiss, N. S. 1972. "Relation of Menopause to Serum Cholesterol and Arterial Blood Pressure." *American Journal of Epidemiology*, 96:237-41.

Wingard, D. L. 1984. "The Sex Differential in Morbidity, Mortality, and Life Style." *Annual Review of Public Health*, 5:433-58.

Wingerson, L. 1981. "Executive Woman – Healthier Than Thou?" *New Scientist*, 92:718-21.

Witkin, H. A., S. A. Mednick, F. Schulsinger, P. Bakkestrom, K. O. Christiansen, D. R. Goodenough, K. Hirshborn, C. Lundsteen, D. R. Owen, J. Phillip, D. B. Rubin, and M. Stocking. 1976. "Criminality in XYY and XXY Men." *Science*, 193:547-55.

Wittelson, S. 1976. "Sex and the Single Hemisphere." *Science*, 193:425-26.

Wittig, M. A., and A. C. Petersen, eds. 1979. *Sex-Related Differences in Cognitive Functioning: Developmental Issues*. New York: Academic Press.

Yung Sun Kang, and Wan Kyoo Cho. 1962. "The Sex Ratio at Birth and Other Attributes of the Newborn from Maternity Hospitals in Korea." *Human Biology*, 34:38-48.

7

POPULATION STRUCTURE AND SEX DIFFERENCES

Eric Abella Roth

Anthropologists have become interested in human population structure relatively recently. Our professional concern with populations, rather than "races" or "types," dates to the early 1960s (Livingstone 1962; Brace 1964) and constitutes "the new physical anthropology." A further result is the creation of "anthropological demography," which encompasses archaeological demography (Hassan 1978, 1981), genealogical demography (Dyke and Morrill 1980), and paleo-demography (Angel 1969, 1975). Anthropological demography has found a valuable niche by focusing attention on the consequences of changes in population on biological and cultural systems. For example, population pressure and disequilibrium have been presented as the driving forces behind the Neolithic revolution, the transition from food gathering to food production in prehistory that began at least 10,000 years ago (Boserup 1965; Binford 1968; Cohen 1977). In the form of "unequal sex ratios," population structure has been proposed as a major determinant in the collapse of the Classic Mayan Empire (Cowgill and Hutchinson 1963). While these are extreme examples, they demonstrate anthropological willingness to integrate biological and cultural variables in demographic analysis. The great strength of anthropological demography is its refusal to restrict itself to a narrow field. Instead, anthropologists recognize the value of demographic studies in producing insights into the social organization of target populations as well as into their genetic systems, health status, and cultural ecology [for examples and reviews of the scope of demographic anthropology, see Swedlund and Armelagos (1976), Ward and Weiss (1976), and Swedlund (1978)].

In this chapter, our goal is to investigate the interaction between sociocultural and biological sex differences and human population processes, structure, and change. To do so, we first introduce demographic methodology applicable to the quantification of sexual differences throughout the human life cycle.

POPULATION: DEFINITIONS, PROCESSES, STRUCTURE

The basic unit of analysis for all anthropologists is the "population." However, differences exist in the definition of human populations. The population geneticist interested in delineating a breeding population or gene pool will delimit this unit by biological kinship. In contrast, the ethnographer may also include those people related by affinal (marital-related) kinship. Anthroplogical linguists define their population by inclusion of speakers of a distinct language or dialect, while the archaeologist views populations as sharing common artifact modes and attributes. Anthropological demographers are not immune from these inconsistencies. Some researchers work with censuses representing a single contemporary community, while others utilize skeletal remains to reconstruct demographic history. The end result is multiple populations, which differ in their spatial and temporal properties.

In this chapter, we touch upon all these different populations and deal with human groups as diverse as those defined by nationalistic boundaries, that is, states and nations, as well as those sharing cultural and/or technological characteristics, for example, bands and tribes. Demography arose in conjunction with the nation-state, and it is for these populations that we have the best demographic records. On the other hand, small human groups held together by kinship ties or a common subsistence pattern are those most often studied by anthropologists, for they most readily allow us to observe the interrelations between biological and cultural parameters.

Emphasis in this chapter lies not in terminology definition, but in defining the processes by which populations change. In demographic terms, this processual view is neatly summarized in the basic demographic equation

$$\Delta = (B + I) - (D + O), \tag{1}$$

where Δ is change, B is births, I is in-migration, D is deaths, and O is out-migration.

While this straightforward equation remains the yardstick by which population processes are measured, it is necessary to introduce the concepts of sex and age to fully recognize population structure. The most basic measure of sexual differences in populations is the sex ratio, defined as

$$\text{Sex Ratio} = (\text{Males/Females}) \times 100. \tag{2}$$

Sex ratios are commonly calculated for three stages of human development. The primary sex ratio denotes the male-female ratio at conception. The secondary sex ratio counts sex frequency at birth, while the tertiary sex ratio is loosely applied to various stages of the life cycle (see Chapter 6).

For large populations where chance fluctuations are smoothed out by large numerical size, the secondary sex ratio commonly exhibits a range of 102 to 108:100, but the primary sex ratio is considered higher (see Chapter 6). Some analyses of interuterine mortality suggest ratios of 170 to 180 males per 100 females (Bernds and Baresh 1979). This picture is complicated by the finding of variable ratios for different timing of spontaneous abortions. Parkes (1974), citing data from Czechoslovakia on fetal abortions, found a ratio of 177:100 for abortions in the second month of pregnancy, 137:100 in the third, and 117:100 in the fourth. This "male disadvantage" is also evident in stillborn and neonatal (here defined as the first 72 hours after birth) mortality, with Naeye et al. (1971) finding a sex ratio of 128:100 for a large U.S. sample.

Overall, then, more males are conceived and die before or at birth than females. The search for factors capable of explaining these phenomena has led to the examination of diverse variables (reviewed by Otten in Chapter 6). In this chapter, we will concentrate on the effect that differing sex ratios may have on population structure.

Figure 7.1 presents three age-sex population pyramids, each showing the composition of a hypothetical human population in standard 5-year age intervals. Each pyramid documents a different population structure, its shape determined by the interaction of the population's fertility, mortality, and migration parameters. In 1907 Lotka developed the model of a stable population, closed to migration and featuring a fixed schedule of fertility and mortality rates. If fixed values prevailed for a significant period of time, say 200 years, then the age composition of the population would assume an invariant, or stable, structure, even though the population might numerically grow, decrease, or remain stationary. Let us assume that the three age-sex pyramids in Figure 7.1 reflect stable populations formed under these conditions. The pyramid labeled "A" may be considered a subset of stable populations denoting a growing population, with the majority of its members in the prereproductive period of the life cycle, aged 0 to 14 years. Pyramid B portrays a declining population, with the majority of its members in the postreproductive period, aged 50+. Pyramid C constitutes a stationary population, with its members distributed uniformly throughout the age intervals. In this simplified example, the effect of fertility and mortality rates on the age composition of a population is clear. In case A, fertility is outstripping mortality, resulting in population growth. The inverse situation is apparent in B, with the result being a future negative rate of growth. In C mortality and fertility rates have achieved an equilibrium, resulting in zero population growth.

Of course, these models are just that – models. In reality, fertility and mortality rates fluctuate over time and no human population is truly closed to migration. The demographer's use of the model of stable population theory is closely analogous to the population geneticist's utilization of the Hardy-Weinberg theorem of genetic equilibrium. No human population satisfies the preconditions of either model, yet without the former demographers would have great difficulty defining demographic parameters, while geneticists would find even the simplest calculation of allele frequencies impossible without the latter.

Demographic methodology will help us explore the effect of the sex ratio and sexual differentials in fertility and mortality on population structure. In 1925 Lotka showed that a stable population will also feature a constant rate of increase, which may be positive (Pyramid A), negative (Pyramid B), or neutral (Pyramid C). Today this measure is termed the "intrinsic rate of natural increase." It is frequently derived from the calculation of a population's net reproductive rate. This last rate is a cohort measure, that is, derived from following a group of people from birth throughout their life span. The net reproductive rate measures the number of daughters a cohort of newborn females will eventually bear during their lifetime, assuming fixed age-specific fertility and mortality rates. In essence, it attempts to determine the rate at which females will "replace" themselves in a population, recognizing that some will die

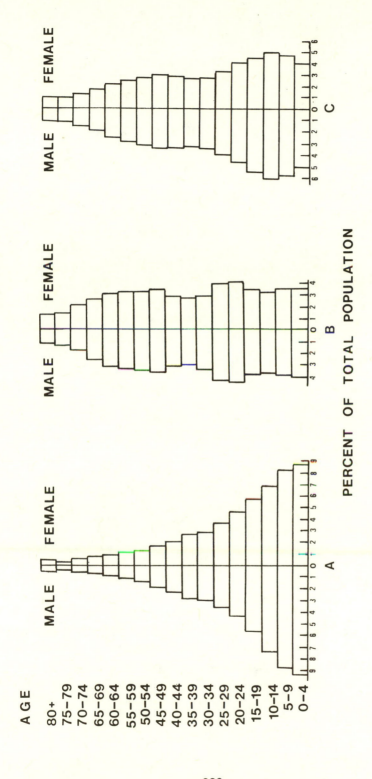

Figure 7.1. Age-sex pyramids representing (A) growing population, (B) declining population, and (C) stationary population.

before reaching the reproductive period, others will die in it, and yet another portion will survive to complete their reproductive period.

Teitelbaum (1972) notes that the net reproductive rate is frequently simplified through the assumption of a uniform secondary sex ratio. Table 7.1 presents data from an introductory demographic textbook that calculates the net reproductive rate based on a constant secondary sex ratio during seven 5-year age intervals spanning the female reproductive period, ages 15 to 49 (Barclay 1958). The second column lists the number of years lived per age interval to a starting cohort radix, or base, of 100,000 women. Owing to reproductive mortality, these person-years decrease throughout the entire period. Age-specific birth rates yield the average probability of giving birth in each age interval. The fourth and final column is the number of births, calculated as the product of age-specific birth rates multiplied by person-years lived per interval. Assuming a constant secondary sex ratio of 105:100, the net reproductive rate is 348,524/205 = 1,700.12. Standardizing this quotient per 1,000 women yields a final net reproductive rate of 1.70012. Since replacement is indicated by a net reproductive rate of 1.0, a figure of 1.7 denotes a rapid rate of growth. That is expected under the ideal conditions of no in- or out-migration and constant birth and death rates for several generations.

TABLE 7.1
Net Reproductive Rate, California, 1960

Age of Mother (years)	Number of Years Lived in Age Interval	Age-Specific Birth Rate	Number of Births
15-19	484,208	0.1028	49,777
20-24	482,693	0.2673	129,024
25-29	480,803	0.1891	90,920
30-34	478,259	0.1034	49,452
35-39	474,665	0.0483	22,926
40-44	469,409	0.0130	6,102
45-49	461,537	0.0007	323
Totals	–	0.7246	348,524

Source: Thompson and Lewis (1965).

However, the secondary sex ratio is not an invariant 105:100. Following Teitelbaum (1972), assume that the population in Table 7.1 is actually composed of two subpopulations, P_1 and P_2, of equal size and identical fertility and mortality. The only difference is now that the secondary sex ratio of P_1 is 104:100 and that of P_2 107:100. Their net reproductive rates would be

Net Reproductive Rate (P_1) = (348,524/204) / 1000 = 1.708   (3)

Net Reproductive Rate (P_2) = (348,524/204) / 1000 = 1.684.   (4)

To determine the effect of these differences on the subpopulation's rates of growth, the intrinsic rate of growth (r) is calculated for each as

r = (log Net Reproductive Rate) $/ T$,   (5)

where T is generation length, here set as 25 years for both P_1 and P_2. The results would be

r (P_1) = 0.00930

r (P_2) = 0.00905.

While holding all other variables constant, even slightly different sex ratios can produce a 2.7 percent difference in the growth rate for the two fixed identical birth and death schedules.

DEMOGRAPHIC TRANSITION THEORY

Differences between populations' vital rates over time are most commonly examined in light of demographic transition theory, a model that arose from the study of relationships between birth and death rates in Europe following the social upheavals of the Industrial Revolution. In essence, this model proposes that in modernization all societies experience the same sequence of demographic change. While a later section of this chapter will return to this central tenet, the basic sequence of the demographic transition is as follows (Bogue 1969, p. 56):

1. Pretransitional – Societies exert little regulation or control of either death or birth rates; they have high vital rates, but almost no growth.

2. Transitional – Death and birth rates are in the process of being lowered; death rates are lower than birth rates, resulting in moderate to rapid growth.
3. Posttransitional – Death and birth rates are low, knowledge of contraceptives is widely diffused, and growth is nearly zero.

Figure 7.2 presents the historical trend in fertility and mortality rates for Denmark's national population, which closely approximates this sequence. Yet the model has not escaped without criticism. Demographers, historians, and anthropologists note that the model was originally developed for the historical sequence of events experienced by Western Europeans, and may not apply to other culture areas. In addition, anthropologists have expressed concern about whether it is applicable to small, "anthropological" groups. Despite these questions, the demographic transition theory contributes a general framework from which to examine demographic change. For prehistoric and historic societies, this framework serves as a useful tool for the investigation of past population dynamics, while for contemporary societies, the distinction between transitional and posttransitional populations is often synonymous with the concepts of "less-developed" and "developed" nations. In the following sections, we incorporate the dynamic model of demographic transition theory with stable population theory to broadly outline human demographic evolution. To do so, we will first examine mortality and fertility parameters separately, with the goal of understanding how sexual differences affect demographic processes.

MORTALITY

Methodology and Measurement

The demographic standard for quantifying mortality is the life table. This technique describes the potential risk and actual occurrence of mortality to a cohort of people moving through the life cycle. The history of this methodology begins with John Graunt's work on mortality patterns for London in 1662 entitled *Natural and Political Observations Made upon the Bills of Mortality*. Thirty-one years later, the noted astronomer Edmund Halley constructed the first modern life table for the city of Breslau. Since then the greatest accomplishment of life table analysis has been the delineation of an overall pattern of general mortality that is comparable for living and extinct populations (Howell 1979).

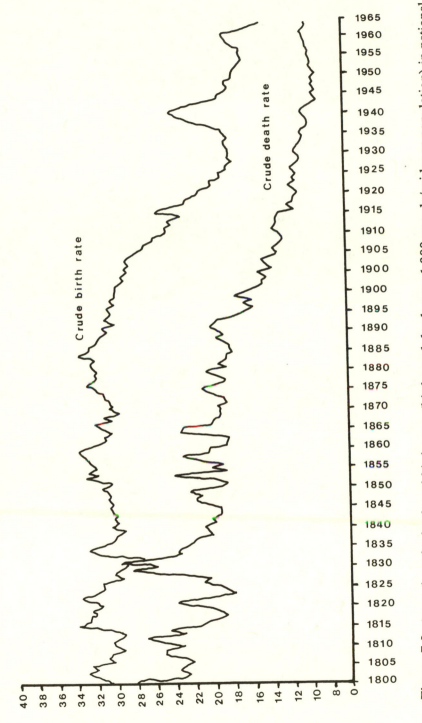

Figure 7.2. Annual crude death and birth rates (births and deaths per 1,000 people/midyear population) in national population of Denmark. [Redrawn from Mitchell (1976, p. 109) and used with permission.]

For example, plotting of mortality curves calculated for human groups will always reveal a J-shaped curve, with mortality pressures high in early infancy and childhood, flattening out through adolescence, and then rising again in old age. This is exemplified in Figure 7.3, which compares mortality curves for two demographically disparate countries, India and Sweden, for the period 1960-61. Essentially these curves depict crude death rates, rough measures of mortality defined as

$$\text{Crude Death Rate} = (\text{Total Deaths/Midyear Population}) \times 1,000 \quad (6)$$

They have been refined to measure mortality in given age intervals on an individual basis. This refinement makes them age-specific death rates calculated as

$$\text{Age-Specific Death Rate} =$$
$$(\text{Deaths to persons of age X})/(\text{Midyear population of age X}) \times 1,000 \quad (7)$$

These curves illustrate the basic similarity in the age pattern of human mortality, even though India has far higher mortality rates. Table 7.2 presents the absolute numerical differences between the two countries, both in terms of age-specific mortality and percentage distribution of deaths. As a final refinement, the two populations can be directly compared through the use of standardized death rates, which compute a weighted average of the age-specific rates in a given population, employing the age distribution of a standard population as the weights. Table 7.3 illustrates this procedure, employing the world population age composition in mid-1960 as the standard population.

Recognition of this general pattern of human mortality led demographers to compile and combine life tables for a multitude of living human populations, which are smoothed by extrapolation to form hypothetical model life tables.

To illustrate the life table format, Table 7.4 presents a sample life table of a hypothetical population living under fairly harsh circumstances. It is based on a sample of 100 individuals, none of whom lived past age 29. Individuals have been classed in 5-year age intervals. As is usual in demography, figures are standardized on a base of 1,000; hence between-population comparisons are facilitated.

The first column identifies age intervals, in our case 0-4 through 25-29. The second column, d'x, lists the raw number of individuals for the

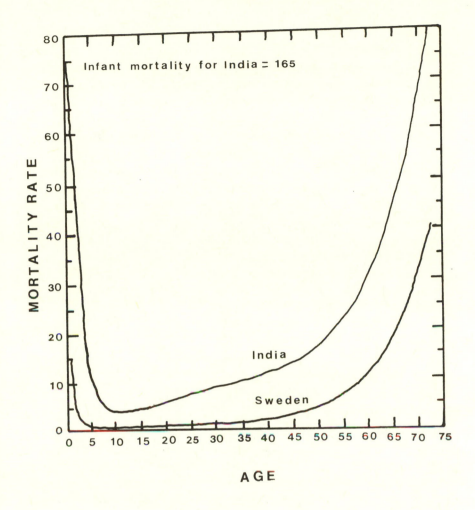

Figure 7.3. Age pattern of mortality, India and Sweden, 1960-61. [Redrawn from Bogue (1969, p. 551) and used with permission.]

TABLE 7.2

Comparison of Age-Specific Mortality Rates of India and Sweden, and Age Distribution of Deceased Persons, 1960-61

Age (years)	Age-Specific Death Rates			Percentage Distribution of Deaths		
	India (A)	Sweden (B)	Difference (A)–(B)	India (D)	Sweden (E)	Difference (D)–(E)
≤ 1	164.9	15.3	149.6	32.6	2.1	30.5
1-4	23.1	1.0	22.1	15.1	0.6	14.5
5-9	5.0	0.5	4.5	3.4	0.4	3.0
10-14	3.8	0.3	3.5	2.2	0.2	2.0
15-19	5.3	0.6	4.7	2.7	0.4	2.3
20-24	7.1	0.8	6.3	3.2	0.5	2.7
25-29	7.9	0.9	7.0	3.2	0.5	2.7
30-34	9.1	1.0	8.1	3.3	0.6	2.7
35-39	10.4	1.4	9.0	3.1	1.0	2.1
40-44	12.2	2.1	10.1	3.1	1.5	1.6
45-49	14.5	3.3	11.2	3.1	2.4	0.7
50-54	19.5	5.3	14.2	3.4	3.7	−0.3
55-59	25.8	8.6	17.2	3.5	5.3	−1.8
60-64	37.7	14.5	23.2	3.8	7.6	−3.8
65-69	53.8	24.5	29.3	3.6	10.6	−7.0
70-74	80.1	49.2	37.7	3.4	14.3	−10.9
75-79	120.1	73.7	46.4	2.0	16.7	−14.7
≥ 80	221.3	167.5	53.8	5.3	31.6	−26.3

Source: Bogue (1969, p. 552).

TABLE 7.3
Standardized Death Rates for India and Sweden, 1960-61, Using Composition of World as Standard

Age (years)	Standard Population (World in Mid-1960) (A)	Age-Specific Death Rates		Expected Deaths in Standard Population	
		India (B)	Sweden (C)	India (A×B=D)	Sweden (A×C=E)
≤ 1	30	164.9	15.3	4.947	0.459
1-4	111	23.1	1.0	2.564	0.111
5-14	226	4.4	0.994	0.994	0.090
15-24	181	6.2	0.7	1.122	0.127
25-44	261	9.8	1.3	2.558	0.339
45-64	146	23.3	0.4	3.402	1.124
65-74	32	64.8	32.7	2.074	1.046
≥ 75	13	159.6	119.9	2.075	1.559
Total	1,000	–	–	19.736	4.835

Standardized rate: India = ΣD = 19.7 × Sweden = ΣE = 4.8.
Source: Bogue (1969, p. 552).

interval in question. The third column, dx, gives the standardized number of individuals per age interval. This is found by dividing the raw number of individuals by the total number (100 in this case) and multiplying by 1,000. The fourth column, lx, is survivorship. It gives the standardized number of individuals alive at the beginning of the age interval. Since 1,000 is the base, 1,000 is the number in the first age interval; the second is found by subtracting dx of the previous age interval from 1,000; the third by subtracting dx of the previous age interval from lx of the second. (Conventionally this would be written $l_3 = l_2 - d_2$; 'x' always takes the place of a specific age interval number.)

Probability of death during a given age group, qx, is the fifth column; it is computed as dx/lx. The next column, Lx, gives the standardized average number of individuals alive during the interval, assuming a normal distribution of deaths during the interval. Lx is found by adding lx of the following interval to lx of the interval in question, and dividing by 2. For example, $L_2 = (1,000 + 600) / 2 = 800$. The next column, Tx, gives the total number of years left that can be lived to the highest age attainable by survivors. It is found by adding all Lx values including and following the interval in question. Tx is used to obtain

TABLE 7.4
Sample Life Table

X Age Intervals	dx Raw Number of Individuals	dx Standardized Number	lx survivorship at Beginning of Period	qx Probability of Death	Lx Average Number of Individuals Alive	Tx Total Number of Years Left	$e^U{}_x$ Mean Number of Years Left
1 (0-4)	40	400	1000	.400	800	2140	10.70
2 (5-9)	16	160	600	.267	520	1340	11.17
3 (10-14)	16	160	440	.364	360	820	9.32
4 (15-19)	8	80	280	.287	240	460	8.20
5 (20-24)	8	80	200	.400	160	220	5.50
6 (25-29)	12	120	120	1.000	60	60	2.50
Total	100	1000	0			0	0

values for the final column, e^{o}_x, which gives the mean number of years left to an individual who enters the age interval. This value is found by the following formula: $(Tx/lx) \times N$. N represents the number of years in the age interval, in our case 5. Thus e^{o}_1 is 10.70; since individuals come into age interval 1 at birth this gives the average life expectancy for anyone born into the population. Life expectancies are produced for all other age categories as well.

Trends in Human Longevity

The life expectancy at birth for the hypothetical prehistoric population in Table 7.4 is very low. While today we take life expectancies of 70+ years for granted, such longevity is a most recent phenomenon. Figure 7.4 plots survivorship curves (*lx* values) for three contemporary pretransitional populations, compared with model life table curves from the Coale and Demeny (1966) series. This last family of model life tables was compiled from large historical samples of mortality recorded from Europe, Asia, Australia, and North America. The three real populations are (1) the Dobe !Kung, a hunting-gathering group of Southern Africa (Howell 1979); (2) the Yanomamo Indians, a South American horticultural (slash and burn) tribe (Neel and Weiss 1976); and (3) the national population of India, 1921, an intensive agricultural (animal traction, irrigation) population (Das Gupta 1971).

The figure shows that age-specific survivorship and hence life expectancies are very low by the contemporary standards of Western industrialized societies. Average life expectancy was even less in prehistory (Acsadi and Nemeskeri 1970; Hassan 1981), with only a recent upswing in the average length of human life span during the last 200 years. Figure 7.5 shows this trend in average length of life. While this sudden increase in average life span is correlated with the onset of the Industrial Revolution in European societies, it was not industrialization per se that was the major causal factor. By far the greatest factor in the transition from high to low mortality rates was the control and eradication of infectious diseases. Modern medical advances in vaccines, antibiotics, and chemotherapy, which generally were preceded by community health and sanitation programs, greatly reduced the impact of infectious diseases in the twentieth century, as exemplified in Figure 7.6. As a result, demographers compiling mortality statistics for the twentieth century noted a shift in the leading causes of death for

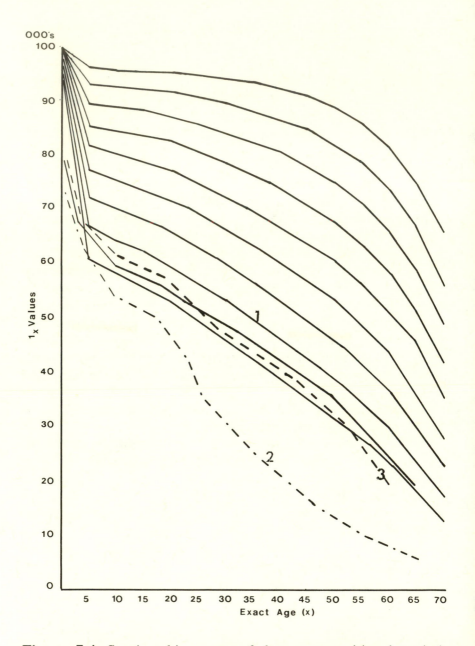

Figure 7.4. Survivorship curves of three pretransitional societies plotted against life table curves representing life expectancies at birth from 30 to 50 years. Real populations: (1) Dobe !Kung (Howell 1979); (2) Yanomamo (Neel and Weiss 1976); (3) Indian national population, 1921 (Das Gupta 1971). (Data used with permission.)

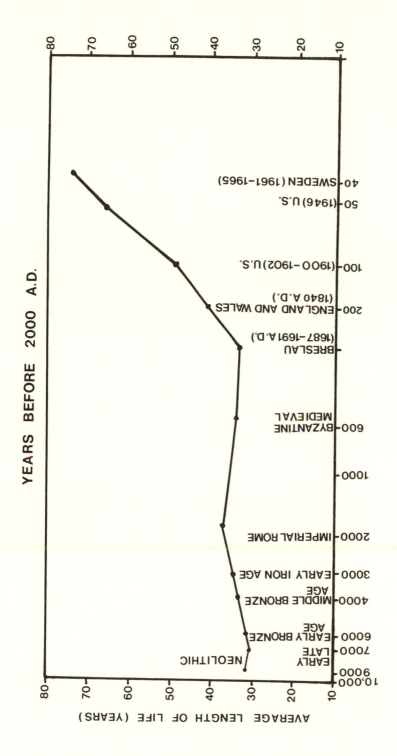

Figure 7.5. Trend of average length of life. [Redrawn from Hassan (1981, p. 122) and used with permission.]

national populations. For the United States in 1900, the leading causes of death were pneumonia, influenza, tuberculosis, and diarrhea, all infectious diseases that accounted for over 31 percent of all deaths. By 1977 the three leading causes of death were chronic diseases much more prevalent in the later stages of the life cycle: heart disease, cancer, and stroke.

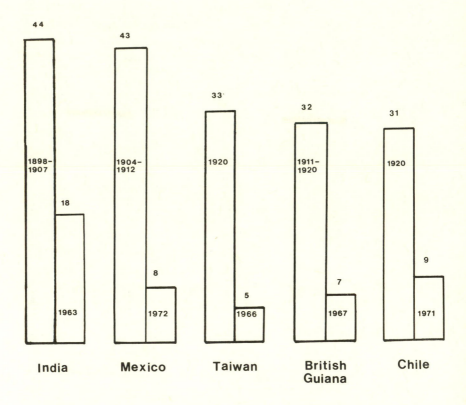

Figure 7.6. Reduction in crude death rates due to infectious disease in the twentieth century, selected national populations. Data include deaths due to typhoid, typhus, malaria, cholera, and influenza-pneumonia. [Data from Preston (1980, pp. 293-94) and used with permission.]

Sex Differentials

Equally dramatic is the recent change in mortality differentials between the sexes (see Chapter 6). Figure 7.7 presents the divergence between adult male and female average longevity, clearly indicating the prehistoric pattern of shorter female life expectancies, a trend that was reversed for almost all human populations during the twentieth century. Since the 1840s, all Western European life tables reveal a higher female life expectancy from any age to the age interval 70 to 74, a differential that appears to be increasing. Retherford (1975) noted that the divergence in life expectancies at birth between the sexes in the United States in

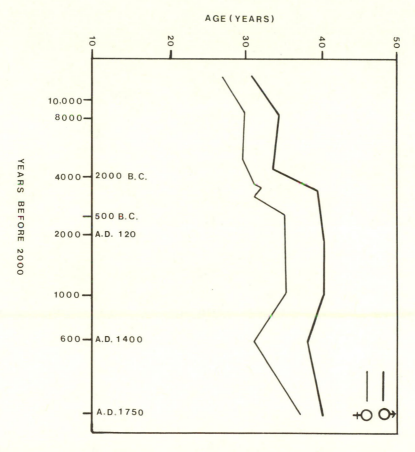

Figure 7.7. Divergence between average length of life of adult males and females. [Data from Hassan (1981, p. 129) and used with permission.]

1910 was 3.5 years (females 52.0, males 48.5), but in 1965 had doubled to 7.0 years (females 73.9, males 66.9).

This change was implemented and maintained by both social and biological factors. Advances in maternal delivery health care obviously favored females exclusively; to a lesser degree, the present high incidence of automobile-related fatalities and cigarette-related morbidity and mortality also favor females over males. In addition, evidence indicates that females possess an innate biological advantage in longevity. In a survey of 75 species, ranging from nematodes, crustaceans, and insects up the evolutionary scale through fish, reptiles, birds, and mammals, Hamilton (1948) consistently found superior female longevity. Likewise for humans, females may have biological advantages at different phases of the life cycle.

Recall the increased male interuterine and neonatal mortality (and see Chapter 6). One commonly cited genetic explanation for this "male disadvantage" (Naeye et al. 1971) pertains to the male sex chromosome constitution, denoted as "XY." Because so-called "sex-linked" genetic material is transmitted almost exclusively on the X chromosome, deleterious or lethal alleles, whether recessive or dominant, will be expressed phenotypically in males, who are hemizygous for the X chromosome (see Chapter 6).

Females have been found to have more reliable supplies of gamma-globulin, the blood fraction containing the body's antibodies against infectious disease (Shettles 1958). During the reproductive period of the life cycle, higher female production of the sex hormone estrogen appears to protect females from coronary heart disease brought about by atherosclerosis of the arteries supplying the heart (Epstein 1965). Besides protection from the normal fatty degeneration of the coronary arterial wall, higher production of the hormone protects females against smoke-induced acceleration of atherosclerosis, and results in lower mortality rates from coronary heart disease than same-age males. This effect appears to be cumulative, affording females protection even through postreproductive age intervals.

Anatomical and physiological differences not specifically linked to disease resistance or longevity include a higher degree of cephalization, a more efficient thermoregulating system, a lower basal metabolism, and a comparatively larger heart. Let us now focus on exceptions to the rule of superior female longevity, examining how cultural factors can overcome apparently innate biological advantages.

"Benign Neglect" of Females

Two notable exceptions to the rule of superior female longevity are the cases of historic nineteenth-century Ireland and contemporary South Asia. In the Irish case, Kennedy (1973) documented a female life expectancy at birth of 29 years, versus 30 years for males, for the year 1841. While this situation was reversed in later time periods, Table 7.5 demonstrates that Irish mortality differentials still lagged far behind those of other Western countries. For South Asia, El-Badry (1969) analyzed census data from India, Ceylon (now Sri Lanka), and Pakistan (now Pakistan and Bangladesh) for the period 1901-64. His data indicated higher female than male mortality in almost all cases.

Although these societies are extremely different, both feature a patrilineal system of inheritance, with familial wealth and property passed along male lines alone. In addition, in both societies females traditionally constitute an economic burden relative to males. Specifically,

TABLE 7.5
Excess of Female over Male Life Expectation at Birth in Years in Ireland, the United States, and England and Wales, 1850 to 1960-62

Approximate Period	Ireland	United States	England and Wales
1850	NA	3.1	1.9
1870-72	1.3	NA	3.2
1880-82	0.5	NA	3.5
1890-92	0.1	NA	3.7
1900-02	0.3	2.9	3.9
1910-12	0.5	3.4	3.9
1925-27	0.5	2.8	4.0
1935-37	1.4	4.0	4.2
1945-47	1.9	5.2	4.7
1960-62	3.8	6.9	5.9

NA, not applicable.

Source: Kennedy (1973, p. 55).

the marriage of a female was often accompanied by the giving of a dowry with the bride. As a result, the males appear to have been treated preferentially throughout their lives, while females were treated with what Cassidy (1980) termed "benign neglect." This discrimination took varied forms.

In historical Irish rural society, women and children did not eat until men and older boys had their fill. While females could thus be expected to be relatively undernourished, they were still expected to work in the fields alongside men during planting, cultivation, and harvesting times. They were also expected to fulfill the traditional female labor roles of cook, housekeeper, and homemaker, duties for which a male would be ridiculed for performing. The result was an overworked, underfed female, a picture entirely congruent with historical Irish mortality rates.

For South Asia, Miller (1981) provided a strikingly similar picture, with special reference to rural North India. Here the practice of bridal dowry was joined by the culturally proscribed low degree of female labor participation. Miller documented sexual differentials in child care including earlier weaning times for female infants, relatively poor nutrition for female offspring, and high male-female ratios for hospital admissions and general medical care.

All of these factors contribute to a particular sex pattern of mortality, associated with competition for scarce food and medical resources. Greenough (1982; cited in Miller 1981) examined data from the Bengal famine of 1943-44 that point to this association. During this period, adult males aged 20 to 40 possessed the lowest mortality rates, while females aged 1 to 5, 5 to 10, and 15 to 20 had much higher mortality rates than males of the same ages. Greenough concluded that, given a harsh economic situation, cultural rules denoting the most valued family members come strongly into play. In the situation of the Bengal famine, these rules dictated that able-bodied males be nourished first, then females.

Systematic neglect of females can also be present in everyday conditions, as the work of Chen et al. (1981) in a rural area of Bangladesh indicated. Previous research in this area noted that male mortality exceeded female mortality in the neonatal period, but that this pattern was reversed for almost all other periods of the life cycle, (see El-Badry 1969). As a result, one important aspect of the researchers' nutritional study was to investigate the possible presence and effect of son preference among families. They observed family feeding patterns, calculated food intake by standard Indian and Bangladeshi food conversion tables, took a battery of anthropometric measurements, and collected data on hospital and health care facility visits. All investigations pointed to female social disadvantages. The study's dietary surveys showed that male per capita food intake, measured in terms of calories and proteins, consistently exceeded that of females. Figure 7.8 presents male-female caloric intake ratios, adjusted for body weight, pregnancy, lactation, and activity levels. Adjustment for these factors negates to some extent the raw caloric differences, but still reveals the age-specific pattern of greater male nutritional levels. This sex differential was confirmed by anthropometric examinations, with 14.4 percent of females classified as severely malnourished versus 5.1 percent of males. The percentage of moderately malnourished girls (59.6) also exceeded that of boys (54.8). Although the study did not reveal strong sex differentials in infection rates, differences were evident in health service utilization, measured in numbers of clinic visits.

These studies point to a relationship between sex-biased health, nutrition, and the long-standing inferior social status of females in widely divergent societies. Such social differentials can override the apparent innate female biological advantages in mortality and longevity.

FERTILITY

Definition and Methodology

As in mortality, demographic measures of human fertility are influenced by both biological and social factors. Unlike mortality, however, traditional fertility measures are applicable only to female reproductive histories, and thus are termed "female-dominant models." Another difference of fertility measurements is that they are usually confined to only one period of the life cycle, the reproductive period, which we earlier defined as between the ages of 15 and 49.

Despite this standard definition, the true boundaries of the female reproductive period are much more difficult to determine. The two physiological limits of menarche, or the first appearance of menstrual periods, and menopause, the final cessation of menstrual periods, are themselves influenced by biocultural factors and vary from culture to culture (see Table 7.6). In addition, these two events may not truly mark the beginning and end of the reproductive period. For menarche Montague (1957) documented on a worldwide basis a period of sterility

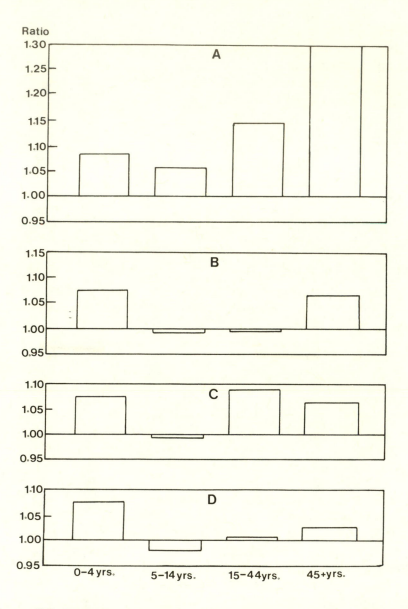

Figure 7.8. Deviation from unity of ratio of male-female caloric intake in relation to requirements by age group: (A) actual; (B) adjusted for body weight; (C) adjusted for body weight, pregnancy, and lactation; and (D) adjusted for body weight, pregnancy, lactation, and activity. [Data from Chen et al (1981, pp. 57, 62) and used with permission.]

TABLE 7.6
Ages at Menarche and Menopause, Selected Populations

Population	Age (years)
Median Age at Menarche[a]	
Cuba (Negro)	12.4
Assam, India (city dwellers)	13.2
Nigeria (Ibo)	14.1
South Africa (Bantu)	15.0
Rwanda	
(Tutsi)	16.5
(Hutu)	17.1
New Guinea (Bundi)	18.8
Mean Age at Menopause	
India (rural Punjab)[b]	42.6
Poland (1925)[c]	44.0
Inuit (Wainwright, Alaska)[d]	44.5
India (rural villages)[e]	44.8
York, England (circa 1845)[f]	47.5
United States (circa 1965)[g]	49.8

[a]All from Johnston (1982).
[b]From Wyon et al. (1966).
[c]From Wolanski (1972).
[d]From Milan (1970).
[e]From Dandekar (1959).
[f]From Whitehead (1847).
[g]From MacMahon and Worchester (1966).

following menarche. This phenomenon, termed "adolescent sterility," appears to be independent of the timing of menarche. As such it represents a good example of primary sterility, or what Howell (1979) called the "not yet state" (p. 125). In this phase, fecundity, the potential to bear children, is not yet established. When this syndrome is prolonged past adolescence, it is referred to as "natural (or absolute) sterility." Table 7.7 presents age-specific percentages of sterility in married women for various populations, illustrating the range of variation in this type of infertility.

TABLE 7.7
Age-Specific Percentages of Sterility in Married Women

Age (years)	European (Historical)[a]	England and Wales (Rural; ca. 1850)[a]	Japan (Rural; ca. 1925)[a]	United States (1955)[b]	!Kung (1968)[c]
20-24	3	4	3	5	12
25-29	5	8	13	9	23
30-34	8	13	23	15	32
35-39	15	21	39	23	54
40-44	32	36	61	NA	78

NA, not available.
[a]From Henry (1965).
[b]From Freedman et al. (1966).
[c]From Howell (1979).

244

Despite these qualifications, the pattern of fertility follows a general course throughout the human life span, much as we have seen for human mortality. Specifically, for noncontracepting, or "natural fertility," populations (Henry 1961), the female fertility curve follows an inverted U shape, with fertility low in the midteens, rising to its zenith in the twenties, and then declining steadily with age thereafter. This pattern is illustrated in Table 7.8, which presents age-specific fertility data for a Kutchin Athapaskan population studied by Roth (1981). Following the format of Howell (1979), these data are presented in matrix form, with rows representing parity (birth order) and columns representing the seven 5-year intervals of the female reproductive period. Summation of each column gives the number of children born per parity level, which also is the number of women who attained that level. Summation of the seven rows yields the absolute number of offspring born per mother's age group.

These absolute values are transformed into probabilities of giving birth through the concept of "risk," defined as the number of person-years lived in a specified period. As the reproductive period is segmented into 5-year periods, risk in any interval is calculated as 5×74 (the total number of women included in the sample) = 370. Division of the number of offspring in each interval by 370 yields age-specific fertility rates, the probability of giving birth per age interval. Summation of the seven age-specific fertility rates followed by multiplication by 5 (recognizing that there are 5 years to each interval) yields the total fertility rate. This is, with numerical rounding, the equivalent of the mean parity of women in the sample, that is, $402/74 = 5.43$.

Evolution of Human Fertility Levels

Until recently, it was commonly conceived that pretransitional populations must have featured extremely high fertility levels in order to achieve population equilibrium with prehistoric and historic high levels of mortality. For example, Rose (1968) proposed that the mean parity of Australian aboriginal females of postreproductive age was about 18. However, studies of contemporary noncontracepting populations with relatively high mortality levels revealed far lower fertility levels than expected. Important examples include the low total fertility rates for the Dobe !Kung (Howell 1979) and for a large sample of Chinese peasant farmers, representing a 1931 census (Barclay et al. 1976). Table 7.9

TABLE 7.8
Fertility Histories of Kutchin Athapaskan Women, Old Crow Village

Parity Number	Age Interval (years)							
	15-19	20-24	25-29	30-34	35-39	40-44	45-49	Total
0								(9)
1	24	31	5	3	2			65
2	8	35	11	2	5	1		62
3		21	20	5	6	2	1	55
4		10	25	9	2	3		49
5		4	18	11	2	5	1	41
6			10	16	5	2	3	36
7			5	10	6	1	1	23
8			3	7	5	3	1	19
9				4	5	5	1	15
10				2	3	5	2	12
11				2	3	3	1	9
12				2		2	1	5
13					2	2	1	5
14					1	1		2
15						1	1	2
16							2	2
Sum	32	101	97	73	47	36	16	402
Risk[a]	370	370	370	370	370	370	370	
ASF[b]	0.086	0.273	0.262	0.197	0.127	0.097	0.043	1.085

Total fertility rate[c] = 5.43. See the text for more details.

[a]Risk is the number of person-years lived in interval i. In this case, n = 74, and each interval is 5 years in length. Risk is thus 74 × 5 = 370.

[b]Age-specific fertility is f_i/risk, where f_i is the absolute number of births in interval i.

[c]Total fertility rate is $5\sum_{i=1}^{7} f_i$.

Source: Roth, 1981.

TABLE 7.9
Age-Specific Fertility and Total Fertility Rates for Contemporary Natural-Fertility Populations, Compared with Hutterite Marital Rates

Age (years)	!Kung (1968)[a]	Chinese Farmers (1930s)[b]	Rural Senegal (1963-65)[c]	Bangladesh (1966-70)[d]	Old Believers (1965-68)[e]	Amazon Indians (1964)[f]	Married Hutterites (1921-30)[g]
15-19	0.135	0.099	0.168	0.169	0.157	0.333	0.300
20-24	0.242	0.247	0.319	0.360	0.478	0.652	0.550
25-29	0.203	0.241	0.308	0.360	0.358	0.450	0.502
30-34	0.152	0.204	0.257	0.332	0.357	0.375	0.447
35-39	0.119	0.143	0.186	0.241	0.348	0.200	0.406
40-44	0.071	0.068	0.096	0.146	0.145	0.082	0.222
45-49	0.016	0.010	0.033	0.035	0.000	0.000	0.061
Total	0.938	1.012	1.367	1.643	1.843	2.092	2.488
Total × 5	4.690	5.060	6.840	8.220	9.220	10.460	12.440

[a]From Howell (1979); [b]From Barclay et al. (1976); [c]From Ferry (1981); [d]From Committee on Population and Demography (1981); [e]From Hall (1970); [f]From Hern (1977); [g]From Eaton and Mayer (1953).

247

presents age-specific fertility and total fertility rates for a sample of twentieth-century natural fertility populations. These are compared with similar rates for married, mid-twentieth century Hutterite women (an Anabaptist religious group of western Canada) whose level and pattern of fertility are one of the highest yet recorded for any human population (Eaton and Mayer 1953) and are frequently cited as representing the maximum potential for human fertility (Coale 1965). Rates of married Hutterite women were used because the rather late mean age of marriage for this population decreases teenage fertility.

The Hutterites represent a well-nourished population taking full advantage of modern medical care. As such, their fertility should not be considered typical of prehistoric populations. Rather, it is better to consider their rates as maximums for modern, monogamous, noncontracepting populations. In contrast, Hassan (1975) estimated the biological parameters for maximum population growth for Paleolithic hunting-gathering populations (see Table 7.10). The important variables are factors determining the average interval between livebirths and female longevity and reproductive span. Employing Hassan's estimates, the total fertility rate would be 5.7 (13 years/27.3 months). Equally important, given an infant mortality rate of 40 to 50 percent, only 3.4 to 2.9 children would survive infancy. The total fertility rate of 5.7 is compatible with the average rate of 5.5 computed from Weiss's compilation (1973) of 17 nonindustrial natural-fertility populations, both well below levels expected of a high-fertility prehistoric population. Figure 7.9 compares the Weiss sample with a sample of eight national populations representing the world's highest fertility levels, 1955-60 (data from DeJong 1972).

While debate continues over fertility levels in Paleolithic hunting-gathering populations, there is consensus that sedentary life-styles in the Neolithic age resulted in elevated fertility rates and a worldwide population explosion. The question of mechanisms remains. Current research on one modern hunting-gathering group, the !Kung of Botswana, who are undergoing the transition to sedentism, introduces two controversial theories of fertility regulation, one concerning lactation and another concerning fat stores of women.

While some of the !Kung are still nomadic hunter-gatherers, others have adopted a more sedentary life, based on cash labor and squatting rights obtained from neighboring farms. Lee (1980) hypothesized that incipient sedentism would alleviate child transport stress (Sussman 1972), that is, the actual stress and strain on females from carrying

TABLE 7.10
Estimated Parameters for Maximum Population Growth for Paleolithic Populations

I. Factors determining birth interval	
Amenorrhea[a]	10 months
Interval before conception	3 months
Interval from conception to birth	9 months
Total birth interval	22 months
II. Parameters determining livebirth intervals	
Birth interval	22 months
Fetal death rate	12 %
Sterility rate	12 %
Resultant livebirth interval	27.3 months
III. Reproductive parameters	
Age at menarche	15 years
Adolescent sterility	1 year
Age at ability to conceive	16 years
Adult female longevity	29 years
Reproductive span	13 years
IV. Mortality parameters	
Maternal mortality	10 %
Infant mortality	40-50 %

[a]Amenorrhea here refers to postpartum amenorrhea, or the period of nonfecundity immediately following childbirth (for more details see text).

Source: Hassan (1975, p. 27).

children over long distances. In the case of the !Kung, this stress is considerable, for females nurse infants for up to 4 years and carry them for long periods in the nomadic !Kung subsistence cycle. Lee thinks that this long nursing period is an adaptive strategy that is the prime factor in the overall low (less than 5) !Kung fertility level. This rests on hypotheses of a relationship between lactation and the duration of postpartum amenorrhea, the period of sterility that follows a birth. Recent evidence suggests the hormone involved in lactation, prolactin, inhibits the production of female gonadotropins, sex hormones necessary for the initiation and continuation of regular ovulatory cycles (see Chapter 6 for a full discussion). Van Ginnekan (1978) claims a strong correlation between the duration of lactation and amenorrhea. While the methodology underlying this relationship has been criticized (Masnick

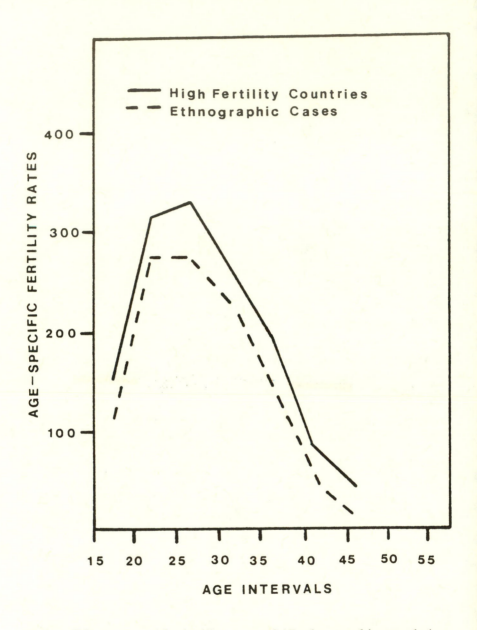

Figure 7.9. Age-specific fertility rates of 17 ethnographic populations, compared with the world's 8 highest fertility countries, 1955-60. [Redrawn from Hassan (1981, p. 135) and used with permission.]

1979), Lee presents data from the !Kung suggesting a selective advantage to the long birth intervals of nomadic !Kung, intervals, which he feels are determined by their long period of breastfeeding. Table 7.11 models the amount of child transport stress for 2-, 3-, and 4-year birth intervals utilizing !Kung infant growth data. These figures and Lee's calculation of transport stress as the product of child weight and distance carried (kilogram × kilometer) point to the advantage of long birth intervals.

Lee's model sees shortened periods of lactation and less intense breastfeeding sessions as the prime determinants of reduced birth intervals associated with sedentism. Alternatively, Howell's research

TABLE 7.11
Model of Child Transport Stress, !Kung Parameters

Birth intervals

	Intervals					
	2 years		3 years		4 years	
Year	Weight (kg)	Child No.	Weight (kg)	Child No.	Weight (kg)	Child No.
1	6.0	1	6.0	1	6.0	1
2	8.8	1	8.8	1	8.8	1
3	17.6	1,2	11.6	1,2	11.6	1,2
4	21.2	1,2	18.4	1,2	12.4	1,2
5	17.6	2,3	8.8	2	6.0	2
Number of children over 10-year period	5		4		3	
Mean weight per year	17.0		12.2		9.2	
Number of years carrying two children	8		3		0	
Work per mother per year (kilogram × kilometer)	32,064		22,824		17,808	

Mean length of birth intervals (months) between successive livebirths

	1963-68	1968-73	1963-73
Nomadic	42.27	36.42	47.63
More sedentary	38.35	29.82	40.12

Source: Lee (1980).

(1979) on the same !Kung population posits another mechanism of fertility regulation, related to the critical weight hypothesis introduced in Chapter 5. This theory was formulated by Frisch (1975, 1978), who in studies of the growth and development in Asian and South American populations noted that menarche and the adolescent growth spurt occurred at approximately the same average weight for different study groups. Estimating the body composition of females at different points of maturation, Frisch and McArthur (1974) posited that a major variable in the inception and maintenance of menstrual cycles is a "critical" amount of body fat expressed as a proportion of total body weight or lean body mass. When this level is attained, the hypothalamus, a specialized area of the brain involved in the secretion of hormones, increases the production of lipid-soluble hormones related to fecundity (for example, estrogen), and menarche is initiated. Once this is achieved, fat deposition must continue in order to maintain menstrual cycles with ovulation. Like the theory emphasizing lactation, the critical weight hypothesis has been criticized on statistical and methodological grounds (Trussell 1978). Evidence to support the hypothesis includes the historic low fertility levels associated with famines, the decline of the average age of menarche in well-nourished modern populations, and reported cases of amenorrhea in anorexic women.

Howell thinks that both the length and rate of childbearing of the !Kung are related to the Frisch-McArthur hypothesis. She interprets the late age of menarche (16.1 years) and high mean age at first birth (20.0 years) as representing difficulty in attaining levels of body fat necessary for regular ovulatory cycles. Likewise, the long birth intervals may represent failure to maintain this critical level, as found in the low mean age at last birth of 34.4 years. As for the recent trend to shortened birth intervals in sedentary !Kung, Howell attributes this to the improved reliability of diet in the cattle outposts where they live.

Neither of these theories has been sufficiently tested in other field situations to determine which biological factors have the greatest impact on fertility. Furthermore, the problem is exacerbated by recent contrasting evidence compiled for !Kung populations. For example, Wilmsen (1979) found that seasonal fluctuations in food availability, individual weight, and fertility varied for hunting-gathering !Kung in accordance with the critical weight hypothesis. Inversely, Konner and Worthman (1980) present evidence that the nursing regimen of !Kung children determines the long average birth interval, directly supporting Lee's contention. Finally, Harpending and Wandsnider's analysis (1982) of nomadic and sedentary postmenopausal !Kung women revealed nonsignificant differences in completed family size.

Despite these last findings, both theories point to increased fertility during the transition from a nomadic to a sedentary life-style. In modernizing societies, the third stage of the demographic transition predicts the fall of fertility levels, following a decline in mortality pressures. Currently, the apparent inability of many of the world's populations to achieve this decline is one of the most striking discrepancies between the "more"- and "less"-developed countries. Before considering this issue, let us first examine the classic transition pattern as it occurred in historical Western European populations. The transition to lower fertility levels is commonly associated with the onset of the Industrial Revolution. Yet England, where industrialization first took hold on a national scale, lagged temporarily behind predominantly agrarian France in the decline of fertility. Indeed, industrialization in some cases actually initiated an increase in fertility, owing to new opportunities for employment and migration (Kleinman 1980).

Figure 7.10 plots the decline of fertility levels for selected Western European countries with different starting times for industrialization. The decline began around 1870, continued with increased momentum until the 1920s, and began to stabilize following the 1930s (Glass 1969, p. 25). The initial decline was facilitated through social mechanisms, such as delayed age at marriage, an increasing degree of celibacy, and coitus interruptus, while the later stages saw the introduction of modern contraceptives. But both featured declining age-specific fertility rates in the later age periods. Figure 7.11 compares a modern contracepting population (Great Britain) with natural-fertility populations. The controlled fertility population exhibits a sharp decline in the first age interval followed by a steady decline, while the natural-fertility regimens decline slowly over the first three age periods.

Fertility declined in Western Europe before modern contraceptives were invented. Likewise, today's transitional populations have used various devices for population control. These include abortions, infanticide, spermicidal agents, and contraceptive drugs and potions. In addition, there exists a wide range of what Wrigley (1978) termed "un-conscious rationality" (pp. 135-37), behaviors that benefit a population without the individual members being cognizant of the advantages. Social norms such as the Indian ban on widow remarriage and the long period of postpartum abstinence practiced by traditional African, American Indian, and Insular Pacific populations are good examples of

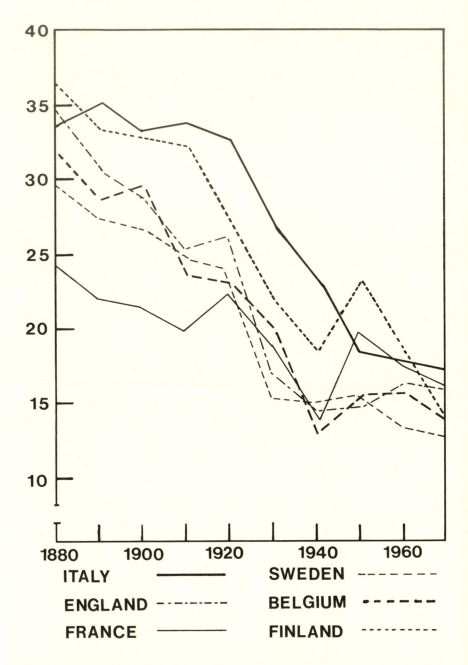

Figure 7.10. Crude birth rates of selected Western European countries with different starting points of industrialization, 1880-1969. [Redrawn from Stolte-Heiskanen (1977, p. 252) and used with permission.]

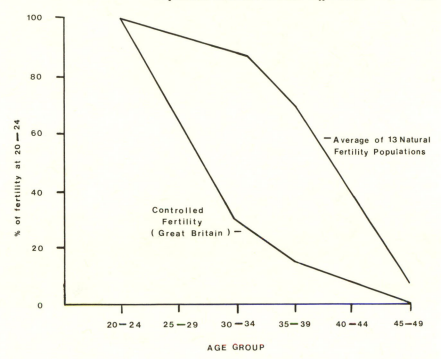

Figure 7.11. Decline of age-specific fertility in controlled (Great Britain) and natural-fertility (average of 13 groups) populations. [Redrawn from Howell (1979, p. 160) and used with permission.]

this phenomenon. That these cultural behaviors can be as effective as modern Western contraceptives is exemplified by a lengthy, intensive, and expensive experiment in population intervention in a rural area of the Punjab, India. Although fertility declined for the target population, the causal factor was not the introduction of modern contraceptives but rather a secular trend toward a higher age at marriage (Mamdani 1972; Wyon and Gordon 1966, 1972).

Demographers are questioning whether the classical demographic transition experience applies to developing countries today. Teitelbaum (1976) outlined differences between developed and developing nations that mitigate against a rapid decline in fertility. Some of these, relative to the historical European situation, are higher fertility levels, fewer opportunities for female labor participation, and fewer opportunities for occupational and rural-urban movement. On the other hand, developing countries have significantly improved contraceptive techniques and international resource programs available to them. Whether this will facilitate a more rapid fertility decline, or a decline at all, remains to be seen.

Woman's Work and Fertility

The possibility of a Third World fertility decline is often viewed as dependent on the entrance rate of women into national labor forces. Only in emphasizing the productive, rather than the reproductive, value of women, goes this argument, will fertility decline. In a similar vein, Hall (1972) predicted two additional stages to the three of the demographic transition to occur only in fully industrialized countries. In the fourth stage, for example, the United States in the 1970s, fertility would be generally low but would vary in relation to economic conditions. For the final stage, which has not yet occurred anywhere, Hall hypothesized that fertility levels would stabilize at a low level as a concomitant of large-scale female participation in the labor force. However, the variance of female fertility would be quite high – some women would have no children while others would have many. More options would be available for women's roles. Subsequent studies in economically developed countries (Kupinsky 1977; Janes 1981) have verified Hall's hypothesis.

Nonindustrial nations of the twentieth century have not moved even into the third stage of the transition, and for them the old models do not work. Instead, these nations frequently demonstrate a positive relationship between fertility levels and female employment rates. The prime example is Sub-Saharan Africa, an area featuring some of the highest fertility rates in the world, where female work force participation is also among the highest globally. Within predominantly agrarian Sub-Saharan Africa, women play the major role in cultivation in more than half of all societies and an equal part in a further quarter (Ware 1977).

How can we explain the North-South dichotomy in relationships between fertility and female labor participation? Part of the answer lies in the Western capitalist economic system in which wage labor provides an individual with control over his/her life. In this type of system, females can gain power by working. However, as others have pointed out, the Western capitalist model pertains to only a small percentage of the world's populations. In the majority of areas, though women must work to ensure personal and familial survival, work does not provide increased freedom of choice. In a survey conducted by Hull (1977) in rural Java, 28 percent of women over the age of 10 were considered as currently employed in agriculture. Revising her wording of the survey, Hull discovered that 53 percent of the same sample reported working during the last harvest. The setting in which labor is performed is highly pertinent. The Western view of labor performed outside the home suggests regimented time periods in impersonal settings, but this is not generally applicable to the developing countries of the world. In the African case, women traditionally work in the family fields, within immediate vicinity of the family home. Children are free to join their mother at work or to roam at will about the work site. Contrast this with the Western setting of an employer's office lacking child-care facilities, and the inherent differences in the phrase "female labor participation" become clear.

Recognition of these differences led to the formulation of the maternal role incompatibility hypothesis (Jaffe and Azuni 1960; Weller 1968), which posits that an inverse relationship between women's work and fertility levels is only as strong as the conflict between the social roles of mother and worker. Ware (1977) summarizes the hypothesis by defining the features of female labor expected to be associated with reduced fertility. Some of these are

1. where alternative child-minding facilities are not available;
2. where children cannot accompany their mothers at work;
3. where children need to be cared for until relatively advanced ages;
4. where women are disadvantaged if they are away from work during pregnancy; and
5. where women formerly had low status compared with men.

While this view is an improvement over the blanket premise that labor participation exerts a negative force on fertility, its predictive value remains contested. One of the most rigorous tests of the model was performed by Mason and Palan (1981) on different ethnic groups in peninsular Malaysia, including Malay, Chinese, and Indian samples within the national population. The Malays constituted 53 percent of the peninsular population in 1970, and represent the traditional sector of Malaysian society, supporting themselves primarily through paddy farming, rubber tapping, and fishing. In contrast, the ethnic Chinese in Malaysia, originally imported to provide labor for peninsular tin mines, today are heavily involved in commerce and trade and are by far the most modernized of the three study groups. The Malaysian Indian community falls inbetween the first two groups, featuring both urban and rural residences and performing both labor and management roles in commerce.

Employing social, economic, and demographic data collected by a peninsular-wide sample of approximately 6,400 females (Malaysian Fertility and Family Survey), the authors constructed mathematical models designed to predict the average number of children ever born to a woman and the mean number of children born in the last 5 years. Their multiple regressions provided estimates of the relative importance upon fertility of independent variables such as the number of years a woman worked since marriage and an indexed measure of the level of maternal role incompatibility. This index included work location, household composition, employment status (employee or self-employed), and the presence of a potential babysitter in the household. Subdividing the three ethnic groups into urban and rural residences, the researchers first attempted to test relationships between female labor and fertility rates posited by the maternal role incompatibility hypothesis. The results, though weak, as shown in Table 7.12, both support and deviate from the hypothesis. In the first regard, a low negative relation exists between work and fertility for all urban segments of the sample. In contrast, an unexpected finding was the negative relationship for the most traditional segment of the sample, the rural Malays. Similarly there is a negative relation for the rural Chinese between fertility in the last 5 years and the same period's work history.

These discrepancies are further highlighted in Table 7.13, which shows the predicted mean number of children ever born by employment-household composition. Both urban and rural Chinese who worked since marriage were predicted to have higher fertility than their nonworking counterparts. Similarly, the study predicted that rural and urban Chinese working away from home and with no potential female babysitter in the household would have more children than those working at home and with potential babysitters in the household composition.

Though the differences in all cases are minor, the results do not support the maternal role incompatibility hypothesis and also speak to problems arising from demographic transition theory. Both models address conditions (including industrialization, education, motivation for social mobility, and labor force participation) that are expected to reduce fertility. Since the expected conditions are not found in many developing

TABLE 7.12
Regression Slope Relating Work Experience to Fertility, for Two Alternative Work and Fertility Measures, by Ethnicity and Residence

Work and Fertility Measures	Malays		Chinese		Others	
	Always Rural	Ever Urban	Ever Rural	Always Urban	Now Rural	Now Urban
Children ever born by years worked since marrying	-0.022	-0.003	0.031	-0.034	0.049	-0.062
Children born in last 5 years by whether worked in last 5 years	-0.078	0.091	-0.108	-0.194	0.078	-0.049

Source: From Mason and Palon (1981, p. 558).

countries, the models do not apply. Thus, exceptions to expected results have become more interesting than the rules. For example, in attempting to account for the higher than predicted fertility of Malay females working outside the home, the authors describe social circumstances in East Malaysia where Malay men rely on fishing for income. Coastal women contribute to the family income by preparing foodstuffs for outside markets. Under these conditions, the birth of an additional child may provide an incentive to increase their market activity. Likewise, Mason and Palon noted that the ethnic Chinese in Malaysia have limited access to fertile land. High fertility may lead Chinese women to engage in commerce outside the home to support growing families.

These examples indicate that human fertility behavior must be analyzed in context, not as an isolated phenomenon. In the following section, we will examine another factor not addressed by general models such as demographic transition theory: conditions in which one offspring sex is preferred, sometimes at the expense of the other sex.

TABLE 7.13
**Predicted Mean Number of Children Ever Born by Employ-
ment-Household Composition Measures, Separately by
Ethnicity and Residence**

Employment-Household Composition Variable	Malays		Chinese	
	Always Rural	Ever Urban	Ever Rural	Always Urban
Employment experience				
Has not worked since marrying	4.36	4.36	4.64	4.26
Has worked	4.33	4.23	5.24	4.52
Occupation/household composition				
Modern occupation and no unmarried woman 16+ years	4.09	3.85	3.97	3.98
Other occupation or household composition	4.33	4.23	5.24	4.52
Class of worker/household composition				
Employee and no unmarried woman 16+ years	4.74	4.44	4.88	4.48
Other class of household composition	4.33	4.23	5.24	4.52
Location of work/household composition				
Away from home and no unmarried woman 16+ years	4.04	4.23	6.23	4.66
Other location or household composition	4.33	4.23	5.24	4.52
Base n	3,416		2,075	

Source: Mason and Palon (1981, p. 567).

Son Preference and Fertility

The strong desire for male offspring, referred to as "son preference,"
is an ancient cultural trait. Its antiquity is attested to in the following
poem written by an anonymous Indian poet about 600 B.C. (from
Williamson 1976):

> In him a father pays a debt
> and reaches immortality
> When he beholds the countenance
> Of a son born to him alive.

Then all the joy which living things
In waters full, in earth and fire,
The happiness that in his son
A father feels is greater far.

At all times fathers by a son
Much darkness, to have passed beyond;
In him the father's self is born,
He wafts him to the other shore.

Food is man's life and clothes provide protection
Gold gives him bounty, marriages bring cattle,
His wife's a friend, his daughter causes pity;
A son is like a light in highest heaven.

This strong preference for sons is still apparent in Hindu culture where male offspring are expected to perform a variety of religious and economic functions. In Hindu cosmology, a son performs the rites of lighting the deceased father's funeral pyre, enabling the father to achieve immortality. In economic terms, the family property and name are transmitted across generations only by male heirs. Male children are welcome additions to the family labor pool and often constitute the sole source of old age assistance for their parents. In contrast, as the poem states, "his daughter causes pity." The traditional Hindu practice of giving a dowry with the bride makes female offspring a future expense. The expense often is not recouped, for complex marriage rules result in a pattern of village exogamy with daughters marrying outside the parental village, providing little or no financial support for their parents. Even in instances of village endogamy, social regulations prevent the patrilocally based married female from aiding her original family (Mandelbaum 1974). No wonder that under these circumstances, a new bride is welcomed into her husband's house by greetings of "May you have seven sons" and "Bathe in milk and you will have lots of sons" (Mamdani 1972).

Son preference is not limited to Indian culture. In Korea, over 30 rituals designed to influence the sex of the next offspring are known today. In Latin America, men with only female offspring are termed "chanceleteros," makers of cheap slippers – a derogatory term for little girls (Stycos 1955).

To quantify cross-cultural preferences for offspring of either sex, Coombs et al. (1975) developed the Coombs scale in which respondents are asked to rank different family size and sex combinations. Based on these rankings, each respondent is assigned a score for sex preference, ranging from one to seven. Seven denotes very strong son preference, one a very strong daughter preference. Figure 7.12 presents a sample cross-cultural comparison taken from four countries. Of the groups shown, South Korea exhibits the strongest son preference, with Taiwan and the United States (in that order) also falling on the side of son preference. Only the Philippine sample shows no sex preference.

Although the almost global pattern of son preference is recognized by demographers, opinion differs as to the extent to which son preference inflates fertility. Those who propose a strong effect cite a high ratio of sons to daughters among Indian men undergoing vasectomies (Poffenberger 1967), shorter birth intervals following female versus male births (Khan 1973), higher acceptance and continued use of contraceptives for women with one or more sons (Cernada 1970), and higher pregnancy rates for women without sons (Freedman and Takeshita 1969). Yet a survey of fertility data from India, Bangladesh, and Morocco (Repetto 1972) found no relationship between offspring distribution and fertility.

To explore the possible effect of son preference on fertility, Heer and Wu (1975) analyzed fertility histories for two Taiwanese townships, Kunglaio and Hsinchuang. The former, a rural township involved in agriculture and fishing, was characterized by higher fertility and mortality levels than the more industrialized Hsinchaung Township, yet both populations preferred male offspring (see Table 7.14, which lists offspring preferences). While far less of the Hsinchuang respondents answered affirmatively that "boys provide more economic support than girls," a greater proportion answered yes to the statement that "boys are more emotionally rewarding than girls" and "tradition and custom require boys." The first response reflected the township's greater involvement with paid labor and the introduction of pension and savings plans. Yet despite this modernizing influence, Taiwanese traditional customs still exerted a strong effect for son preference. In particular, the role of son as heir and source of old age assistance remained strong in both communities.

To compare the effect of son preference on subsequent fertility, Heer and Wu devised a multiple regression model in which the dependent variable was the number of subsequent births among currently married women of third parity or higher (see Table 7.15). In Run A, one independent variable was the number of survivors of the first three

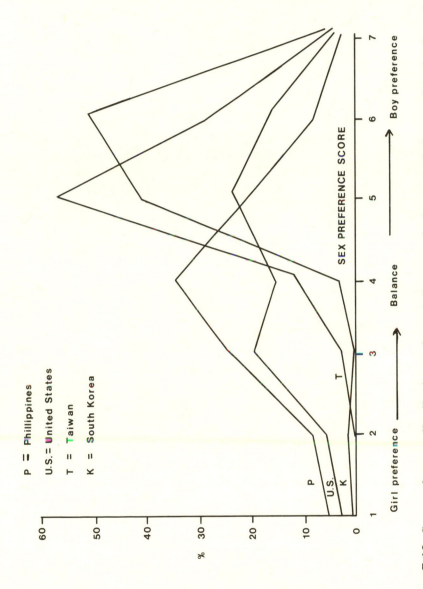

Figure 7.12. Sex preference distributions of married women in four populations, using the Coombs scale. [Data from N. Williamson (1978, p. 12) and used with permission of the Population Reference Bureau, Inc.]

TABLE 7.14

Reasons of Taiwanese Women and Men for Preferring Boys or Girls

	Sex of Respondent	Township	
		Kungliao (%)	Hsinchuang (%)
Boys provide more economic support than girls	F	64	36
	M	48	38
Girls provide more economic support than boys	F	0	0
	M	1	1
Boys are more emotionally rewarding than girls	F	11	15
	M	7	13
Girls are more emotionally rewarding than boys	F	0	2
	M	0	0
More boys are needed to insure against possible deaths of sons	F	0	1
	M	0	2
Tradition and custom require sons	F	13	20
	M	13	20
Other reasons	F	2	4
	M	10	10
No answer	F	10	22
	M	20	17
Total	F	100	100
	M	100	100

Source: N. Williamson (1976, p. 144), reprinted with permission of Sage Publications.

livebirths. In Run B, the independent variables specified the sex as well as number of offspring. The most important variables predicting subsequent fertility were the biological factors of birth interval, length of lactation, and age. Next were township and education, followed by number and sex of survivors, in Runs A and B, respectively. Although preference for sons still ranked lower, it was a better predictor than six other social and economic variables. Overall, this survey indicated that sex preferences, expressed in current offspring number and composition, exerted some pressure on fertility.

Results such as these led national governments and private organizations interested in population planning to address the issue of son preference. In the 1970s, Singapore utilized a poster of a young girl and boy with the motto "Boy or Girl, Two Is Enough," to assist in lowering the country's fertility (N. Williamson 1978). Similarly, the Planned Parenthood Federation of South Korea from 1970 to 1974 adopted the motto "Daughter or Son Without Distinction – Stop at Two and Bring Them Up Well." In China, son preference is viewed as a lingering aspect of the male superiority ascribed to Confucian tradition, and is denounced throughout the media. Despite such efforts, the real eradication of son preference can come about only through social change designed to reverse what Caldwell (1976) termed the "intergenerational flow of wealth and services." If this flow runs from children, representing sources of income, labor, and old age assistance, to parents,

TABLE 7.15
Number of Subsequent Births Among Currently Married Women of Third Parity or Higher and with Third Birth at Least One Year Prior to the Interview

	Run	
Rank of Each Predictor	*A*	*B*
Elapsed reproductive interval since third birth	0.820	0.820
Mean length of lactation of all livebirths beginning with the third	0.156	0.154
Age	0.141	0.139
Township	0.078	0.077
Educational attainment	0.076	0.076
Number and sex of survivors of the first three livebirths at one year following the mother's third livebirth	–	0.062
Number of survivors of the first three livebirths at one year following the mother's third livebirth	0.046	–
Preference for sons	0.040	0.039
Husband's income	0.032	0.032
Educational aspirations for nephew	0.031	0.030
Perception of child survival	0.028	0.029
Labor force status	0.027	0.028
Husband's occupation	0.027	0.027
Birth control knowledge	0.006	0.005

Number of cases, 3,898; mean, 2.729; standard deviation, 2.261.

Source: Reprinted by permission of the publisher from *Population and Development in Southeast Asia*, edited by Jan F. Kanter and Lee McCaffrey (Lexington, MA: Lexington Books, D. C. Heath and Co., copyright 1975, D. C. Heath and Co.).

then large families will remain a logical strategy for survival. Since most of the world's societies are patrilineal, it is likely that males will remain the preferred choice of offspring. Only by reversing this flow will small families be the norm and the third stage of the demographic transition be realized.

The recent radical decline of fertility in China (Aird 1981) provides a good example of how son preference and a child-to-parent flow of wealth go hand in hand. Observing the slow progress of family planning in the rural areas of China in 1970, Chairman Mao Tse-tung observed:

> In the countryside, a woman still wanted to have a boy child. If the first and second were girls, she would make another try, if the third one came and was still a girl, the mother would try again. Pretty soon there would be nine of them, the mother 45 or so, and she would finally decide to leave it at that. (Katugiri and Terao 1972, p. 2)

To combat this problem, the government introduced a generous retirement pension for urban industrial sections, coupled with the "five guarantees" – food, clothing, shelter, medical care, and burial – for childless old couples in rural communes. "All of this has resulted in a highly equitable income distribution pattern, and helps reduce the need for sons as old age security" (Chen 1974, p. 14). Other developing countries, in contrast to the Chinese example, have adopted a more laissez-faire approach to son preference, hoping that economic and social changes concomitant with modernization and industrialization will act to limit son preference. In the case of Taiwan, these changes have not overcome the long-standing preference for sons, with Coombs and Sun (1978) noting no significant changes in family composition preferences in spite of very dramatic and rapid modernization.

INTEGRATION OF FERTILITY AND MORTALITY: A COMPUTER SIMULATION APPROACH

Computer Simulation

Thus far, we have treated fertility and mortality separately. In the following section, an attempt to integrate them is made through computer simulation, an experimental analytical tool that anthropologists have successfully employed since the 1960s [for examples see MacCluer

(1973), Dyke and MacCluer (1974), Wachter et al. (1978), and Hammel (1980)]. The great strength of simulations is that they allow for the exploration of complicated biological and/or social systems, the mechanisms and interactions of which otherwise would be difficult, if not impossible, to study. As the name implies, simulations model or "simulate" real situations by utilizing specific input parameters to generate possible scenarios; they tell the outcome of specified processes or rates. They are very much like model populations or summary rates mentioned earlier (for example, the net reproductive rate), with the added feature of dynamism: Computer simulations allow processes to interact with each other and to change over time.

Simulations may be either prospective or retrospective. In the former, populations may be projected into the future to examine changes in size and composition. Retrospective simulations may reconstruct population history while simultaneously testing the internal consistency of the input parameters. A further distinction is that simulation may be either deterministic, stochastic, or a combination of the two. In the first, the simulation is the result of an algebraic equation or mathematical statement that assigns invariant values to the input parameters. By contrast, stochastic simulations incorporate the element of chance fluctuations, or stochasticity – so important in the study of small populations – into their basic programs. Input data are treated as a probability statement, so that runs with identical input may yield nonidentical results. Stochasticity is usually incorporated into the programs by the generation of random numbers in relation to age- and sex-specific input variables. To quote an example from MacCluer (1973, p. 221), a stochastic simulation may be programmed to generate a random number R and compare it with an age- and sex-specific probability of dying, D. If $R \leq D$, the simulated individual dies, or if $R \geq D$, the "person" survives to the next age interval. Such techniques are frequently termed "Monte Carlo," likening the generation of random numbers to an elaborate roulette wheel.

Simulations may be further distinguished by whether the entire study population, or only one individual, is the basis for decision making. If the former, then the program is a macrosimulation, or macromodel. Inversely, if age- and sex-specific decisions are made individually for each member of a start population, the program is a microsimulation or micromodel. In the following sections, the usefulness of computer simulation to demography is examined with specific regard to the problems of human infanticide, son preference, and sex preselection of offspring.

Systematic Female Infanticide

Infanticide, the killing of infants either through overt actions or the "benign neglect" described earlier, conjures up images of savage societies. In reality, infanticide has been practiced in almost all the world's societies. The reasons for infanticide are varied, with examples including spacing childbirths to ensure proper nutrition for living infants, regulating future adult sex ratios, eliminating infants with congenital defects, eliminating multiple births, either out of superstition or to ensure the survival of one of the infants, and eliminating motherless and/or illegitimate births (L. Williamson 1978). While infanticide is not an indiscriminate practice, it has traditionally discriminated against females.

Although it is accepted that infanticide has been practiced in diverse societies, the question of how much female infanticide a population can sustain without facing the threat of extinction has long remained unsolved. A case in point is female infanticide in Arctic Inuit (Eskimo) populations. Here ethnographers commonly reported systematic female infanticide, with Inuit exhibiting strong son preferences related to the male role as hunters. Females were viewed as economic burdens, and were allegedly killed in the belief that the time spent suckling them would delay the mother's next conception, which might result in a male offspring. Despite the large literature on female infanticide in Inuit populations, this phenomenon was observed directly only once. Far more common was the ethnographic practice of ascribing infanticide from census data. For example, one study of Canadian Arctic Inuits reported that of a total of 116 births, 38 allegedly ended in female infanticide. Assuming an equal sex ratio at birth, this was interpreted as representing a female infanticide rate of 66 percent (38 of 58).

To test whether this high rate of infanticide would threaten the existence of a small, closed population similar to historic Inuit, Schrire and Steiger (1974) constructed a simulation model. Theirs is a stochastic, or Monte Carlo, model, in which no migration is allowed to occur to the initial population of 500. Age-specific fertility levels were constructed to sum to a total fertility rate of 7.2, closely matching earlier ethnographic reports of Inuit fertility. Likewise, age-specific mortality rates mirror those derived from historic records, depicting a life expectancy at birth of about 40 years. The model generates random numbers to determine if liveborn infants will live or be subjected to infanticide, with rates of infanticide adjusted to different levels on different runs.

Table 7.16 presents the results of this model, simulated for 500 years at different levels of female infanticide. The initial start population shown here is divided between adults and children as recorded commonly by early ethnographers, though more precise age categories were utilized in the actual model. Although random fluctuations make the population larger at some points, the picture for all levels of infanticide points to population extinction. This is shown in Figure 7.13, depicting fluctuations in population composition and size for infanticide rates of 10, 15, and 20 percent. These show that even at a 10 percent female infanticide rate, the population would be heading for extinction.

Based on these results, Schrire and Steiger reached several basic conclusions. The first was that an effective upper limit of 8 percent exists for systematic female infanticide. Therefore, they viewed female infanticide not as a meaningful cultural practice intended as a means of population and economic control, but rather as a response to short-lived periods of environmental stress. In addition, the authors expressed the belief that the commonly cited preponderance of males among juvenile children for Inuit societies, together with a preponderance of females among adults, may reflect the observers' consistent overestimation of the age of juvenile females. This could have been due to their younger age at marriage, if marriage was used as a criterion for the division between juveniles and adults.

This model was criticized by Chapman (1980), who held that Schrire and Steiger neglected one important facet of infanticide:

> All women in their hypothetical Eskimo population were subject to the same fertility rates, regardless of whether their previous child had been killed at birth or allowed to live. Evidence cited below, however, indicates that the cessation of lactation following infanticide would significantly decrease the expected interval before the next pregnancy. Women whose previous infants had been killed at birth would thus be more fertile than women whose children had lived. (P. 318)

The already noted relationship between lactation and postpartum amenorrhea could be particularly strong in a population like the Inuit, which features long lactation periods. Thus, the death of a still-nursing infant might shorten the period of postpartum amenorrhea. Chapman modeled this relationship by using previously derived equations (Ginsberg 1973) relating the effect of prolonged breastfeeding to no breastfeeding, given as

TABLE 7.16
Results of Various Infanticide Rates for a Hypothetical Population

	Time (years)					
Rate	*0*	*100*	*200*	*300*	*400*	*500*
10 percent						
B	79	90	77	60	39	43
G	79	68	54	40	37	39
M	204	224	167	136	112	91
F	204	201	153	117	91	92
15 percent						
B	79	62	50	53	35	30
G	79	57	40	44	29	25
M	204	196	148	119	81	82
F	204	165	125	113	88	77
20 percent						
B	79	48	29	20	10	12
G	79	33	16	11	9	17
M	204	134	70	42	26	33
F	204	89	54	33	31	37

B, number of boys (0-14 years); G, number of girls (0-14 years); M, number of males; F, number of females.

Source: Schrire and Steiger (1974, p. 174).

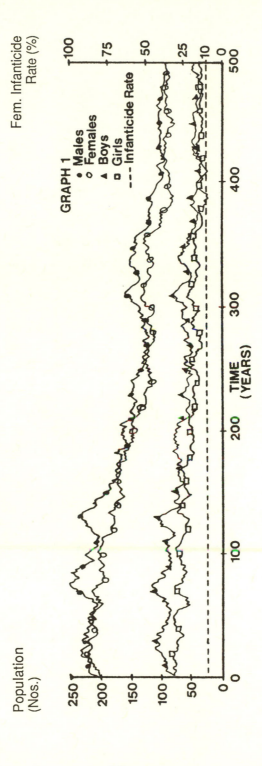

Figure 7.13A. Variations in population size and composition, under 10 percent rate of female infanticide. [Redrawn from Shrire and Steiger (1974, pp. 182-83) and used with permission.]

271

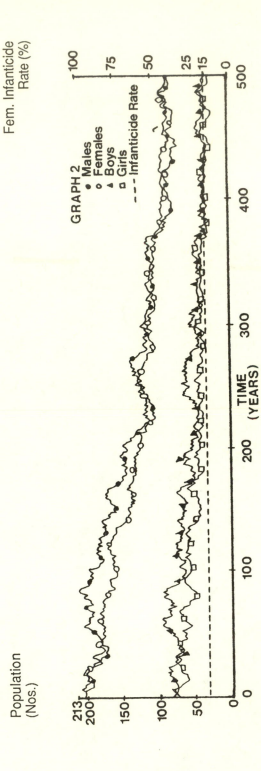

Figure 7.13B. Variations in population size and composition, under 15 percent rate of female infanticide. [Redrawn from Shrire and Steiger (1974, pp. 182-83) and used with permission.]

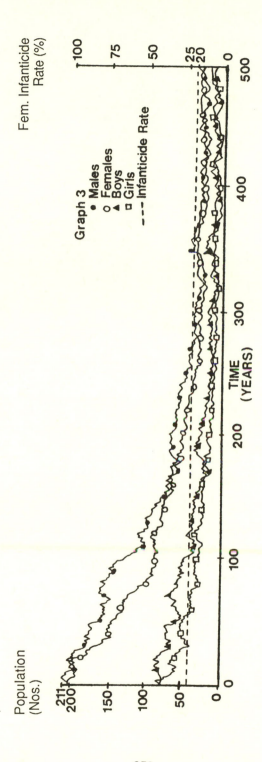

Figure 7.13C. Variations in population size and composition, under 20 percent rate of female infanticide. [Redrawn from Shrire and Steiger (1974, pp. 182-83) and used with permission.]

$$I^* = G + 1.2 + A + T \tag{8}$$

$$I = G + 1.2 + 5.5A + T, \tag{9}$$

where I^* is the expected birth interval in months under conditions of no nursing (that is, following infant mortality) for women of age j, G is the period of gestation, A is the anovulatory period, and T is the waiting time until conception, given the resumption of ovulation for a woman of age j. These equations may be simplified by substituting known estimates of G and A, namely, 9 months for G and, based on a survey of nonindustrial populations, 4 to 5 months for A. For $A = 4.5$ months, the equations would read

$$I^* = 14.70 + T \tag{10}$$

$$I = 34.95 + T. \tag{11}$$

Therefore, prolonged or full nursing in the absence of infant mortality would extend the predicted birth interval by the amount

$$I = I^* = 20.25. \tag{12}$$

The effect that this difference would have in total fertility is found by comparing the summed fertility of women who practiced infanticide versus those who did not. For the latter group, the total fertility rate was set at 7.66. For the former, the total fertility rate was 15.69, over twice as high. Other assumptions in this model included constant fertility and mortality rates (with the latter identical to the Schrire and Steiger simulations), no in- or out-migration, and a start population of 100 males and 100 females. Table 7.17 presents the mean and range values of survivors for ten stochastic replications. As with the Schrire and Steiger model, the age-sex composition is presented in terms of boys, girls, men, and women. Unlike the previous model, the results of these simulations suggest that populations could survive with infanticide even up to 30 percent. Only under conditions of 40 percent systematic female infanticide is the population threatened with extinction, according to the Chapman model.

The paradox is that up to a certain point, the effects of differential mortality in the form of female infanticide are compensated for by increased fertility. Contrary to the Schrire and Steiger model, Chapman's adjusted simulations point to the possibility of systematic female infanticide as an effective means of long-term population control, even for small hunting-gathering populations such as the historic Inuit. As Chapman notes, this practice may not have been consciously viewed as a means of population control. Instead, it may have constituted what we earlier called "unconscious rationality," behavior beneficial to a population without the individual members being cognizant of its benefits.

The directly contrasting results of the two simulations exemplify the strengths and weaknesses of computer simulation methodology. Simulations are only as valid as the input parameters that lie at their base. In this case, adjustment of only one input variable – the length of amenorrhea due to lactation – spelled the difference between population extinction and survival. The fact that we as programmers can easily and effectively alter the outcome of simulations should always be kept in mind when interpreting the results of simulation exercises. Yet this very manipulative nature of simulation methodology also proves to be its strong point. In the above example, the basic research design could be, and was, altered to better reflect observed biological parameters. The result was that the model became more "real."

Note, though, that neither research design conclusively proved that the Arctic Inuit ever practiced systematic female infanticide. That was never the question. The question in point was whether small, reproductively isolated populations, such as the historic Inuit, could sustain high levels of female infanticide without facing the threat of population extinction. The ethnographic record, as we saw, cannot answer the question. Yet this paucity of hard data has not stopped ethnographers from postulating that systematic female infanticide was widely practiced among Inuit populations. Perhaps this is the sort of unusual, gruesome cultural practice, such as reports of cannibalism, that early ethnographers seized on as evidence that other cultures were indeed "primitive." Once established in the ethnographic literature, female infanticide, or more precisely the specter of it, proved difficult to displace. Any deviation from the expected tertiary sex ratio among Arctic native populations was routinely ascribed to the practice of female infanticide, even if the resultant quantification of these deviations led to estimates of female infanticide rates of over 60 percent.

Although differing in their estimates of the upper limit of infanticide, both simulations recognize that rates of 60 percent or greater are well beyond the upper limit of infanticide compatible with population survival.

TABLE 7.17
Mean and Range (in Parentheses) Numbers of Survivors for Ten Replications of Simulated
Population Growth

Infanticide Rate	Age-Sex Group	Elapsed Time (years)					
		0	100	200	300	400	500
20 percent	Boys	32	59.9 (36-89)	86.4 (60-118)	152.4 (99-220)	250.3 (143-435)	453.9 (222-799)
	Men	68	105.9 (85-122)	148.0 (99-205)	257.2 (174-375)	404.5 (218-664)	736.5 (410-1257)
	Girls	32	46.7 (34-60)	66.8 (41-96)	115.6 (67-172)	195.0 (116-337)	342.4 (205-640)
	Women	68	80.4 (62-103)	114.2 (89-156)	188.8 (116-292)	326.9 (192-537)	570.4 (320-963)
30 percent	Boys	32	59.0 (38-89)	63.8 (37-96)	66.7 (14-107)	80.7 (35-134)	80.5 (41-136)
	Men	68	99.9 (67-150)	117.0 (67-175)	135.7 (38-198)	144.7 (64-240)	153.0 (81-233)
	Girls	32	37.6 (23-63)	41.0 (28-55)	47.0 (20-77)	51.8 (29-79)	50.2 (33-95)
	Women	68	70.4 (51-110)	74.4 (37-102)	84.2 (30-135)	100.8 (46-164)	101.2 (53-161)

40 percent						
Boys	32	32.8 (12-48)	25.3 (8-68)	18.8 (3-43)	13.6 (3-39)	13.0 (0-30)
Men	68	75.9 (45-98)	57.9 (22-69)	39.7 (6-86)	26.5 (1-70)	26.8 (0-44)
Girls	32	20.3 (12-29)	16.1 (1-44)	11.7 (1-33)	8.7 (0-18)	9.6 (0-22)
Women	68	41.7 (22-54)	30.7 (7-57)	23.2 (3-54)	16.1 (3-29)	19.3 (0-37)

Source: Chapman (1980, p. 323).

Herein lies the power of computer simulations: the ability to test hypotheses by modeling the interaction of random and nonrandom events and processes. While these models do not fully reflect the richness and complexity of real world situations, they can make us examine basic premises in the anthropological literature.

This is not to say that simulations offer the only means of reexamining old concepts and exploring new ones. Chagnon et al.'s reexamination (1979) of infanticide rates and causes among the Yanomamo Indians of Brazil is a good case in point of an empirical, nonsimulation exploration of this subject. In this careful, honest analysis, Chagnon and colleagues examined Yanomamo demographic data previously thought to support the notion of high female infanticide rates. Their analysis revealed that in Yanomamo culture, infanticide, while present, is related to child and maternal health status, marital relationships, food resources, and other specific factors, rather than to a preference for male children. Data indicated that infanticide was not sex specific, and did not vary according to the status of the parents, as the model predicted.

Son Preference and Son Survivorship Motivation

Son survivorship motivation describes a logical consequence of son preference. Unlike infanticide, where unwanted female babies are killed, son survivorship motivation has as its goal the continued survival of male offspring. As found throughout traditional societies, this behavior recognizes two important biocultural factors. The first is the already described importance of males in traditional culture; the second is the recognition that under conditions of high mortality, male offspring may not survive to fulfill any of these roles.

Recognition of these factors may lead parents to adopt fertility plans designed to maximize the chances of male offspring survival. Two specific models of these are those termed "replacement strategy" and "insurance (hoarding) strategy" (Preston 1978). In the former, parents intend to have x number of offspring alive at the end of their reproductive period. The insurance or hoarding strategy recognizes that some proportion of sons may die after the parents' reproductive period, making replacement impossible. Therefore, the parents attempt to bear $x + n$ children, as insurance against son loss.

Son survivorship motivation probably has a long history, as reflected in folk sayings and proverbs. For example, "One son is no son, two sons are an undependable son, and only three sons can be counted as a real son," reads a Chinese proverb. More blunt is an Iranian saying: "The first two are for the crows" (Harrison 1981, p. 220).

Today the importance of son survivorship motivation lies in its relation to falling mortality levels in traditional societies where this behavior is found. In these circumstances, parents may continue to plan their families in traditional ways, ignoring the recent phenomenon of declining mortality pressures. The result is accelerated population growth.

To explore the possible consequences of such a scenario, Venkatacharya (1978) examined son survivorship motivation through a Monte Carlo simulation model featuring different behavioral rules and varied mortality and fertility levels. He employed Coale and Demeny (1966) model life tables, West series, which represent different life expectancies at birth. Table 7.18 presents the basic parameters of these mortality schedules. Fertility parameters provided three levels of total fertility. The first generated total fertility levels close to recent Indian national levels (total fertility rate of 6.0), while the second and third yielded on average two and four additional births, respectively, per simulated marriages spanning the female reproductive period. In Figure 7.14, which shows the effect of mortality improvement in combination with several fertility levels, note the large percentage increase in both living children and living sons caused by stable fertility levels and declining mortality pressures.

Two rules for son survivorship were added to this basic model. In the first, a couple is assumed to continue childbearing until one son reaches the age of 10. Under the next set of rules, a couple ceases childbearing after the birth of a second or third son, provided a previous son is alive. Failing to meet these criteria, the couple continues childbearing, stopping only if, after the birth of a fourth son, both the third and fourth sons survive for a minimum of 10 years. Failing this, the couple continues to procreate until the end of the female reproductive period. Table 7.19 shows the results for the first of these variations under different mortality regimens. Although far lower than the previous set of runs without son survivorship rules, the average number of sons per children increases with reduced mortality. Venkatacharya solves this apparent puzzle by noting that although fertility is terminated once a son reaches 10, this denotes a period of at least 10 years of undisturbed

Number living

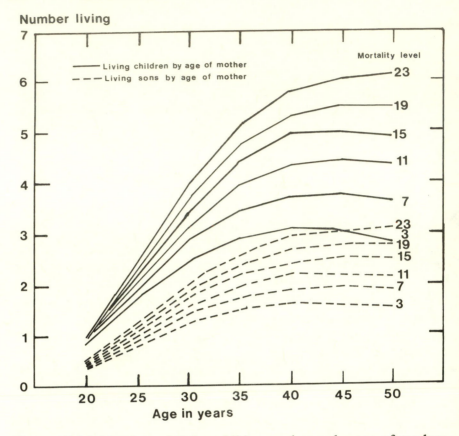

Figure 7.14. Number of living children and sons by age of mother, different mortality levels, total fertility rate = 6.0 [After Venkatacharya (1978, p. 245) and used with permission.]

fertility. As Table 7.20 shows, the percentage increase in the mean number of living sons and children (as a result of mortality improvement) is substantial. The identical picture of an increased burden of children under improving mortality is evident for the second set of rules, where mortality improvement from level 11 to 23 is accompanied by a 33.3 percent increase in the number of living children.

Table 7.21 presents essential demographic rates for the three models: (1) no son survivorship motivation, (2) fertility cessation when one son reaches age 10, and (3) subsequent fertility dependent on survivorship of two previous sons. While the "stopping rules" associated with each fertility strategy cause a decline in overall fertility levels, they do not avert

TABLE 7.18
Indexes of Mortality Input, Coale and Demeny (1966) West Series

	Level of Mortality					
Life expectancy	3	7	11	15	19	23
Males (^oe_o)	22.85	32.48	42.12	51.83	61.23	71.19
Females (^oe_o)	25.00	35.00	45.00	55.00	65.00	75.00
Life Table Infant Mortality (1,000 q_o) by Level						
Males	351.3	248.2	171.7	111.4	62.9	21.4
Females	305.5	213.9	146.1	93.4	49.9	15.2
Life Table Childhood Mortality (1,000 q_1) by Level						
Males	214.4	145.5	94.4	51.1	21.0	3.4
Females	215.5	145.6	93.7	50.5	19.0	2.4

Source: Venkatacharya (1978, p. 242).

TABLE 7.19
Effect of Mortality Improvement on Number of Living
Children and Sons for Women in Surviving Marriages at Age
50 Under Three Different Fertility Levels

	Total Fertility		
	10.00	8.00	6.00
Mortality Level [Coale-Demeny (1966) Designation]			
11			
Living sons	3.53	3.02	2.09
Living children	7.39	6.08	4.26
23			
Living sons	5.22	4.32	3.02
Living children	10.21	8.47	6.03
Percentage Increase			
Living sons	48	43	45
Living children	38	39	42

Source: Venkatacharya (1978, p. 245).

TABLE 7.20
Mean Number of Living Children and Sons of Women Age
50 Under Various Mortality and Fertility Regimens in Which
Procreation Is Assumed to Stop When One Son Reaches Age
10

	Total Fertility		
	10.00	8.00	6.00
Mortality Level			
11			
Living sons	1.978	2.121	1.654
Living children	3.709	4.351	3.186
23			
Living sons	2.411	2.804	2.261
Living children	4.840	5.610	4.428
Percentage Increase			
Living sons	22	32	37
Living children	31	29	39

Source: Venkatacharya (1978, p. 249).

TABLE 7.21
Intrinsic Growth Rate, Birth Rate, Death Rate, and Other Measures Under Various Input Combinations

(per 1,000)

Input Combination	Mortality Level	Growth Rate	Birth Rate	Death Rate	Total Fertility Rate(TFR)	Net Reproductive Rate
No son survivor motivation, TFR = 6.0	3	6.63	50.28	43.65	6.08	1.19
	7	17.90	52.87	34.96	6.08	1.62
	11	25.70	53.89	28.19	6.08	2.00
	15	31.63	54.32	22.70	6.08	2.35
	19	36.14	54.34	18.21	6.08	2.65
	23	39.18	53.88	14.70	6.08	2.89
Fertility ends as soon as a son lives to 10 years of age, TFR = 6.0	3	1.57	42.29	40.73	5.13	1.04
	7	12.77	45.04	32.27	5.03	1.37
	11	20.34	46.07	25.73	4.95	1.66
	15	26.16	46.68	20.52	4.87	1.91
	19	30.39	46.60	16.21	4.78	2.10
	23	32.97	45.71	12.74	4.70	2.24
Fertility ends as the present and two previous sons are living, TFR = 6.0	3	-5.94	32.04	37.98	4.21	0.86
	7	5.37	34.94	29.56	4.15	1.14
	11	12.10	35.16	23.06	3.99	1.34
	15	17.49	35.53	18.04	3.89	1.52
	19	20.63	34.45	13.82	3.72	1.64
	23	23.08	33.65	10.57	3.64	1.73

Source: Venkatacharya (1978, p. 252).

a progressively accelerated rate of growth with each improved level of mortality.

Taken together, the simulations demonstrate that improvements in mortality may increase family dependency burdens, population growth rates, and net reproductive rates, when son survivorship fertility strategies are in place. If the global reduction of mortality cannot overcome son survivorship motivation along with its concomitant problem of accelerated population growth, then will fertility levels remain high for those populations exhibiting strong son preference rule? Venkatacharya's simulations would appear to answer this question in the affirmative.

Sex Preselection

One potential alternative to high fertility rates associated with son survivorship motivation is the predetermination of offspring sex. This idea is not as futuristic as it may sound initially. Research into the predetermination of human sex dates to the 1950s, and at present at least three approaches exist. As reviewed by Williamson (1978) these are (1) timing of sexual intercourse, (2) separation of male- and female-bearing sperm followed by artificial insemination, and (3) selective abortion after fetal sex determination.

The first approach has received the most publicity. In 1970 the American gynecologist Landrum Shettles suggested that boys would be the predominant offspring when coitus was close to ovulation. The basis of this suggestion was that sperm carrying the male Y chromosome are faster but shorter lived than their female counterparts. Copulation at ovulation presented an opportunity when the cervical mucus would favor easy penetration, and hence favored the Y-bearing sperm. A similar approach was then proposed by Guerrero (1975), who suggested a rhythm method based on changes in the basal body temperature associated with ovulation. Figure 7.15 presents the differences in timing of intercourse that purport to preselect offspring sex, as suggested by the two researchers. At present, conflicting reports concerning the validity of both techniques abound (see Chapter 6). The researchers each claim success rates of over 80 percent, while independent studies on the techniques most often note that the great majority of women tested did not correctly follow the timing instructions, thereby nullifying results. For example, only 6 percent of a German sample and at most 2 percent of a Singapore group were deemed to have followed the Shettles technique as instructed.

The strongest proponent of the second approach, sperm separation and artificial insemination, is the reproductive physiologist Ronald Ericsson. His technique centers on the separation of Y-bearing sperm via repeated filtering through different dilutions of human serum albumin, a protein found in human blood. According to Ericsson, the Y-bearing sperm have the greatest motility and move to the bottom of the solution. Repeating the method is reported to result in a solution containing up to 90 percent Y-bearing sperm (Ericsson et al. 1973). As in the case of the Shettles-Guerrero approaches, the final test of the Ericsson technique has not yet been made. Early results include three human infants conceived through artificial insemination: one girl, one boy, and one spontaneous abortion.

The third approach to sex preselection, that of selective abortions, is technologically feasible in the form of amniocentesis. With this technique, fluid from the amnion, the innermost membrane surrounding the fetus, is withdrawn by a hollow needle during the fourth month of pregnancy and tested for sex determination. The technique could facilitate late abortions if the "wrong sex" is discerned *in utero*. At present, however, amniocentesis is virtually restricted to the search for chromosomal abnormalities in the fetuses of older mothers or women with a familial history of genetic disease.

Despite a tradition of social scientists predicting the imminent arrival of readily available techniques for sex preselection, such is still not the case. The concept has retained its appeal for many, including some family planners who view it as a means of reducing high fertility levels caused in part by strong son preference. In support of this view, they cite the 1,000 women who immediately volunteered to test the Shettles technique in Singapore (Williamson 1978) and the first trials of a new Chinese method to determine fetal sex followed by selective abortions. This test resulted in a total of 30 abortions, 29 of which were female fetuses.

Possible demographic effects of sex preselection could be modeled via computer simulation if we imagine that an effective, inexpensive means of sex predetermination had filtered down to a grass-roots level. What, then, would be the overall effect on a small (village) population with traditionally strong son preference? To explore this question, the stochastic microsimulation AMBUSH (Howell 1979) was used. Two sets of simulations, each consisting of ten replicates modeling a 100-year period, were completed. Set 1 consisted of fertility parameters mirroring

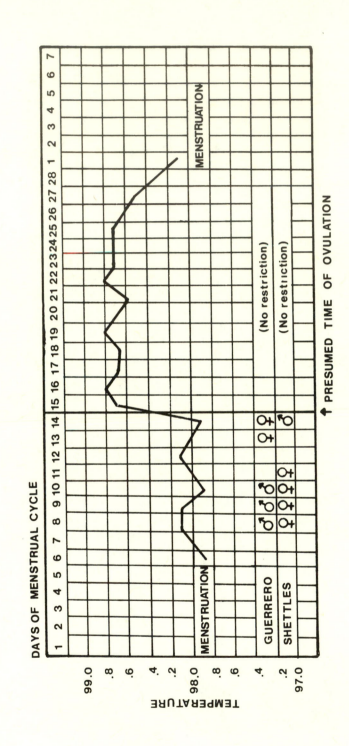

Figure 7.15. Comparison of recommended timing of intercourse for sex preselection: Guerrero versus Shettles. [Redrawn after N. Williamson (1978, p. 23) and used with permission.]

current Indian fertility levels (total fertility rate, 5.6) with the secondary sex ratio set at 105:100. For set 2, idealized sex ratios and family sizes given by married Indian women of childbearing age (Freedman and Coombs 1974) were utilized. In this report, the ideal mean number of children was 3.58, with the ideal number of sons 2.15, yielding an ideal sex ratio of 150:100. For both sets, mortality schedules were identical, representing the Coale and Demeny (1966) model life tables, West series, level 12 for females (e_0 = 47.5), and level 14 for males (e_0 = 49.6). The start population for both sets consisted of a village population of 500 composing an Indian tribal population previously analyzed by Roth et al. (1982).

Results of both simulation sets are shown in Table 7.22. Mean figures from the replicate runs demonstrate that the lower fertility levels of the set 2 simulations resulted in far slower population growth, as shown by the lower crude birth rate and mean population size for the entire 100-year period. The higher sex ratio also played a role in slowing down population growth. In these simulations, identical input variables determine the proportion of women and men who enter a marriage eligibility pool per year. Once in this pool, males search for females who are younger than themselves and who are not related through common ancestry. Eligibility in this mate pool continues until a marriage match is attained, or until an individual is deemed too old to remain a viable marriage choice. This last parameter is age 45 for females and 60 for males. Simulated persons removed from this pool are labeled and counted as "never married." In Table 7.22, the effect of high male sex bias is evident in the large number of males who fail to find a mate in the second set of simulations. This number is even more striking when one considers that far fewer males were born and entered the pool in this set than in that with a higher total fertility rate. The excess of males also results in an increase in the mean age at marriage and the age differential between spouses, factors that are due to the simulation rule of preference for older males in mate selection. The relative scarcity of females means that older, preferred males are the most successful in marriage matches.

Comparison of the two sets points to possible benefits of sex preselection in reducing population growth by the decrease in "excess" fertility intended to produce male offspring. However, this is not the full picture. One feature of AMBUSH is the program's ability to perform egocentric kinship counts by 10-year age intervals for different kinship categories. To determine the effect of the reduced fertility levels on son survivorship, AMBUSH calculated the percentage of fathers with at least

TABLE 7.22
Characteristics of Two Simulated Models of Differing Total Fertility Rates (TFRs) and Secondary Sex Ratios, Ten Replicate Runs per Simulation Set, 100 Years

Input Parameter	TFR = 5.6 105:100	TFR = 3.6 150:100
Crude birth rate	37	21
	(34-40)	(17-25)
Crude death rate	17	18
	(16-19)	(15-25)
Mean population size	1,387	629
	(1,287-1,475)	(571-673)
Females never married	28	23
	(20-53)	(16-31)
Males never married	23	194
	(0-76)	(131-240)
Age difference of spouse ($\male$)	4.9	6.9
	(3.9-6.1)	(6.6-7.2)
Mean age at marriage	21.6	28.6
	(21.2-22.3)	(27.8-29.7)

Values are means, with ranges in parentheses.

one living son for the entire 100-year simulation period. Figure 7.16 presents a comparison of the two simulation sets for this aspect of family composition. As can be seen, the idealized rates, despite the higher male sex ratios, yield lower percentages of fathers with living sons. This is particularly important for parents at older age intervals, for it is during this period that sons may constitute the sole source of support and old age assistance.

In addition to these short-term disadvantages, simulation of the idealized parameters for longer time periods indicates population instability and the threat of extinction. This is shown in Table 7.23, which records population sizes for five replicate simulations for a period of 400 years. As was the case with the Schrire and Steiger (1974) Inuit simulations, the populations initially increase in size, only to decline dramatically later. Unlike the Inuit model, this decline is caused not by an absolute scarcity of women in the childbearing years, but rather by a scarcity of these women relative to the number of eligible males. As time goes on, this scarcity will, of course, become an absolute one, as fewer women are born owing to the altered sex ratio.

Simulation of sex preselection leading to a male bias in the secondary sex ratio for small, closed populations suggests that alteration of the sex ratio may produce quite striking changes in population composition and demographic rates in a relatively short time, as well as harbor long-term effects. While preselection may reduce fertility levels that are inflated owing to son preference, simulations indicate that the reduction could not be as great as that modeled here (a 36 percent reduction in total fertility from 5.6 to 3.6) and still result in a comparable degree of sons able to care for their elderly parents. Not, that is, unless the sex ratio were increased even further in favor of males. Yet, as we have seen above, this causes a true dilemma, as the raising of the secondary sex ratio appears to initiate population decline and instability. Although sex

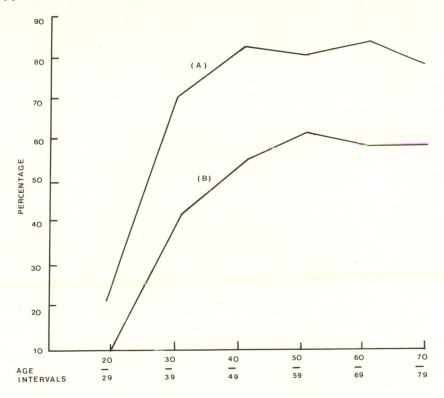

Figure 7.16. Percentage of fathers, by age group, having one or more living sons, as determined from 100-year simulation: (A), total fertility rate = 5.60; (B), total fertility rate = 3.59.

TABLE 7.23
Population Sizes of Five Replicate Simulations Representing
400 Years with Total Fertility Rate of 3.59 and Secondary
Sex Ratio of 150:100

Run Number	Years							
	50	100	150	200	250	300	350	400
1	721	635	500	430	376	328	225	196
2	685	667	591	511	367	343	298	261
3	681	645	575	531	466	375	346	318
4	647	626	649	621	509	418	420	363
5	665	635	602	537	468	432	401	350

preselection is still not feasible, these simulations suggest that the time to consider the questions of its possible ramifications in both biological and social terms is now.

SUMMARY

The major tenet of this chapter is that human population processes and structures respond dynamically to sex differences and to the values that societies place upon them. To explore this hypothesis, basic demographic methodology and a brief review of demographic history have been presented in the context of stable population and demographic transition theory.

Population sex differences, which are so often assumed to be invariant, exert large and quantifiable effects on other demographic parameters. We have seen this to be true from the early example of the calculation of the net reproductive rate through to the final problem of sex predetermination and its possible consequences for future populations. We have also observed that these sex differences are not "givens," but rather that they can respond to changes in population size, technology, medicine, religious and/or marital rules, cultural ecology, and many additional biological and sociocultural variables. Rather than representing a static class of phenomena peripheral to demographic studies, the examples in this chapter point to sex differences as vital, dynamic components of human population structure.

Traditional demographic investigations stress biological at the expense of cultural variables, with the view that belief and value systems do not lend themselves to quantitative analysis. Examples and discussions in this chapter demonstrate that the latter view is not correct. We repeatedly saw that these factors, simply by being sex selective and specific, exhibit a biological effect on demographic rates.

By examining articulations between cultural and biological variables, we can observe that there is nothing mystical about their interaction. While terms such as "status" or "role" remain vague, we have seen mechanisms that clearly differentiate the sexes socially, with effects on the biological composition of human populations. Included here are the overt actions of systematic female infanticide, the more covert form of "benign neglect" found in cultures as diverse as historic Ireland and contemporary South Asian populations, the interrelated phenomena of son preference and son survivorship motivation, and the looming specter of sex preselection. That cultural variables and phenomena are capable of quantification is evident throughout the chapter, from the empirical analysis of anthropometry and food intake conducted by Chen et al. (1981) to the simulation exercise of son survivorship motivation by Venkatacharya (1978). Furthermore, that these social practices can actually overcome or reverse inherent biological properties is shown in the case of reversed sexual mortality differentials for historic Ireland (Kennedy 1973) and modern South Asian populations (El-Badry 1969; Miller 1981), despite the evidence showing that females possess innate physiological and biological advantages that usually manifest themselves in longer average female longevity relative to males.

This chapter also has noted topics that are receiving continuous study and that have not been resolved: the natural regulation of the primary sex ratio; the relative effect of lactation versus nutrition on fertility levels; the relevance of demographic transition theory to the less-developed nations of the world today; the effect of female labor participation on subsequent fertility; the absolute amount of systematic female infanticide a small, endogamous population can sustain without fear of extinction; and the effectiveness of already developed techniques of sex preselection. All of these topics represent fertile ground for future research.

Finally, I want to note two important research topics that this chapter has not reviewed: the literature on the costs and benefits of children in different societies (see Nag 1981) and the influence of different family structures and mating systems on fertility (see Shain and Jennings 1980). These demographic topics, closely linked to sexual differences, remind us that there is still much to be done in documenting significant sexual differentials as well as delineating their biological and sociocultural causes. The onus is on us to uncover and analyze these differences in relation to human demography and population structure.

ACKNOWLEDGMENTS

I want to thank Brian Muir and the Oregon State University Department of Anthropology for preparing the figures for my chapter.

REFERENCES

Acsadi, G. Y., and J. Nemeskeri. 1970. *History of Human Life Span and Mortality*. Budapest: Ackademiai Kiado.

Aird, J. 1981. "Fertility Decline in China." In *Fertility Decline in the Less Developed Countries*, edited by N. Eberstadt, pp. 119-28. New York: Praeger.

Angel, J. 1969. "Paleodemography and Evolution." *American Journal of Physical Anthropology*, 31:343-53.

___. 1975. "Paleoecology, Paleodemography, and Health." In *Population Ecology and Social Evolution*, edited by S. Polgar, pp. 167-90. The Hague: Mouton.

Barclay, G. 1958. *Techniques of Population Analysis*. New York: Wiley.

Barclay, G., A. Coale, M. Stoto, and T. J. Trussell. 1976. "A Reassessment of the Demography of Traditional Rural China." *Population Index*, 42:606-35.

Bernds, W., and D. Baresh. 1979. "Early Termination of Parental Investment in Mammals, Including Humans." In *Evolutionary Biology and Human Social Behavior*, edited by N. Chagnon and W. Irons, pp. 487-505. North Scituate, MA: Duxbury Press.

Binford, L. 1968. "Post-Pleistocene Adaptations." In *New Perspectives in Archaeology*, edited by S. Binford and L. Binford, pp. 313-41. Chicago: Aldine.

Bocquet-Appel, J. P., and C. Masset. 1982. "Farewell to Paleodemography." *Journal of Human Evolution*, 11:321-34.

Bogue, D. 1969. *Principles of Demography*. New York: Wiley.

Boserup, E. 1965. *The Conditions of Agricultural Growth*. Chicago: Aldine.

Brace, C. L. 1964. "A Non-racial Approach Towards the Understanding of Human Diversity." In *The Concept of Race*, edited by A. Montague, pp. 103-52. New York: Collier Books.

Caldwell, J. 1976. "Toward a Restatement of Demographic Transition Theory." *Population and Development Review*, 1:321.

Cassidy, C. 1980. "Benign Neglect and Toddler Malnutrition." In *Social and Biological Predictors of Nutritional Status, Physical Growth, and Neurological Development*, edited by L. Greene and F. Johnston, pp. 109-42. New York: Academic Press.

Cernada, G. 1970. *Taiwan Family Planning Reader: How a Program Works.* Taiwan: Chinese Center for International Training in Family Planning.

Chagnon, N. 1977. *Yanomamo: The Fierce People*, 2nd ed. New York: Holt, Rinehart and Winston.

Chagnon, N., M. Flinn, and T. Melacon. 1979. "Sex-Ratio Variation Among the Yanomamo Indians." In *Evolutionary Biology and Human Social Behavior*, edited by N. Chagnon and W. Irons, pp. 290-320. North Scituate, MA: Duxbury Press.

Chapman, M. 1980. "Infanticide and Fertility Among Eskimos: A Computer Simulation." *American Journal of Physical Anthropology*, 53:317-27.

Chen, L., E. Huq, and S. D'Souza. 1981. "Sex Bias in the Family Allocation of Food and Health Care in Rural Bangladesh." *Population and Development Review*, 7:55-70.

Chen, P. C. 1974. "The 'Planned Birth' Program of the People's Republic of China, with a Brief Analysis of Its Transportability." Paper presented at the Southeast Asian Development Advisory Group of the Asia Society, Indonesia.

Coale, A. 1965. *Factors Associated with the Development of Low Fertility: An Historical Survey.* Belgrade: United Nations World Population Conference Paper, WPC/WP/94.

Coale, A., and P. Demeny. 1966. *Regional Model Life Tables and Stable Populations.* Princeton, NJ: Princeton University Press.

Cohen, M. 1977. *The Food Crisis in Prehistory.* New Haven, CT: Yale University Press.

Committee on Population and Demography. 1981. *Estimation of Recent Trends in Fertility and Mortality in Bangladesh.* Washington, D.C.: National Academy Press.

Coombs, L., C. Coombs, and G. McClelland. 1975. "Sex Preference Scales for Number and Sex of Children." *Population Studies*, 29:273-98.

Coombs, L., and T. H. Sun. 1978. "Family Composition Preferences in a Developing Culture: The Case of Taiwan, 1973." *Population Studies*, 32:43-64.

Cowgill, U., and G. Hutchinson. 1963. "Sex-Ratio in Childhood and the Depopulation of the Peten, Guatemala." *Human Biology*, 35:90-103.

Dandekar, K. 1959. *Demographic Survey of Six Rural Communities.* Bombay: Gokhale Institute of Politics and Economics.

Das Gupta, P. 1971. "Estimation of Demographic Measures for India, 1881-1961, Based on Census Age Distributions." *Population Studies*, 25:395-414.

DeJong, G. 1972. "Patterns of Human Fertility and Mortality." In *The Structure of Human Populations*, edited by G. Harrison and A. Boyce, pp. 32-56. London: Clarendon.

Dyke, B., and J. MacCluer. 1974. *Computer Simulation in Human Population Studies.* New York: Academic Press.

Dyke, B., and W. Morrill. 1980. *Genealogical Demography*. New York: Academic Press.

Eaton, J., and A. Mayer. 1953. "The Social Biology of Very High Fertility Among the Hutterites." *Human Biology*, 25:246-64.

Eberstadt, N. 1981. "Recent Declines in Fertility in Less Developed Countries and What Population Planners May Learn from Them." In *Fertility Decline in the Less Developed Countries*, edited by N. Eberstadt, pp. 29-71. New York: Praeger.

El-Badry, M. 1969. "Higher Female than Male Mortality in Some Countries of South Asia: A Digest." *Journal of the American Statistical Association*, 1234-44.

Epstein, F. 1965. "The Epidemiology of Coronary Heart Disease: A Review." *Journal of Chronic Diseases*, 18:735-74.

Ericsson, R., C. Longevin, and M. Nishino. 1973. "Isolation of Fractions Rich in Human Y Sperm." *Nature*, 246:421.

Ferry, B. 1981. "The Senegalese Surveys." In *Child Spacing in Tropical Africa: Tradition and Change*, edited by H. Page and R. Lesthaeghe, pp. 265-74. London: Academic Press.

Freedman, R., and L. Coombs. 1974. *Cross-Cultural Comparisons: Data on Two Factors in Fertility Behavior*. New York: Population Council.

Freedman, R., and J. Takeshita. 1969. *Family Planning in Taiwan: An Experiment in Social Change*. Princeton, NJ: Princeton University Press.

Frisch, R. 1975. "Demographic Implications of the Biological Determinants of Female Fecundity." *Social Biology*, 22:17.

Frisch, R. 1978. "Nutrition, Fatness and Fertility: The Effect of Food Intake on Reproductive Ability." In *Nutrition and Human Reproduction*, edited by W. Mosley, pp. 91-122. New York: Plenum Press.

Frisch, R., and J. McArthur. 1974. "Menstrual Cycles: Fatness as a Determinant of Minimum Weight for Height Necessary for Their Maintenance or Onset." *Science*, 185:949.

Ginsberg, R. 1973. "The Effect of Lactation on the Length of the Post-Partum Anovulatory Period: An Application of a Bivariate Stochastic Model." *Theoretical Population Biology*, 4:276-99.

Glass, D. 1969. "Fertility Trends in Europe Since the Second World War." In *Fertility and Family Planning: A World View*, edited by S. Behrman, L. Corsa Jr., and R. Freedman, pp. 25-74. Ann Arbor: University of Michigan Press.

Greenough, P. 1982. *Prosperity and Misery in Modern India: The Bengal Famine of 1943-44*. Oxford: Oxford University Press.

Guerrero, R. 1975. "Type and Time of Insemination Within the Menstrual Cycle and the Human Sex Ratio." *Studies in Family Planning*, 6:367-71.

Hall, R. 1970. *Population Biology of the Russian Old Believers of Marion County, Oregon*. Ann Arbor, MI: University Microfilms.

Hall, R. 1972. "The Demographic Transition: Stage Four." *Current Anthropology*, 13:211-15.

Hamilton, J. 1948. "The Role of Testicular Secretions as Indicated by the Effects of Castration in Man and by Studies of Pathological Conditions and the Short

Lifespan Associated with Maleness." *Recent Progress in Hormone Research*, 3:257-324.

Hammel, E. 1980. "Experimental History." *Journal of Anthropological Research*, 36:274-91.

Harpending, H., and L. Wandsnider. 1982. "Population Structures of Ghanzi and Ngamiland !Kung." In *Current Developments in Anthropological Genetics*, edited by M. Crawford and J. Meilke, pp. 29-50. New York: Plenum Press.

Harrison, P. 1981. *Inside the Third World*. Middlesex: Penguin Press.

Hassan, F. 1975. "Determinants of the Size, Density and Growth Rates of Hunting-Gathering Populations." In *Human Population, Ecology, and Social Evolution*, edited by S. Polgar, pp. 27-52. The Hague: Mouton.

Hassan, F. 1978. "Demographic Archaeology." In *Advances in Archaeological Method and Theory, Vol. I*, edited by M. Schiffer, pp. 49-103. New York: Academic Press.

Hassan, F. 1981. *Demographic Archaeology*. New York: Academic Press.

Heer, D., and H. Y. Wu. 1975. "The Effect of Infant and Child Mortality and Preference for Sons upon Fertility and Family Planning Behavior and Attitudes in Taiwan." In *Population and Development in Southeast Asia*, edited by J. Kantner and L. McCaffrey, pp. 253-79. Lexington, MA: Lexington Books.

Henry, L. 1961. "Some Data on Natural Fertility." *Eugenics Quarterly*, 8:81-91.

Henry, L. 1965. "French Statistical Research in Natural Fertility." In *Public Health and Population Change*, edited by M. Sheps and J. Ridley, pp. 333-50. Pittsburgh: University of Pittsburgh Press.

Hern, W. 1977. "High Fertility in a Peruvian Amazon Village." *Human Ecology*, 5:355-68.

Howell, N. 1976. "Toward a Uniformitarian Theory of Human Paleodemography." In *The Demographic Evolution of Human Populations*, edited by R. Ward and K. Weiss, pp. 25-40. New York: Academic Press.

Howell, N. 1979. *The Demography of the Dobe !Kung*. New York: Academic Press.

Hull, V. 1977. "Fertility, Women's Work and Economic Class: A Case Study from Southeast Asia." In *The Fertility of Working Women: A Synthesis of International Research*, edited by S. Kupinsky, pp. 35-80. New York: Praeger.

Jaffe, A., and K. Azuni. 1960. "The Birth Rate and Cottage Industries in Under-Developed Countries." *Economic Development and Cultural Change*, 9:52-63.

Janes, E. 1981. "The Impact of Women's Employment on Fertility in the U.S., 1970-75." *Population Studies*, 35:161-74.

Johnston, F. 1982. *Physical Anthropology*. Dubuque, IA: W. C. Brown.

Katugiri, T., and T. Terao. 1972. "Family Planning in the People's Republic of China. Report on the First IPFF Visit." *IPFF Medical Bulletin*, 6:1-3.

Kennedy, R. 1973. *The Irish: Emigration, Marriage and Fertility*. Berkeley: University of California Press.

Khan, M. 1973. "Factors Affecting Spacing of Births." *Journal of Family Welfare*, 20:54-67.

Kleinman, D. 1980. *Human Adaptation and Population Growth*. New York: Allaheld.

Konner, M., and C. Worthman. 1980. "Nursing Frequency, Gonadal Function and Birth Spacing Among the !Kung Hunter-Gatherers." *Science*, 207:788-91.

Kupinsky, S. 1977. *The Fertility of Working Women: A Synthesis of International Research*. New York: Praeger.

Lee, R. 1980. "Lactation, Ovulation, Infanticide and Woman's Work: A Study of Hunter-Gatherer Population Regulation." In *Biosocial Mechanisms of Population Regulation*, edited by M. Cohen, R. Malpass, and H. Klein, pp. 321-49. New Haven, CT: Yale University Press.

Livingstone, F. 1962. "On the Non-existence of Human Races." *Current Anthropology*, 3:279-81.

Lotka, A. 1925. "On the True Rate of Natural Increase." *Journal of the American Statistical Association*, 20:305-39.

MacCluer, J. 1973. "Computer Simulation in Anthropology and Human Genetics." In *Methods and Theories of Anthropological Genetics*, edited by M. Crawford and P. Workman, pp. 219-48. Albuquerque: University of New Mexico Press.

MacMahan, B., and J. Worchester. 1966. *Age at Menopause: United States, 1960-1965*. Series 11, No. 19. Washington, D.C.: National Center for Health Statistics.

Mamdani, M. 1972. *The Myth of Population Control*. New York: Monthly Review Press.

Mandelbaum, D. 1974. *Human Fertility in India: Social Components and Policy Perspectives*. Berkeley: University of California Press.

Masnick, G. 1979. "The Demographic Impact of Breastfeeding: A Critical Review." *Human Biology*, 51:109-25.

Mason, K., and V. Palon. 1981. "Female Employment and Fertility in Peninsular Malaysia: The Maternal Role Incompatibility Hypothesis Reconsidered." *Demography*, 18:549-76.

Milan, F. 1970. "The Demography of an Alaskan Eskimo Village." *Arctic Anthropology*, 7:26-43.

Miller, B. 1981. *The Endangered Sex: Neglect of Female Children in Rural North India*. Ithaca, NY: Cornell University Press.

Mitchell, B. 1976. *European Historical Statistics, 1950-1970*. New York: Columbia University Press.

Montague, A. 1957. *The Reproductive Development of the Female, with Especial Reference to the Period of Adolescent Sterility*. New York: Julian.

Naeye, M., L. Burt, D. Wright, W. Blanc, and B. Tetter. 1971. "Neonatal Mortality: The Male Disadvantage." *Pediatrics*, 48:902-06.

Nag, M. 1981. "Economic Value and Cost of Children in Relation to Human Fertility." In *Fertility Decline in the Less Developed Countries*, edited by N. Eberstadt, pp. 274-94. New York: Praeger.

Neel, J., and K. Weiss. 1976. "The Genetic Structure of a Tribal Population, the Yanomamo Indians: XII. Biodemographic Studies." *American Journal of Physical Anthropology*, 42:25-52.

Parkes, A. 1974. "Sexuality and Reproduction." *Perspectives in Biology and Medicine*, 17:399-410.

Petersen, W. 1975. "A Demographer's View of Prehistoric Demography." *Current Anthropology*, 16:227-46.

Poffenberg, T. 1967. "Age of Wives and Number of Living Children of a Sample of Men Who Had the Vasectomy in Meerut District, U.P." *Journal of Family Welfare*, 13:48-51.

Preston, S. 1978. *The Effects of Infant and Child Mortality on Fertility*. New York: Academic Press.

Preston, S. 1980. "Mortality Declines in Less Developed Countries." In *Population and Economic Change in Developing Countries*, edited by R. Easterlin, pp. 289-361. Chicago: University of Chicago Press.

Repetto, R. 1972. "Son Preference and Fertility Behavior in Developing Countries." *Studies in Family Planning*, 3:70-76.

Retherford, R. 1975. *The Changing Sex Differential in Mortality*. Westport, CT: Greenwood Press.

Rose, F. 1968. "Australian Marriage, Land-Owning Groups and Initiation." In *Man the Hunter*, edited by R. Lee and I. DeVore, pp. 200-08. Chicago: Aldine.

Roth, E. 1981. "Community Demography and Computer Simulation Methodology in Historic Village Population Reconstruction." *Journal of Anthropological Research*, 37:279-301.

Roth, E., A. Ray, and B. Mohanty. 1983. "The Delineation of Fertility Strategies in an Indian Tribal Population of India: The Koyas of Koraput District, Orissa." *Journal of Anthropological Research*, 39:265-76.

Schrire, C. and W. L. Steiger. 1974. "A Matter of Life and Death: An Investigation into the Practice of Female Infanticide in the Arctic." *Man*, 9:161-84.

Shain, R., and V. Jennings. 1980. "Family Structure and Fertility." In *Fertility Control: Biological and Behavioral Aspects*, edited by R. Shain and C. Pauerstein, pp. 290-98. Hagerstown, MD: Harper and Row.

Shettles, L. 1958. "Biological Sex Differences with Special Reference to Disease Resistance and Longevity." *Journal of Obstetrics and Gynecology of the British Commonwealth*, 65:288-95.

Shettles, L. 1970. "Factors Influencing Sex Ratios." *International Journal of Gynaecology and Obstetrics*, 8:643-47.

Stolte-Heiskanen, V. 1977. "Fertility and Woman's Employment Outside the Home in Western Europe." In *The Fertility of Working Women: A Synthesis of International Research*, edited by S. Kupinsky, pp. 250-80. New York: Praeger.

Stycos, J. 1955. *Family and Fertility in Puerto Rico*. New York: Columbia University Press.

Sussman, R. 1972. "Child Transport, Family Size and Increase in Human Population During the Neolithic." *Current Anthropology*, 13:258-59.

Swedlund, A. 1978. "Historical Demography as Cultural Ecology." *Annual Review of Anthropology*, 7:137-73.

Swedlund, A., and G. Armelagos. 1976. *Demographic Anthropology*. Dubuque, IA: W. C. Brown.

Teitelbaum, M. 1972. "Factors Associated with the Sex Ratio in Human Populations." In *The Structure of Human Populations*, edited by G. Harrison and A. Boyce, pp. 90-109. Oxford: Clarendon Press.

Teitelbaum, M. 1976. "Relevance of Demographic Transition Theory for Developing Nations." *Science*, 188:420.

Thompson, W., and D. Lewis. 1965. *Population Problems*. New York: McGraw-Hill.

Trussell, J. 1978. "Menarche and Fatness: Reexamination of the Critical Body Composition Hypothesis." *Science*, 200:1506-09.

Van Ginnekan, J. 1978. "The Impact of Prolonged Breast Feeding on Birth Intervals and on Postpartum Amenorrhea." In *Nutrition and Human Reproduction*, edited by W. Mosley, pp. 179-97. New York: Plenum Press.

Venkatacharya, K. 1978. "Influence of Variations in Child Mortality on Fertility: A Simulation Model Study." In *The Effects of Infant and Child Mortality on Fertility*, edited by S. Preston, pp. 235-57. New York: Academic Press.

Ward, R., and K. Weiss. 1976. *The Demographic Evolution of Human Populations*. New York: Academic Press.

Ware, H. 1977. "Women's Work and Fertility in Africa." In *The Fertility of Working Women: A Synthesis of International Research*, edited by S. Kupinsky, pp. 1-34. New York: Praeger.

Weiss, K. 1973. "Demographic Models for Anthropology." *American Antiquity*, 38, Part 2, Memoir 27.

Weller, R. 1968. "The Employment of Wives, Role Incompatibility and Fertility." *Milbank Memorial Fund Quarterly*, 46:507-26.

Whitehead, J. 1847. *On the Causes and Treatment of Abortion and Sterility*. London: John Churchill.

Williamson, L. 1978. "Infanticide: An Anthropological Analysis." In *Infanticide and the Value of Life*, edited by M. Kohl, pp. 61-75. Buffalo: Prometheus Books.

Williamson, N. 1976. *Sons or Daughters: A Cross-Cultural Survey of Parental Preferences*. Beverly Hills, CA: Sage.

Williamson, N. 1978. "Boys or Girls? Parents' Preference and Sex Control." *Population Bulletin*, 33:1-35.

Wilmsen, E. 1979. "Diet and Fertility Among Kalahari Bushmen." Working Paper No. 14. Boston: African Studies Center, Boston University.

Wrigley, E. 1978. "Fertility Strategy for the Individual and the Group." In *Historical Studies of Changing Fertility*, edited by C. Tilley and L. Berkner, pp. 135-54. Princeton, NJ: Princeton University Press.

Wyon, J., S. Finner, and J. Gordon. 1966. "Differential Age at Menopause in the Rural Punjab, India." *Population Index*, 32:328.

Wyon, J., and J. Gordon. 1972. *The Khanna Study: Population Problems in the Rural Punjab*. Cambridge, MA: Harvard University Press.

8

ISSUES FOR THE FUTURE

Roberta Hall

This text has emphasized the interdependence of cultural patterns and biological sex differences. Yet each society must choose its own means of dealing with anatomical and physiological differences between males and females: It can exaggerate them, it can distort them, or it can ignore them. The choices a society makes affect the structure of its social life and mold the perceptions that its members hold of their own and of the opposite sex.

A crucial choice concerns the age at which males and females reproduce. Physiological differences are remarkably clear-cut. For women, reproduction must occur between the ages of 15 and 45, but for men it theoretically can occur at any time during adult life. Among some cultures, for example, the Russian Old Believers who immigrated into western Oregon in the 1960s, little difference exists in the age of marriage or in the reproductive patterns of the two sexes. Both sexes usually marry before the age of 20, live monogamously, and follow identical reproductive courses (Hall 1970). This culture demonstrates that it is possible for a society to ignore the potential for male-female differences in reproductive pattern.

Other societies exaggerate the biological differences between the sexes. For example, within many traditional African cultures, the age at which a person marries, as well as the reproductive pattern, differ greatly for men and women. Among the traditional Gikuyu, women marry between the ages of 15 and 20, but men do not marry until at least age 25. This produces a disparity in the adult sex ratio, which reinforces a particular marriage system. Kenyatta (1973) wrote: "Thus, in every

299

generation there are more women of marriageable age than men, which helps to balance the system of polygamy" (p. 290). In many polygynous societies, restraints upon marriage of males are economic – generally, older men are expected to have the resources with which to maintain their families. But there may be social rules as well. Among the Mossi, for example, a boy could not marry until his father died (Skinner 1973).

Societies with marriage rules such as these magnify biological male-female differences in the life cycle and reproduction. Yet in such societies women are not necessarily less free or independent than elsewhere. Among most traditional West African societies, women have a significant economic role to play and a measure of economic independence, even though they usually perform these roles in the married state. Though their economic activities are associated with those of their husband, they are not submerged in his. Each wife maintains control over her own hearth, garden produce, and children.

In most traditional societies, there exist patterned differences between males and females, and a member of such a society is imbued with specific beliefs regarding differences in the biology, emotional outlook, and social behavior of men and women. It is difficult for members of Western industrial societies to imagine that such a structure might not rank members of one sex higher than the other nor provide more choices to members of one sex than to another. In fact, most traditional societies do not permit either sex to make many choices. Neither the monogamous Old Believer society, in which men and women follow a single pattern in mating and reproduction, nor the West African polygynous societies, which exaggerate male-female differences, permit either sex to choose its own life-style. Both sexes have significant restrictions, and the roles of the two are expected to be complementary rather than competitive. Yet in most traditional societies, the issue of sex differences is not divisive.

Instead, it is in industrial societies of the last quarter of the twentieth century where consensus regarding sex roles is conspicuously lacking, and in these industrial societies, the issue of sex ranking looms large. As the electorate is anything but unified on the topic, candidates' views concerning sex roles and the issue of women's rights have swayed elections. Contrary opinions are embraced by groups that include both men and women as adherents, and each side believes it represents the side of morality, however differently each defines it.

What is of the deepest concern to me as a scientist and a humanist is whether we can use our scientific tradition in a liberating manner. The issue of sex differences confronts each of us personally, as individuals struggling to maintain a personal identity in the face of impersonal forces. Profound disagreement concerning validation of views of male-female differences may be the most important element explaining why the issue of male-female differences is so heated and protracted. Our individual and corporate dilemma in the last part of the twentieth century concerns our ability to integrate humanitarian values and scientific commitments. How can we be sure that our heart is not misleading our head, or our head misleading our heart? The history of science is full of stories in which well-meaning individuals have perpetrated both types of errors.

In this final chapter, I want to share some personal reflections upon our topic and its meaning within our own society. Our goal has been to examine the biosocial bases of male-female differences by considering specific data and explanations for them. We have considered socialization of boys and girls into sex roles, mating strategies of both sexes from an evolutionary viewpoint, differences in sensory abilities and the effects of these differences on cognitive styles, size and body proportion differences between the sexes, genetic and hormonal processes associated with sex, and the interaction of social and demographic effects in respect to sex and gender. While we wanted to consider a variety of cultures in our analysis – and in two chapters have included animal populations as well – we have drawn heavily on studies in U.S. society. In part, this focus reflects the residence of most of our authors, but it also reflects a tension within U.S. society arising from the absence of consensus regarding sex roles. This text has given little attention to the individual personality, and has concentrated upon social behavior and cultural patterns. In considering the meaning of these studies, particularly their significance for our individual-centered culture, I see the need to introduce the individual.

At the conscious level, most members of industrial societies of the present day reject arguments about gender based solely upon theology or upon cultural traditions. Yet, at the unconscious level, these forces insinuate themselves into our behavior patterns and our sense of our own self-images. Many times, this occurs through key individuals who have left an impression upon us. My own mother's greatest fear was that she or her children would be considered nonconformist by the middle-class society in which she was steeped. Her neurotic fears prevented her from making contributions to society and from enjoying the creativity of her own children. These personality traits, which in a milder form represent the cultural ideal for U.S. females who were born, as she was, in the first quarter of the century, were so extreme that even as a child I implicitly rejected them. Even so, in times of crisis, the pattern has haunted and tempted me. The rejection I experienced as a child because I did not conform to her concept of appropriate female behavior, and the lack of empathy between myself and my mother during my adult years, have inhibited my relations with other women. Certainly there is nothing unique about my own experience. Many women and men, perhaps even a majority of them, carry emotional scars from life experiences in which they were forced to separate from family members or family patterns in order to respond to life as it presents itself. As scientists and scholars, our tradition is to remove ourselves personally from the phenomena we are studying. Hence, the tendency of the authors of this book, and probably most of its readers as well, is to discount their individual experience, even though it may offer valuable insights. Instead, validation for our analysis of sex differences comes from observations performed, recorded, and analyzed according to accepted scientific principles.

Evolutionary theory, the most important and pervasive theory applicable to biobehavioral studies in this book, guides the perceptions of many social scientists as well as those of students of natural history. Yet many times we overlook its lessons. One of the most impressive facts that an evolutionary approach offers is the recognition that many potential solutions may be found for any problems that life imposes upon its subjects. Which solution is ultimately "chosen" by a given species, and the rules that have operated in any particular instance, are empirical questions, which cannot be deduced *a priori*. Diversity, opportunity, and innovation are integral to living systems – not just incidental by-products.

Some of the most insightful comments on variability in human personality appeared in a popular anthropology book published in 1934. The author was Ruth Benedict, and the title of the book *Patterns of Culture*. It is best remembered for its metaphor of culture as an individual human personality, but more enduring are the author's insights concerning the individual and society. Benedict's work has always implied to me that there is a spontaneous and hopeful untamability in humanity that does not submit entirely to any social pressures. Within this innate biological capacity for diversity and innovation lies the power of the species to preserve itself. Benedict (1934) wrote:

> Most human beings take the channel that is ready made in their culture.
> If they can take this channel, they are provided with adequate means of

expression. If they cannot, they have all the problems of the aberrant everywhere. (P. 106)

No culture yet observed has been able to eradicate the differences in the temperaments of the persons who compose it. It is always a give-and-take. The problem of the individual is not clarified by stressing the antagonism between culture and the individual, but by stressing their mutual reinforcement. . . . We have seen that any society selects some segment of the arc of possible human behavior, and insofar as it achieves integration its institutions tend to further the expression of its selected segment and to inhibit opposite expressions. But these opposite expressions are the congenial responses, nevertheless, of a certain proportion of the carriers of the culture. (P. 220)

It is clear that culture may value and make socially available even highly unstable human types. If it chooses to treat their peculiarities as the most valued variants of human behavior, the individuals in question will rise to the occasion and perform their social roles without reference to our usual ideas of the types who can make social adjustments and those who cannot. Those who function inadequately in any society are not those with certain fixed "abnormal" traits, but may well be those whose responses have received no support in the institutions of their culture. The weakness of these aberrants is in great measure illusory. It springs, not from the fact that they are lacking in necessary vigor, but that they are individuals whose native responses are not reaffirmed by society. They are, as Sapir phrases it, "alienated from an impossible world." (P. 233)

The person unsupported by the standards of his time and place and left naked to the winds of ridicule has been unforgettably drawn in European literature in the figure of Don Quixote. Cervantes turned upon a tradition, still honored in the abstract, the limelight of a changed set of practical standards, and this poor old man, the orthodox upholder of the romantic chivalry of another generation, became a simpleton. (P. 233)

For some traditional arrangements it is obvious that very high prices are paid, reckoned in terms of human suffering and frustration. (P. 234)

Tradition is as neurotic as any patient; its overgrown fear of deviation from its fortuitous standards conforms to all the usual definitions of the psychopathic. This fear does not depend upon observation of the limits within which conformity is necesary to the social good. Much more deviation is allowed to the individual in some cultures than in others, and those in which much is allowed cannot be shown to suffer from their peculiarity. It is probable that social orders of the future will carry this tolerance and encouragement of individual difference much further than any cultures of which we have experience. (P. 234)

Some readers of Benedict think she believed in the unlimited power of a culture to mold individuals to its pattern. A more careful reading suggests a different message – the view that individual differences are intrinsic to humanity. They are a part of the human biogram, and a culture's ability to mold the individual, though impressive, is limited. I have quoted passages at length to demonstrate that respect for the individual human personality is integral to the book *Patterns of Culture*, even though this theme is not the one that made it famous. In Benedict's view, a wise society, by permitting diversity, reduces the level of conflict between the individual and the society. By reducing the anxiety individuals feel concerning their own bodies and personalities (for example, their anxieties concerning gender identity), societies could more effectively tap the innate skills for survival with which each person is endowed at birth.

What guidance can this bio-cultural approach to male-female differences provide? It offers no behavioral dogmas, but tells us that in many societies, issues of sex and gender identity are not divisive as they are in our own, and suggests they need not divide us. Just as cultures at other times and places have worked out their own solutions, ours will also. Because we are a heterogeneous society in which the individual personality is revered above all, our solution will have to be built upon that unique base. Unlike the traditional societies that give neither sex many options, ours will have to provide many options for both – a much more difficult assignment. We have yet to produce the wise society, which Benedict envisioned, that provides a generous scope for its members. Perhaps, though, it is not yet too late.

The biocultural approach tells us that we have a unique, individual biology in addition to the endowments given universally to all members of the species. The key to our individual destiny requires acceptance of a dynamic interplay between our own biology and the sociophysical environment that supports us. Our first goal as scientists must be to increase the level of respect with which all men and women regard each other, and themselves.

REFERENCES

Benedict, R. 1934 (reprinted 1946). *Patterns of Culture.* New York: Mentor Books.

Hall, R. L. 1970. *Population Biology of the Russian Old Believers of Marion County, Oregon.* Ann Arbor, MI: University Microfilms International.

Kenyatta, J. 1973. "Marriage System." In *Peoples and Cultures of Africa*, edited by E. P. Skinner, pp. 280-96. Garden City, NY: Doubleday.

Skinner, E. P. 1973. "Intergenerational Conflict Among the Mossi: Father and Son." In *Peoples and Cultures of Africa*, edited by E. P. Skinner, pp. 326-34. Garden City, NY: Doubleday.

INDEX

ACTH, 168, 169, 178
adaptive radiation, 133
adolescent growth spurt, 146, 147
adolescent sterility, 245, 251
allometry, 131
amenorrhea, 149, 251, 271
amniocentesis, 287
androgens, 171, 175-78
aneuploidies, 179-84
athletic ability of males and females, 149-51, 154-56
Australia antigen, 192
Australopithecus, 29, 41-43, 45, 47, 53-55, 139, 142
autoimmune disorders: sex differences in, 207

baboon model of human evolution, 135
Barr bodies, 164, 181
Benedict, Ruth, 304-06
benign neglect (*see* infanticide), 241-43, 270, 293, 298
binocular rivalry, 68
binocular vision, 83-84, 127
bioenergetic model, 16, 135, 153
birth control, 264, 266-67, 299
birth order, 194
body composition, 2, 85, 129, 148-52, 154
brain damage, 105, 120, 121
brain lateralization, 88, 112-14, 116, 124-26, 128, 172, 173
breast feeding, bottle feeding, 44, 155, 170, 171, 266, 271, 293, 296, 298

cancer: differential risks by sex, 202
cardiovascular disease: differential risk by sex, 203, 204
carnivores: sex differences in, 133, 135, 139
chimerism, 185
cognitive processes, 2, 59, 95-96
color blindness, 82
computer simulations, 268-80, 281-86, 287-92, 295, 298

Darwinian fitness, 31
demographic transition theory, 227, 258-61, 292, 294, 296, 300
Down's syndrome, 181
dyslexia, 114-18, 121-31, 128

endocrinology, 165-73
estrous cycle, 30, 37, 38

familial studies, 114-19
father-absent households, 10-11
female dependency hypothesis, 29, 30, 49, 50
fine motor system, 85-86, 88-89, 103
Freud, Sigmund, 151
Fulari, 9

gender (*see* sex roles), 10, 123, 211
genetic drift, 187
genome, 160
global developmental lag theory, 77
gross motor system, 86

habituation, 65, 122, 127
Hardy-Weinberg theorem, 224
hemizygosity, 164, 190, 240
H-Y gene, 161-63, 173
homemakers: susceptibility to disease, 210
hyperactivity, 120, 121

immunoglobulins, 206
inclusive fitness, 28, 38
infanticide (*see* benign neglect), 23, 39, 197-99, 270-80, 293, 295, 300
intelligence, 97-98, 124, 128
introns, 158

junk DNA, 158

karyotyping, 159, 163, 183, 186
Klinefelter's syndrome, 181-82
!Kung, 7, 8, 42, 44, 54, 247, 249, 250, 251, 253, 254, 297, 298, 300

lactation (*see* breast feeding)
language, 59, 89, 92, 98, 103, 113, 114, 118, 222
life table, 228, 230, 233-35, 281, 287, 295
Linnaean hierarchy, 134, 137
longitudinal studies, 77, 109, 127, 145, 146, 183
loudness: sex differences in perception, 71-76

maternal role incompatibility, 259-61, 298, 300
mathematics and sex differences, 106-11, 119, 120, 123
meiosis, 158
memory, 94, 99, 102, 104, 123
mitosis, 158
mosaicism, 164, 184, 185
Müllerian duct, 174

Neanderthal, 141-43, 156
Neolithic, 142, 221
Net Reproductive Rate, 224, 226, 286, 292
nutritional stress: effects on sexual dimorphism, 143, 147, 149, 153, 155

osteoporosis: differential risk by sex, 204, 205

parasitic genes, 158
parental investment, 19, 28, 32-34, 40, 45, 47, 50, 187, 294
placenta, 170, 174
polygamy, 33, 34, 45, 131, 302
population pyramid, 223, 225
prepared learning tradition, 2, 5, 12, 21
punctuated equilibrium, 138

race, 195, 196, 221, 294
rank in primates, 17, 37, 38
reading, 98-102, 104, 105, 116, 118, 120, 121, 122-25, 127
reproductive isolation, 158, 277
Russian Old Believers, 249, 296, 301, 302, 307

seed eating hypothesis, 41
sex abnormalities, 164, 174, 176, 177, 179-86
sex preselection, 269, 286-94, 300
sex ratios, 34, 116, 156, 157, 186, 221, 223, 226, 227, 289, 290, 292, 293, 295, 296, 299; primary, 189-93; secondary, 193-200; tertiary, 201
sex role, 2, 5-12, 14, 15, 20, 23, 24, 43, 303
sexual selection, 31-34, 52, 54, 129, 157, 131, 153
socialization in sex roles, 68, 107-10, 120, 211
sociobiology, 14, 27-58, 131, 188
son preference, 262-69, 280, 282, 286, 293, 299
spina bifida, 190
stable population theory, 223, 224,

292
stationary population, 224
statistical significance, 61-62

territoriality, 35, 36, 39, 70
tfm genes, 161, 162, 175, 177
Turner's syndrome, 181

Type A/Type B personality, 209

visual persistence, 78-79

work roles: differentiated by sex, 6-7,
48

ABOUT THE EDITOR AND CONTRIBUTORS

ROBERTA HALL – Department of Anthropology, Oregon State University, Corvallis, Oregon. Dr. Hall organized and edited *Sexual Dimorphism in Homo Sapiens: A Question of Size* (Praeger), wrote *The Coquille Indians: Yesterday, Today and Tomorrow* (Smith, Smith, and Smith Publishers), and with Henry Sharp prepared *Wolf and Man: Evolution in Parallel* (Academic Press).

PATRICIA DRAPER – Department of Anthropology, University of New Mexico, Albuquerque, New Mexico. Dr. Draper earned a Ph.D. at Harvard University in social anthropology with special interests in child development. She has done field research in Africa.

MARGARET E. HAMILTON – Division of Postgraduate Education, Los Angeles College of Chiropractic, Whittier, California. Dr. Hamilton holds a Ph.D. in biological anthropology from the University of Michigan. Research interests include human sexual dimorphism, both skeletal and behavior.

DIANE McGUINNESS – Department of Psychology, Stanford University, Stanford, California. Dr. McGuinness has research interests in sex differences in perception and cognition, learning disabilities, computers in education, and social dynamics. She is a research associate at Stanford University and vice-president of the Education Division of Treemark, Inc., of Sunnyvale, California.

CHARLOTTE M. OTTEN – Professor Emeritus of Anthropology at Northern Illinois University, DeKalb, Illinois. Dr. Otten has made research contributions in many areas of biological anthropology and has served as an officer in the Human Biology Council and the American Association of Physical Anthropologists.

ERIC A. ROTH – Department of Anthropology, University of Victoria, Victoria, BC, Canada. Dr. Roth's research interests encompass the demography of traditional societies, with an emphasis on subarctic North American and South Asian populations.